EDUCATING MESSIAHS

to end religious conflict
From the series of essays written for

CHILDREN FOR AN HONEST, JUST, AND FAIR WORLD

Colin Hannaford

First a soldier, then a teacher

Order this book online at www.trafford.com
or email orders@trafford.com

Most Trafford titles are also available at major online book retailers.

Printed in the United States of America.

ISBN: 978-1-4669-9401-0 (sc)
ISBN: 978-1-4669-9403-4 (hc)
ISBN: 978-1-4669-9402-7 (e)

Library of Congress Control Number: 2013908810

Trafford rev. 11/05/2013

 www.trafford.com

North America & international
toll-free: 1 888 232 4444 (USA & Canada)
fax: 812 355 4082

FOREWORD

There can be no greater gratification for a teacher than to hear gracious and encouraging words from former students. All of us who stand at the front of a classroom like to think, and wish to believe, that our efforts with our students have borne productive fruit. Colin Hannaford has for many years dedicated his life to that always challenging and critically important task of pointing students in the direction of broader horizons and of leading them step by step to new discoveries and to life-changing commitments.

When a group of graduates from the European Union School in Culham near Oxford, England, invited him to a reunion for former students and teachers, Colin was greeted with a surprising and career-affirming request that he write a series of essays to appear on Facebook to *"tell the world what you taught us in your classroom."* What more genuine and humbling words could any teacher ever hope to hear?

What you are about to read is the faithful product of many long hours and many restless nights devoted to meeting the challenge laid down by his students. What could he say of significance about how to help our children learn to defuse the explosive dynamite of the absolute certainties and their accompanying intolerances held and defended by religions and governments and societies the world over that threaten, in the end, to be our collective undoing?

"We kill to defend our idols," he suggests, and he encourages us always to think it possible that, contrary to our unquestioned convictions, we may find the wisdom at long last to acknowledge that in some critically destructive way we just might be wrong. What hideous results of our refusal to acknowledge our mistakes might we discover some sad and awful day lying at our collective feet on our own political and theological doorsteps? What, you may ask, does he have to offer by calling into question the madness that all too often passes for defending "the truth" against error or for protecting and ensuring our clearly parochial way of life?

Could it be that, as the author suggests, the most powerful weapon of nonviolence is "the refusal to accept shabby lies as certain truths"? Could it be that we often confuse our habits and traditions with morality? Could it be that it is to our children that we must look to help us out of what Colin courageously identifies as "Satan's trap"?

As you read the pages that follow, you will most likely find yourself drawn into the delightful and sometimes sobering continuing dialogue between a thoughtful and beloved teacher and an admiring group of former students, many of them now parents with children of their own. He writes them letters and sends them emails, and he makes them all available to you, the reader, as he thinks his way, with his students and with you, through the dark labyrinth of failed ideas and, with hope, into the light of new possibilities.

"Quo vadis?" he wonders. Where are you going? Or more importantly, perhaps, where are *we* going? And if we need to change directions, is it perhaps too late?

You may not like or agree with everything you read here, and that's perfectly okay. But if you don't, that probably means, more importantly, that you are doing some thoughtful and careful thinking, and I am confident that nothing could please Colin Hannaford more than to know that you have taken seriously what he is trying with such fervent conviction to say.

Duane E. Davis, PhD
Professor Emeritus, Religion and Philosophy
Mercer University, Georgia, USA

An explanation

"And what is truth?"

This question appears only in the testimony of John, not in any of the other gospels. According to his report, Jesus and Pilate were alone.

If they were alone, only Jesus or Pilate could have reported it later. Roman justice was swift. Within hours Jesus was stripped and scourged. He was unlikely to have been capable of passing on any such details. If it was not Pilate, who was the witness?

*

The Army had taken over a particularly ugly four-story modern tower block for its headquarters. In the long hours of the night there was a need for some distraction in the operations room. Lit by a glaring wall of illuminated maps, in a silence broken by the squawk of radios sending regular reports, and only occasionally more excited chatter, it was my solitary kingdom from late evening to early morning. When the rest of the operations staff arrived, after I had delivered my report of the previous twenty-four hours to the general, sometimes together with his brigade commanders, I was free to breakfast and sleep.

It was rare for the general to ask me what to do next. In fact, he never did ask me: thus missing a valuable opportunity. I was hardly an important cog in his army. In contrast to his soldiers on the street, I was as safe as in a submarine. I was desk-bound, a scribbler. No-one ever shot at me. I was never required to shoot back at anyone. As I left my place, another officer would take over in front of the maps, the radios, the telephones, and the tape-recorders. I was bored.

Perhaps one of the Army padres left a Bible there, intending to save another soul. Four decades later, I am now able to realize: this is where it started.

Within five miles of my kingdom, Christians were killing Christians. The Catholics, known as and calling themselves Taigs, were killing Protestants. The Protestants, known as Prods, were killing Taigs. All of this was happening in a ferment of religious hatred not known for centuries in Europe.

Why is it so easy, we simple soldiers were caused to wonder, to turn fervent belief in a loving, compassionate, and merciful God into hatred of others? What is the mechanism? Where is the lure? Where are the trip wires in the mind?

Can it only be: as less optimistic humanists maintain, that there is a monster waiting in all of us, a beast, always hoping for an excuse, however feeble, to rape, to torture, and to murder?

How close is this beast to you: right now?

I leafed back a page or two. A few days before his arrest Jesus had told his followers: *"When the Spirit comes who reveals the truth about God, he will lead you all into the truth. He will not speak with his own authority, but will tell you what he hears and will tell you of things to come."* And yet, when Peter with his drawn sword tried to prevent the arrest: *"Do you not think that I will drink the cup of suffering which my Father has given me?"*

If arrested by Romans, Jesus must know that he will be interviewed by Pilate himself. Only Pilate could order him killed. But crucifixions were as common to Rome as road kill is common to us. No-one would notice yet another wretch slowly dying on a cross. At his end only his women sat below his cross to watch him die.

But this ending was too banal. Although I did not agree with everything Jesus was said to have done or said, he was too bright to commit himself to such a dismal end! There is no flair; it lacks fizz. A much bigger story is needed.

Although having repeatedly to placate the Jewish mob, always especially volatile in Jerusalem, Pilate was no friend of Jewish customs or sensibilities.

Since that crucial day Christians have been taught that no-one has ever had more confidence than Jesus. What, then, might persuade Pilate to interview him after his first arraignment? Could

Jesus then convince Pilate of the nature of this Spirit *'which reveals the truth about God'*?

What would that mean? Still more important: if this *'truth'* was the most important message that Jesus intended this *'Spirit'* to reveal *'about God'*, where the hell (perhaps literally) is it now? Why was this not recorded? If it was ever once recorded, who would have an interest in erasing it?

Apart from writing my daily reports of bombs, murder, kidnapping, and punishment by torture and murder, I had weeks in which to write an account of their private interview: in my imagination, remarkably similar men; quick-tempered, impatient of sloppy ideas; on occasion given to violent action; above all, both immensely sure of themselves.

They differed in only one aspect.

Pilate has been brought up to honour Rome's laws, and is now required to uphold them. The truth that he believes is already written and codified. It has only to be applied: with justice, if possible; without, if not. He is, in the end, a lawyer. He can interpret, not change.

Jesus has been brought up to honour Jewish beliefs: although, as I now discovered, he held only two essential. At some early time in his life, he had broken free from the most pervasive, most powerful, and most limiting of all Jewish customs: their fascination with all the exact rituals that underpin Jewish identity. In his time there were several rabbinical factions competing to codify these rituals. Theirs was good business. Jesus annoyed them all.

I called my play *'Game'*. It really isn't a very good play; but in it I try to show Jesus attempting to persuade Pilate that truth is never something to be fixed, codified, incorporated into customs and rituals; that although fixity of truth is insistently demanded by virtually all cultures, it cannot be the true end of intelligence, of inquiry; it cannot even be real knowledge. Truth must be forever increasing and expanding, so that one day, even if in the next millennium, our future generations may even know what it is to know God.

In my story, he fails. No shame is attached. It would be very difficult—as you will see—to do this even now. Despite a further two thousand years of promises of peace world-wide, the beast in men is still very active.

My first concern in these essays was to identify its true nature. They are printed here privately in order to preserve a record of what is, and should be, an endless quest, and they are dedicated to my ex-pupils, without whose encouragement they would not have been written.

My thanks are due to them.

Colin Hannaford, Oxford, September 2013

AN INTERVIEW WITH COLIN HANNAFORD
by
**Professor Michael Shaughnessy,
Senior Correspondent of EducationNews.org,
September 26th, 2011**

Colin, in my report of our conversation, I have called you 'A Prophet without Honour in His Own Land'. After attending a reunion at your old school, you created a Facebook page to which there has been a remarkable response. What prompted you to do this?

All my friends were telling me I was getting nowhere in trying to persuade our ministers of education that whilst children in authoritarian societies can learn well from being told what to think, children in more open societies do not. They learn best by being encouraged to talk, about their ideas, their feelings, even about the direction of their societies. This, of course, is what an 'open society' means. I was exhausting myself and should just give up. Then in the summer I attended my old school's final reunion of staff and pupils. I had never been to any of these before. I was surrounded by former pupils, some now in their 30s and even 40s, who greeted me with so much pleasure that I was astonished. Of course, when children have no-one with whom to compare their teachers whilst they are being taught, they are not likely to regard anyone as particularly special. Thirty years later they have more experience. They had used Facebook to organize their reunion and urged me to join. I decided to make one last effort. It looks like this:

To my Class of 2011

Okay, folks: time to get serious. I want to recruit you all into the most dangerous game on Earth. Just a few years before I became a teacher, a man for whom I had great respect told me that I might be a new messiah. I retorted that I was not such a fool. Lately I have realized that a messiah is simply someone who is honest and asks awkward questions.

But this is always a dangerous business. Such people used to be called iconoclasts: smashers of idols. Idols encourage division, hatred, and violence. Many messiahs in many countries are currently being beaten, tortured, and murdered for attempting to show others that they are worshipping idols. As a mathematics teacher I decided that my first duty was to help you to preserve your honesty and to be unafraid to ask questions. Now I wish I had been more forthright. Today the world needs not one individual messiah but an entire generation of messiahs. It took me some years to learn this. There are currently 750 million Facebook users. If just one percent begins to tell their children to reject dishonesty and to ask awkward questions, we can make a start on a cleaner, fairer, kinder world.

How have your pupils responded?

In the First Week

Penny wrote:

"Love it Mr. H."

Gabriella wrote:

"If just one percent begins to tell their children to reject dishonesty and to ask awkward questions, we can make a start on a cleaner, fairer, kinder world." I like this phrase. I've always lived my life this way, especially asking awkward questions ☺*, but the*

majority of people never answer and fear civil confrontation and acceptance of diversity. It's like Don Quixote fighting the windmills."

Tania wrote:

"I love the idea! It's up to us to live in honesty, even if it's just that one percent for now! Great text, Mr. Hannaford!"

Giulia wrote:

"I love your writing, used to love your lessons full of passion for honest learning. You are touching a very difficult subject here in Italy where many of us are not happy with the so-called honesty of our government. I try to teach my kids honesty and always encourage discussion and question posing, but I ask myself if this is enough?"

Lucy wrote:

"Thank you for sharing this with us, Colin! Amazing writing, as usual.☺ I recall things you've taught me every day with my son—and try to teach him as you did me! And I will share this with as many people as possible! xx"

Karen wrote:

"Goodness me, I remember your teaching s-o-o-o well. On one particular occasion you jumped around the class pretending to be a molecule heating up!!! I respect your writing and I agree that honesty is probably the most important thing we can teach our children today. Thank you so much."

Peter wrote:

"Thanks, Colin. At 9.30am on 07/07/05, just as a series of bombs were going off on the London Underground, I was sitting

on a train pulling into Paddington Station, looking at a guy dozing opposite me, wondering, 'If this man was the messiah, would I recognise him? How would I recognise one when I next come across her?' On that day the bombers probably thought they were messiahs (or some such word), and some of the victims may have been too. Why aren't we?"

Natalie wrote:

"I do agree with this idea! You'd think it would not be so hard to ask questions and expose the truth. Sadly this ability is often crushed from early childhood on. Asking awkward questions of your parents is one of the most difficult challenges. For example, a simple truth like 'pain hurts' very often goes unheard in a culture where you are told 'it's for your own good'; in the end you no longer know what you truly feel . . . . We can all start by really listening and hearing our children, and addressing their questions (this includes babies' crying) thereby encouraging them to ask. Schools also often seem to discourage thought in children . . . . I'm looking forward to reading your articles in EducationNews! All the best for now!"

Anica wrote:

"I love both of these articles. They are insightful and have some promising ideas. I can understand why a lot of people would have a problem with these ideas as I think implementing the changes that are so badly needed would be a huge task. There are so many things to say about the subject you have chosen to address and talk so passionately about. I am glad someone is fighting for an ever failing educational system. You were my favourite teacher because you listened and encouraged us to use our own voices and talk about what we truly felt. Our moral lessons were the only classes Lucy and I looked forward to. I remember thinking once it was the only time the whole class actually got involved. Everybody listened, everybody got to say their piece! Sometimes we argued but surely a good discussion cannot pass without a hitch! You were always alive

and passionate about what you discussed with us. Thank you, Mr. Hannaford. You taught me more than you know☺. x"

Veronica wrote:

"Dear Colin, you are definitely a New Messiah, when it comes to teaching maths to children all over the world through Logic. Not being the most logical of people, I admire you!
Love, Veronica xxx."

Rob wrote:

"My two older girls love maths and I spend time with them doing it. Much of it has to be credited to you and your methods. I love maths and think my 2-year-old will too. Big respect, Colin. Robert."

Erica wrote:

"I think honesty is only a word that can be used where you remain true to yourself and your own personal beliefs, providing they do not encroach on others'. We teach our sons to work hard, to the extent of their ability, learn from mistakes as well as success, be kind, thoughtful, etc . . . . I think we have all turned out just fine and our children will do too. In this way, we spread the word little by little."

And so, this is how it started: without their encouragement I would never have begun. Nor, at the time, did I know where it would end. You don't believe in miracles? I think you should.

In the Second Week

There has been a great amount of interest in our first week for 'Children for an Honest, Just, and Fair World'. Our numbers have already increased ten-fold!

Please continue to help as much as you can by spreading the word, involving others, asking questions, and suggesting other organisations we can link to ours!

With your encouragement, I would also like to return to writing a more complete account of where these ideas have come from. It has been a long hard slog, but at the end we can now explain to children how they can help the world to be a more honest, just, and fair place.

In the Third Week

Once the sky was thought to be like a great tent. Outside was the glory of Heaven: inside were the shades of the Earth. According to Hindu myth, from time to time an incarnation of the supreme god, a messiah, would open a flap in the roof of the tent, come down from Heaven and cleanse the Earth of human corruption and violence.

There have been nine messiahs. We are waiting for a tenth.

It is much harder to believe today that the sky is just a tent. And so stubborn and violent have modern differences of opinion become that if a messiah could now step through the roof of the sky, it is likely that he would be attacked as an alien.

Much of the certainty with which beliefs are expressed, modern and old, is bluff.

Unfortunately, certainty will always justify cruelty, and unlimited certainty will justify unlimited cruelty. Despite the certainty of some scientists, we have hardly begun to understand what questions we humans can ask: or what answers we might understand.

Where is the tenth messiah to save us from our corruption and our violence?

The answer, we have realized, is that we need an entire generation of messiahs to show us the way to a more honest, just, and fair world.

The certainties for children are their need of shelter, security, and love: and, that they must ask questions.

The world changes. To adapt to its changing, children must ask questions.

Recently I attended a meeting that was protesting at the situation in a country in which all effective power is held by a tiny fraction of the people. These few people control education; the media; the political process; create the laws; control industry; decide who shall be regarded as enemies of the state, etc.

The meeting was exciting. We were shown film of other meetings, equally exciting.

Finally I took one of the organisers aside, away from the noise, to tell him: *"Look at what I see. I see one group of people, absolutely certain that they are morally right, protesting that another group of people, several thousand miles away, also absolutely certain that they are morally right, is wrong. This is no good. Give me paper and a pen!"*

He did so, rather puzzled. I drew an outline of a great fortress. I gave it three massive high towers, connecting them by a great wall. I labelled the towers: 'OBEDIENCE'; 'DISHONESTY'; 'FORCE'. Above the wall and the towers, I wrote 'POWER'.

"That," I said, *"is what you have to defeat. It looks impregnable. It is not. There are many within it as there are without who can pull it down. Here they are outside".* I drew many children below. *"And there are many more within, for those within have children too. All these children want to be honest. They all want to ask questions. They will breach those walls, and pull down the towers."*

He took my drawing away, promising to show it to his superiors. I wonder if he did. No-one really likes children who question their certainties.

What I did not say to him, of course—as you may have detected—is that both sides see the other hiding behind massive walls whose towers are also labeled 'OBEDIENCE'; 'DISHONESTY'; 'FORCE'.

All powers can be humbled by children asking: Why?

It is time to begin.

Colin

In this third week we found that another group had associated itself with ours. Conscience House, in Arabic 'Wjdan House', had then around 3,500 members, mostly writing in Arabic, many declaring that they are agnostic or atheist.

Dear Wjdan House,

Thank you for your interest in our group 'Children for an Honest, Just, and Fair World'. Our wish is to engage everyone who agrees that encouraging children to be honest and to ask questions can help to bring peace to our dangerously divided world in which mutually distrustful hegemonies are continually striving to dominate others. We hope you agree with our aim; but there is an obvious difficulty in exchanging views about this, since ours are exclusively in English and yours are in Arabic. We have tried the Google translation service, but the result is very difficult to understand.

We will try to find an Arabic speaker who can translate the gist of our exchanges. If you agree on the importance of this, can you do the same for us by translating Arabic into English?

If this is not possible—or, if you do not agree with our aim— it would seem only sensible for our groups amicably to separate again.

With best wishes,

Colin Hannaford

9ᵗʰ October 2012

Dear Mr. Colin Hannaford, first of all I would like to thank you for this initiative, and in the name of the members of Wjdan House (conscience-house) we would like to cooperate with your group seeking for encouraging children to be honest and be able to bring peace to our societies and of course to our world. We also hope that the quintessence of this cultural cooperation is to achieve the real aims we are seeking for. We do realize the differences between our cultures, but these differences mean nothing when we deal with themes like cultural exchange, honesty, human moral values and peace. Even the language is not an obstacle which prevents this initiative! We also do believe and "hold these truths to be self-evident, that all men are created equal, that they are endowed by their Creator with certain unalienable Rights, that among these are Life, Liberty and the pursuit of Happiness." So let us begin . . . .

Best wishes—Wjdan House

From Mara Alsaffa:

. . . Please show us the way to help your group to do the best for children . . . and you [are] welcome.

From Aimer Aljashaeme:

Do not cost yourself a translation, we will do so.

9ᵗʰ October 2012

From Saif Albasri:

Dear Mr. Colin Hannaford, the part you are trying to point out is also a part of our enlightenment policy. We are trying our best to publish our messages to the members and outside this group, and we do need any support especially from enlightened people like you. So what do you suggest, how should we begin this cooperation? Do you have a certain Program or concept? We agree with you and this group is opened to every thought!

From Abbas Alkabbi:

Work in silence, and let your work speak louder.

In the Fourth Week

Saif suggests that we can try to learn from each other, and asks if we have a programme which Wjdan House might follow. Veronica asked: What are children to do when their questions are ignored, or—a worse, but entirely likely possibility—if they are punished simply for asking?

Abbas offers the splendid comment: 'Work in silence, and let your work speak louder.'

Let me try to respond all at once. It seems to me that Veronica's is the most vital question. To explain why I think so completely would take a little too long, but children certainly soon get used to their parents not being able to answer questions like: *"Why is the sky blue?"* They will simply save questions like these for later. If, however, they are punished for asking, they will first realize that these adults want to appear strong but must be weak in being unable to answer. If the ban is even more serious, eventually the children refused answers to any question may ask: *"Who will recognize me, and my right to ask questions, if my society will not?"* And this, of course, will take them to the very threshold of enlightenment.

Learning from each other is always going to be difficult. To some extent, we are all embedded in our own cultural hegemony. This always makes what we hear rather different, and sometimes completely different, from what is meant and what is said. I first began to understand this from a thoughtful lecture here in Oxford by HE Sheikh Abdullah Bin Mohamed al-Salami of Oman. He spoke of the need for 'a new basis' to reduce the great dangers to us all of continuing hegemonic rivalry. We shook hands as he left the Taylorean lecture room, and later I gave one of his officers my card. On it I had written that we have 'the programme that you have asked for, Saif.' I have had no response from Oman, but these are early days.

It is essential to realize that hegemonies are composed of many inter-dependent organisations. No-one actually controls them all. The President of the United States does not control the military-industrial-congressional complex of the United States. The Pope does not control the Catholic Church.

Hegemonies are powerful only because no-one dares question their right to power. As soon as this begins to happen—as in Tripoli, as in Egypt, and now on Wall Street—their power is seen to depend, as usual, on unthinking obedience, on deliberate dishonesty, and, ultimately, on force to frighten and suppress.

So, I think the answer to your question, Saif, therefore echoes Abbas' advice. The work of mothers in their homes will eventually speak loudest, when they quietly tell their little ones: "You can always be honest with me: and, when you are bigger, never be afraid to be honest with others and to ask questions. If anyone beats you for asking, that person is simply too frightened to be as honest as you are."

Best wishes,

Colin

In the Fifth Week

On Tuesday of this week, 11 October, I was invited to an address by the Speaker of the Iraq Parliament, HE Osama Al-Nujaii, in the University's Examination Schools. A tall dignified figure, speaking in Arabic, His Excellency gave a remarkably candid account of the present situation in Iraq. Questions were then asked about Iraq's relations with Syria and Iran, about Sharia, the freedom of religion and expression, nepotism, the developing Iraqi economy, etc.

His audience numbered at least seventy. It is understandable for questions to be first invited from university scholars and other known experts. I was therefore agreeably surprised when the moderator, Sir Jeremy Greenstock, a distinguished British diplomat, invited the second question from me. He also asked that I say who I am.

This surprised His Excellency's interpreter. *"Did you say the Institute for Democracy from—from mathematics?"*

His Excellency was also surprised. He asked aloud, in English: *"How are they connected?"*

I asked: *"How confident are the young people of Iraq of a democratic future?"* This received a cautiously optimistic reply, but he also noted that the future does not entirely depend on young people. Having received this response, I continued: *"Now I will answer Your Excellency's question."* And this, I was telling myself, had better be the shortest and the best lecture you have ever given in your life.

"Your Excellency," I explained, *"mathematics can be taught in two very different ways: either as instruction to be obeyed"*—and as I spoke *"obeyed"* I pointed at him forcefully as if demanding obedience—and then I closed my fist, opened my hand, palm upwards, and spoke more gently—*"or mathematics can be offered as an argument"*—I drew back my hand as if inviting agreement—*"to be agreed."*

His Excellency nodded thoughtfully. But the whole of the room responded, even more remarkably, with a muted but concerted "Mmmm". Short IS sometimes more effective.

As I was leaving the Examination Schools twenty minutes later I was met by the Iraqi TV interviewer and his cameraman. The interviewer asked if I would repeat all that I had said to His Excellency. I did so. But I added: *"You see, when children are offered mathematics as argument, the question is not only whether you agree"*—I pointed to the interviewer—*"but whether she agrees"*—pointing to one side—*"and whether he agrees"*—pointing to the other side—*"and she, and she, and he. In this way children learn together critical, constructive, and, above all, receptive discourse. They learn to accept, even to value, different opinions."*

Unfortunately, it isn't possible to watch Iraqi TV in Oxford. If any of you see the interview, I would be very glad to know what was made of it! But let it be in English, please!

15ᵗʰ October 2012

About The Socrates Workbook

Dear Friends,

It is not at all difficult to help children to think independently. Unfortunately, school classes are generally addressed by teachers as if the whole class is thinking alike at the same time. The main reason for this is, of course, tradition, but the reason for its continuation in modern schools is explained in my article in EducationNews.org entitled 'The Bad Boy of British Education', where I single out one exceptional school for praise.

All parents know that children have very different minds; that they think and learn in different ways. To help my own youngest pupils to understand how their minds can learn independently and far more effectively, I produced a 30-page colouring book called the Socrates Workbook. It is in several major languages, including Arabic and Russian, and there is a Teachers' and Parents' Guide, although this is only in English.

Originally its title declared that it was 'for 9 to 11 year-olds', but one of our senior pupils—they made most of the translations, for which I paid a pound per page—told me: "Mr H., this title's wrong. It should say 'for 9 to 19 year-olds'. We all need to learn what's in this book!"

It will give any child who works through it (but not gallop through it, please!) a distinct advantage in learning to think and learn independently, but they may also wish to show it to their teacher, explaining that it can inexpensively increase the learning ability of an entire class: even of an entire school.

If you use it, either privately or publicly, I will naturally like to know if it is successful.

Bon chance!

Colin

21ˢᵗ October 2012

Dear Friends,

"What is truth?" Pilate asked.

Truth is the direction in which we are able to learn more.

And this, it seems to me, is what all the fighting is about: whether to learn more, or not.

Since my ex-pupils asked me to begin this venture, I have been both delighted and appalled by Facebook. I have been delighted to discover that others are excited by the prospect of raising a new generation of messiahs who will always want to be honest, to ask questions, and thereby always to learn more.

I have been delighted as well to have been shown so many beautiful babies and children. It is entirely possible that what they learn will not only be more comprehensive, but simpler too. This is the lesson of science. There is no reason why it may not be true of life itself.

Have you ever noticed how one's mind may notice something entirely unimportant and make it piquantly relevant? I was driving out of London one day last week when this happened to me. My attention was suddenly triggered by an advertisement. I think it was actually for fashionable clothes. What is important is that it told me: "Tomorrow is a luxury you do not have".

This afternoon I took a call from Herte Diamant, a celebrated Jewish poet, now in her eighties. When I told her once how lonely thinking sometimes makes one feel, she told me: *"But if you have climbed higher than anyone has climbed before, you shouldn't be surprised if you find yourself on the summit of a mountain, alone."*

Facebook has greatly relieved this fearful sense of being alone. At the same time, I have often been appalled by what it has brought into my life.

I live alone in a small but comfortable house in a quiet corner of the usually peaceful and well-ordered city of Oxford. I share my home with three bears, a giant rabbit, a platypus, a small gorilla, a miniscule elephant, and several others. They are all stuffed. They are company, but do not argue. To find an argument, I have only to cycle for ten minutes to find a most satisfyingly contrary opinion in a lecture or a seminar.

What is absolutely certain about my quiet, comfortable, lonely but well-ordered life is that however passionately others may disagree with me, or however passionately they may disagree with each other, the results will not resemble any of the images that you have shown me, especially, but not only, those sent by Wjdan House.

There have appeared images of terrible mutilations, rows of carbonised bodies, destroyed homes, destroyed lives, and most recently a truly terrifying image of a small girl, of about eight or nine years of age, with a burnt face and splints on both arms, painfully scrawling 'FUCK YOU GOD' with a pen gripped awkwardly in her only partly bandaged right hand.

Tomorrow is a luxury we do not have. To help people to learn not to destroy those who disagree with them, and to do so as hideously and violently as possible, it will not be enough to give children the notion that God is responsible for such obscenities. I have realised that many of you would like to believe that God does not exist. In this respect, I will be of little comfort to you. Where perhaps I can help is by offering a much more comprehensive and yet simpler understanding of who—or what—God is.

I will do this in the next few days.

Best wishes,

Colin.

25th **October 2012**

Dear Friends,

In my previous letter I described how Facebook has delighted me by vastly enlarging my circle of friends: indeed, by informing me that I have many more friends than I knew; but that it has also appalled me, by bringing into my quiet and comfortable life images of a cruel, ugly, and ultimately disastrously divided world.

These images have also made even clearer that to help people to learn not to want to destroy everyone who may disagree with them, we must start with the children.

The reason is to be found in Genesis 2:16-17. It contains the very first statement of moral law: the warning against certainty most ignored by cultures throughout history, as it is ignored today.

The little injured girl painfully scrawling 'FUCK YOU GOD' should really be accusing the many who suppose they have been appointed guardians of moral certainty. Most are simply demonstrating the fact that they have no faith in God: nor, indeed, any in human intelligence.

The more deeply inspired look instead for better ways to convince: through friendship and through reason.

Unfortunately, the majority of adults have eaten sufficiently of the tree of the knowledge of good and evil to be sure that they know precisely what—and who—is good and evil. They are unlikely to think themselves evil. They are unlikely to change their minds. The older they are, the more likely they are to be prepared to prove the truth of their morality by sending younger adults to war.

There is still hope, however, that the younger adults, especially those who have just become parents, can be persuaded that the future of their children will be more promising if the children of their enemies are as less likely to make war as theirs are.

This has been my aim for almost forty years. I began by attempting to show education authorities, actually their governments, that obliging the majority of children to learn to pass exams without understanding, and without ever admitting that they do not understand, is the easiest way to teach children to be dishonest and to be reluctant to ask questions. When successful deceit is considered socially acceptable—and even, as in some religions, socially necessary—the ultimate consequences are socially disastrous.

My first attempt failed. I do not believe that my analysis is wrong. What I had failed to notice is that it also predicts how governments will behave. Since they will contain many whose advancement has been won through deceit, they do not want children to be encouraged to be honest and to ask questions. Honest people are inevitably a threat to secretive cabals. As I write this, large numbers of people are protesting against the dishonesty of their banks and governments. They have at last begun to question. They probably admire Mahatma Ghandi, but Che Guevara too. They need to know how to stop children being taught to be dishonest.

I applauded Abbas Alkabbi when he wrote: *'Work in silence, and let your work speak louder.'* I have been attempting to work in silence for forty years. I do not regret this time. About half-way through it I was amused to realize that I was behaving very like the brave and foolish young men in the age of the most romantic chivalry, who set out to find the Holy Grail in order to lay it at the feet of their beautiful lady. Unfortunately, they did not really know what the Grail really is. It was a mystery. They only knew that it was of unique importance.

There is a beautiful lady to whom I wish to present my Grail. I have discovered that it is simply the gift of peace to the world.

I have loved her for many years, and was deeply saddened when she refused my discovery; but the images which Facebook has shown me have also shown why silence is no longer an option. To help those in harm's way, I must be prepared to place myself in harm's way with them.

The experience that my old friend Cecil King believed so uniquely important is briefly described in a chapter of my earlier book '473959'. It was he who told me 'You could be a new messiah', and it was to him that I said 'I'm not such a fool.'

We agreed, therefore, about its importance. We disagreed how it should be used. I had been an atheist since I was twelve. Within minutes of its occurring I knew who it was who told Moses: "I am that I am". I understood why Jesus referred to God as his Father. I knew that the Prophet Muhammad had indeed been embraced so tightly by an angel—as he reported—that he could not breathe.

God certainly exists. He is greater and more powerful than all but a very few have been able to envisage. He may be guiding the evolution of intelligent life throughout a universe of trillions of galaxies, every one composed of billions of stars.

And he does this in a manner so comprehensive and so simple as to be almost absurd.

The failure to obey, however, is not at all absurd. It is extinction.

I will return to my promise next, to what and who—in my belief—God is.

Entracte

Recently I have been asked to decide, in effect, which religious sect I believe to be more virtuous than others. This I will not do. The founders of every major religion always offered a reason for people to unite. Usually, often within a very short time, their once united followers have found reasons to divide: then to divide again, and to divide again.

It is very easy to find reasons for division. It is harder to show why people should discard their differences, and see themselves as one. It can be done. Here is an example.

Last week I was invited to the Jewish celebration marking the end of the annual reading of the Torah. This is when the Torah scrolls are removed from their usual enclosure and carried around in a very joyful and very noisy dance by the men whilst they are being pelted with sweets by the children.

It was an entirely happy festivity, and so I was more than a little surprised when my host, who a few minutes before had been dancing with his smallest daughter shrieking with laughter on his shoulders, paused for breath and, indicating me, told the other dancers, as they also paused for breath: *"He wants to change the world!"*

He was obviously serious, so that one of the younger rabbis at once asked me the obvious question: *"How will you change the world?"*

Still somewhat surprised, I explained what we have been discussing here: that it will require an entire generation of messiahs.

"That," said my questioner thoughtfully, *"is very interesting",* and the other young Jews nodded. But when later I reported to the lady, the light of my life, she, being always ready to challenge my temerity, wanted to know why I thought this might be important.

She refused to think so. Her own religion tells her that the Messiah has visited our world already, and is now in Heaven. Why, she repeated, did this response of a Jew, even of a rabbi, matter?

Trembling, as you will imagine, with a mixture of rage and sorrow, I was then bound to ask myself the same question. Eventually, I replied:

"Well, almost certainly the Jews have the most highly developed sense of survival of any culture. They might see immediately that my suggestion can increase their children's chances of survival: as, indeed, it can."

After the Torah celebration, my host the rabbi had more time to reflect.

"Of course," he murmured, *"in the Jewish faith, there is in everyone a spark of the Messiah."* He paused. *"So yours is really a Jewish idea."*

27ᵗʰ October 2012

Dear Friends,

"When I was a child, I spoke as a child, I understood as a child, I thought as a child: but when I became an adult, I put away childish things." (I Corinthians 13:11)

The world seemed so much simpler when the sky was the roof of a great tent and the Earth was enclosed beneath it; when God, although occasionally given to angry commands of genocide, was otherwise a cheery old gentleman who created everything and was always ready to comfort and protect. Heaven was just above the roof. Hell was down below the floor. Despite plagues, famine, war, flood, drought, conquest and earthquakes, the world was simpler and more complete. It was ruled everywhere by men. God was a man. God was a warrior. God gave over the world to men. Lilith was dismissed for being disobedient. After her, Eve gave Adam the right to decide right or wrong.

Our world is very different. How different have **we** become?

Today we are obliged to explain to our children that the whole of our history has been lived on a speck of dirt orbiting a not-very-unusual star on the edge of a not-very-unusual galaxy. Its vast vortex, containing up to four hundred billion stars, is revolving like a pinwheel in a universe containing billions more galaxies, some containing trillions of other stars. Our own, like many others, is believed to have a massive discontinuity at its centre, drawing everything close enough into itself, reducing its atoms to pure energy and perhaps, we think—but how can we know?—spewing it out somewhere, perhaps into an entirely different dimension of reality.

Although Arab and Persian philosophers believed many centuries before Galileo that the specks of light in the night are stars, the true magnitude of our universe has only been realised in the past few hundred years. Even before Darwin, many began to believe that the scale of everything then being discovered was just too vast to be directed, let alone that it could all be created by God.

More recently many have been ready to question whether God is necessary at all. Since Galileo first declared, and as Isaac Newton seemed to prove, that the universe can be understood only through mathematics, much of the confidence of modern thinkers has been based on the apparently illimitable success of mathematics and now on its dependent sciences.

Even more recently it has been realised that there are limits to what even mathematics can prove. The man who has done most to show this, G. J. Chaitin, writes: '*Most people believe that anything that is true is true for a reason [but] some things are true for no reason at all.*'

More violent, unpredictable, and fragile than it has ever been believed before, our world is no longer a happy place for nine-tenths of our children to grow up in. We are too many to feed properly, to house adequately, to educate at all. As the Irish poet W. B. Yeats wrote of a far less anxious time: '*Things fall apart; the centre cannot hold . . . . The best lack all conviction, whilst the worst are full of passionate intensity.*'

What are we to do? Shall we throw up our hands and encourage children to believe in the games of the past? We have all played these games. The ones in which we invented special rules and names and passwords, rituals to which we admitted only our very special friends, telling others of fearful penalties for their trespass or disclosure.

In my primary school my friends and I made a headquarters for our game in an old air-raid shelter left beside the playground. Into its dark and smelly passages we would drag tiny tearful juniors to initiate them by smearing a magic poison on their left arm. This was actually nail varnish. As we smeared it on their arm, we would tell them that if they ever betrayed our secrets, or tried to wash it off, their arm would first turn black, then shrivel and fall off—and then they would die.

Our average age would have been between eight and nine. It is a humbling thought that there may be at least one seventy-year-old in the Manchester suburbs whose left arm is still unwashed.

Similar games as these today hold many hundreds of millions captive. How can they escape? Many will not want to. What they believe may give them a sense of comfort, security, and purpose that they cannot live without. It may require them to kill and die. This may be a price they are prepared to pay.

How can we offer hope to our children in this new, vast, terrifying universe? How can we explain to our children that those who use violence to demonstrate their power are only adult versions of the bullies in their playground?

We can begin by showing them the images of our common ancestors made by the Dutch twin brothers Adreie and Alfons Kennis (www.kenniskennis.com/index2.html). The earliest, *Australopithecus africanus*, lived from three to two million years ago. Then came *Homo habilus*, two million years ago; then *Homo erectus*, then *Homo heidelbergensis*, then *Homo neanderthalensis*, and, finally, or almost finally, we *Homo sapiens* arrived on the scene some 200,000 years ago.

We may show them the evidence of our Earth's fragility: the Ice Ages, the several super-eruptions, the many asteroid strikes, the rise and fall of the oceans, the cyclic switching of the Earth's magnetic poles, the wobble of its axis. Life, we can explain, had to survive all of these.

We should point to the trillions of stars now visible through the great rents that old Galileo began to make in the roof of the tent; to explain that there are good reasons to suppose that a fraction of their number, say a trillion or two, host worlds like ours; and that there may be even more universes, equally uncountable, in whatever other dimensions the black holes open onto.

Then we can ask our children's opinion! So, go ahead and ask them!

If there are intelligent beings on some of those worlds, what do they think all such beings, together with every other form of life, must share in order to survive?

Let them look again at our ancestors: at the fact that they have changed.

The principle of survival was explained by that wonderfully modest man, Charles Darwin. But his explanation involves a curious bias. Not challenged at the time, it is not challenged now.

Darwin proposed that some individuals of species change from time to time, always at random. The environment selects those changes which best suit the survival of the offspring of one of the slightly altered individuals. This whole process is mechanical.

You—and they—may notice the bias. It was anathema in Darwin's time—and still is—to suppose that a species might *actively* offer different forms of itself to be selected for survival by its environment. We might call this an active strategy rather than passive.

In our own case, as humans, we might call it being honest.

To make this strategy fit some other curious experiences that our species has had from time to time, we might recognize that every one of the games that people are still playing sets a high value on being honest.

And this honesty is said, invariably, to be by the direct command of God.

Love to all,

Colin.

Next: How God drives evolution.

31ˢᵗ October 2012

Dear Friends,

It never occurred to me and my friends that we might be causing our younger initiates any lasting mental or psychic harm in the mock initiation ceremony that we obliged them all to experience in the malodorous dark of our derelict air-raid shelter.

Although some squeaked and trembled on being anointed, others were stoic, others gleeful, some were ecstatic at the punishment we promised if ever they betrayed our secrets. But eventually, sadly, our nail varnish dried out completely, and the first of our games came to an end. We found almost immediately, however, that we had prepared an even more exciting diversion!

It had the advantage of being in the open air. It could involve the whole junior school. The infants we had baptized were only too eager to throw themselves into battles against the unbaptized. They joined enthusiastically in our holy wars until the Christmas holiday.

After Christmas we had snow-ball fights in which everyone was so muffled up with coats and scarves that all differences were forgotten. The year after that, I think, I must have passed the exam for grammar school, where life took another turn away from those childish joys.

Despite my wilful impiety, as it certainly was in practice, I do not believe my early atheism began this early. It emerged a few years later. My parents were different Christians. They decided I should be allowed to decide. I was sent to alternate churches on alternate Sundays.

The effect was disconcerting. Although both declared the same text to be sacred, there were some seriously different interpretations of its meaning. It seemed to me that an omnipotent divinity could have managed much better.

But then there was the deeper puzzle that this particular divinity was said to be simultaneously a son and his own father. He was said to have been born to a mother who was eternally virgin. He had been tortured and had died as a man. He then went to Heaven, where he is separate from his father, yet not separate, and both are accompanied by something called a Holy Ghost.

Most worrying in both was the requirement not to question, not to criticize: in essence, not to think. Faith, it was hammered into us, was all the reason that we would ever need for belief. Obedience was expected. Understanding was not required.

None of these seemed to me respectable demands from any divinity, far less from one I was supposed to thank repeatedly for making me capable of free will.

Consequently, at the age of eleven or twelve, I made a decision. I decided that I would not believe in anything that made no sense to me. This included the nonsense that both churches insisted was the sole defence against eternal punishment.

I remember being frightened at the thought of being alone. Thirty or more years I would be amused on passing my eyes over a

Baccalaureate exam paper in philosophy, and reading the demand: *'Describe and discuss the origin of existential anguish.'*

On the verge of adolescence, there can be a very real sense of existential anguish: of gaining independence, but of no-one really caring for one anymore. I decided to wait until I was a little older before making a definite break with God.

Instead, I discovered science: a world which encourages inquiry; in which people, even if they most passionately disagree, are drawn to work together; a world in which one is actually encouraged to disagree. I left behind my worries about His Holy Ghost.

I know now, of course, that science also has its heresies, its own rules; its own observances. It likes routines; conformity; regularity; order. It even has its own thought-police, although they are not much liked, because of their habit of pursuing vindictively.

Science does not admit to the value or importance of emotions. Science is supposed, above all, to be inhumanly dispassionate. This is nonsense, of course. Dispassionate discoveries may be possible by computers: but not by a human mind. Many scientists report a sudden sharp sense of emotional certainty, essentially of joy, just before rational certainty is sure. (See *Descartes' Error*, Damasio, A., 1994)

The general problem, therefore, is not to understand why religions screw up so much that an angry, injured little girl can be found defiantly writing 'FUCK YOU GOD'.

The solution to this general problem is that she has been fucked up by men, not God: specifically by men persuaded that they have a special dispensation to fuck up other people.

Such men can be recruited from all nations. Behind all the arguments for their violence will always be the most addictive pleasure known to man. It is the power of destroying lives.

This pleasure should never be ignored. It is the major male prophylactic against—of course—existential anguish. The only way to remove that anguish is to show how to open the doors to paradise without the keys of violence and destruction. I will look at that possibility in my last essay.

The special problem is much easier. It is to persuade scientists that the intense emotional and intellectual relief fundamental to a scientific discovery is exactly the equivalent to the intense emotional and intellectual experience fundamental to a spiritual discovery.

The difference is that in scientific discovery the emotional relief is comparatively minor. This is why, as we have seen, scientists could dismiss emotions as distraction.

The emotional relief in spiritual discovery is commonly so overwhelming that it is rational explanation that may be thought unnecessary.

These barriers create Stephen J. Gould's famous 'non-overlapping magisteria' of equally majestic but undemanding prolixity.

Solving our special problem requires a little more experience and a little more thought.

Reality is certainly not an illusion. If we pretend too much that it is, we die.

On the other hand, what we perceive as reality we now know is a mélange of sensations continually composed and recomposed by our minds.

Continually, and not continuously, because our awareness of it lags behind.

It takes an appreciable time to assemble all the parts and put them together. Ordinarily this is much easier because the reality we want to understand is much the same for all of us. This wish can be usurped only when unpredictable events pile in too fast.

The rational adventurer's attention is invariably focused on this solid-seeming reality. He is not attentive to anything else. He is, in this sense, distracted. He can expect only a relatively tiny change in this reality significant to him, and then significant to others.

The spiritual adventurer has to stake everything on one throw: sanity, future, life. He is likely to be in a dangerous situation, and yet, most paradoxical of all, he has to be calm: even if angry, still determined.

Deep in the bowels of a huge idol worshipped as reality by an entire people, the spiritual adventurer jerks open a hidden door, and is pitched without warning into a realm of immense energy and forces of which his mind has no previous experience. It happens so fast that his mind can seize only familiar images to convey to his conscious mind what is happening.

This is an important process. It can explain reports of many similar experiences.

Let me try to illustrate it from my own experience. Having reported, as briefly as possible, what seemed to be happening, I will then try to interpret these experiences sequentially.

There was first the clearly impossible perception of being carried through the entire universe to its outer limit: passing through galaxies, as I wrote for the Epiphany Philosophers in Cambridge University three years later, "like streamers of mist, radiating faint heat."

Then, a brief pause: looking into total darkness.

Then, that huge presence, expanding as it is rushing forward.

Then, the violent, crushing embrace.

Then, the assurance of kinship: **"You are of me!"**

Then, the audible advice I had asked for.

Then, the abrupt return.

Then, the residual image, but this I discovered only the next day.

Total interval: not more than fifteen seconds. I slept well. In the morning, at my first formal interview, I took the advice given. It has directed my life ever since.

Now the interpretation:

1. There is another reality far larger than ours;
2. It is home to an immeasurably powerful intelligence akin to ours;
3. It encourages us to survive;
4. It tells us how to survive;
5. It has many more forms of life to help survive;
6. You have a job to do: '***Go back and tell them***'.

When, at the end of my three weeks in his hospital I described the experience of the first night to its military director, he flicked the air as if at a fly. *"We don't want <u>that</u> in your record!"* he declared. The record shows I was there for hearing tests.

Vast sums have been spent on the SETI programme: on the belief that several million years ago a far more advanced civilization than ours began sending information to other civilizations how to save themselves from extinction; that we will be able to receive this information, will be able to understand it, and will be able to communicate it worldwide.

In contrast, my report was received, in somewhat unusual, but probably necessary, circumstances, by the ultimately most essential communication device that we humans possess: a healthy human mind. My report could hardly be easier to understand. It is equally easy to communicate.

To survive into the future, our children need to know that they have the right to be honest, and that they have the right to ask questions.

That's all.

I will next try to answer a final, very different question.

Colin.

Next: Check-point Charlie.

Entracte: On brevity!

Last Sunday I attended a conference on the future of Syria organized by the Next Century Foundation in the Initiatives for Change Centre in London.

The current situation is stark. Either the Assad regime prepares for democracy or there will be chaos and civil war. War will involve Turkey, Iraq, Israel, probably Iran. It will spread.

The deeper complexity in Syria was described by NCF director, William Morris. The population is divided into at least a dozen groups—regional, tribal, religious, and secular: Turkomen; Druse; Armenian; Ismaili; Christian; Jews; Alawite; Sunni; Palestinian. There is also the Kurdish nation, divided between

Syria, Turkey, Iraq, and Iran. At first there seemed little that I could say, and as usual I was nervous (believe me!), but encouraged by a lady in the audience who pointed me out repeatedly to the chairman. I first introduced myself and then said:

"There is an expression in English that refers to 'a sea change'. If you know the sea, you will know how quickly its moods can change. At present, the mood in this room is for war. Most of you can see no alternative. You need a sea-change. Of all the groups that I have heard spoken of in Syria, there is one that I have not heard mentioned, although it is more numerous than all the others combined. What is this group?"

I waited, hoping. After a moment, someone in the room responded: **"Women!"**

"Thank you." I continued. *"Women: women and children make up far more than half of the population of any country. There are two very simple principles that women, as mothers, can teach their children: two principles which, when understood by a majority, will automatically produce a democratic society."* I paused. *"The first principle is that they must always be as honest as they are able."* I paused: longer this time. *"And the second principle is that they must always know that they have a right to ask questions."*

I had to leave an hour before the end. As I did, I was met by three young men who had spoken passionately in earlier discussions. *"Come back!"* they requested. *"You have made more sense today than anyone else!"* Sadly, it was impossible for me to stay. But there was also no more to be said. Tell the women to tell their children: the future is theirs to make.

Penny Swann McBride, commenting on the ideas offered in the preceding **Entracte**: *"Absolutely brilliant!"*

Entracte:

One of the great mysteries of reflective thought is that from time to time one feels the presence of others. Usually their inspirations are recorded in books which one has had neither time nor inclination to read. Then it is often as if a ghostly librarian is plucking at one's sleeve to murmur: *"I really think you MUST notice this."*

Often this is just exasperating, for it may happen only after great effort. Sometimes, however, it is exhilarating. Here is an instance of the second kind.

I came to France for two weeks intending to try finally to bridge all the gaps between scientific reality, as currently understood, and my own impossible experience as a much younger man; the necessity to understand God as truly universal: that is, as encouraging all life everywhere to evolve ever more satisfactorily to be in an honest relation with its environment; the suggestion that the mind can interpret its perceptions of its immediate reality only in forms most familiar to it; that the 'black holes' of Wheeler, Hawking, et al., in being both exits and entrances to our reality, may constitute that which previous seers have perceived and interpreted—as, incidentally, I did—as entrances and exits of heaven; and, finally, but only in the final essay, that what I will call the idols of identity are the final barrier that children must be made aware of to be honest enough to evolve to the next natural level. Whether grinding these idols of identity to dust will immediately entitle them to 'enter heaven'—and whatever that may mean—I will leave it to others to decide.

The hardest line to write is always the first. In the first week I covered pages of scribble in vain, attempting to find my first line. I was close to despair.

But before leaving Oxford, I had bought a book from the Oxford University Press bookshop in the High for the sake of a quotation of Blaise Pascal.

Some of you will know that Pascal had some kind of experience aged 31, clearly a dangerous age, which caused him to abandon his earlier scientific studies to devote the rest of his short life to philosophy and theology. He died, aged 39, without ever being able to describe fully what that experience meant to him. Since he wrote in 17th-century French, I will venture to suggest how he might write it today:

"We do not content ourselves with the life we have in ourselves and in our own being; we desire to live a life in the mind of others, and for this purpose we endeavor to shine. We labour unceasingly to adorn and preserve this life in other minds at our own expense."

The OUP book has a horrible title: *'The Unimaginable Mathematics of Borge's Library of Babel'*, almost designed to deter most readers, and is in addition an extremely clever mathematics book, much of it beyond my dwarfish mind. Its author is a mathematics professor, William Bloch, who is, incidentally, also given to encourage his readers by referring to himself as Blockhead. Some intellectuals will stoop very low!

Looking for distraction, I found in Bloch's text another quotation by someone called Charles Sanders Peirce: 'Thus we may define the real as that whose characters are independent of what anybody may think them to be.'

I had never heard of Charles Sanders Peirce. In defence of my own ignorance, he was much concerned with logic and mathematics, and appears to have been much neglected by many others, although Bertrand Russell called him: "Beyond doubt . . . one of the most original minds of the later nineteenth century, and certainly the greatest American thinker ever," and Karl Popper is recorded as declaring Peirce to have been "one of the greatest philosophers of all times."

So, on the Sunday afternoon of my first week in France, I printed the 34 pages of the Stanford Encyclopaedia's account of Peirce's life's work in order to sit on my host's balcony to read through them all in the November sunshine whilst smoking my new meerschaum, wearing my beanie, my scarf, two vests, a fleece jacket and padded trousers, and marked the following, occasionally laughing out loud with pleasure: p. 11: 'For Peirce, the entire universe and everything in it is an evolutionary product.' *p.* 12: '. . . At any temporal point in the process of scientific inquiry we are only at a provisional stage of it and cannot ascertain how far off we may be from the limit to which we are somehow converging . . . . He called his first principle of reason: "Do not block the way of inquiry!"' p. 14: '. . . At the other end of the spectrum [of the nearly law-like behaviour of large physical objects] we see in human processes of imagination and thought an almost pure freedom and spontaneity.' p. 15: 'Peirce called his doctrine that chance has an objective status in the universe "tychism" . . . or "what the gods happen to choose to lay on one." . . . The most fundamental engine of the evolutionary process is not struggle, strife, greed, or competition. Rather it is nurturing love, in which an entity is prepared to sacrifice its own perfection for the sake of the well-being of its neighbour.' p. 16: '. . . The related sort of thinking that constituted for Herbert Spencer and others a supposed justification for the more rapacious practices of unbridled capitalism, Peirce referred to in disgust as "The Gospel of Greed".' p. 23: '. . . mind pervades all of nature in varying degrees; it is not found merely in the most advanced animal species.' p. 24: 'Whenever the representing relation has an instance, we find one thing (the "object") being represented by (or: in) another thing (the "representamen") and being presented to (or: in) a third thing (the "interpretant").'

I found this in an earlier reading of the entry on Peirce in Wikipedia, which is more entertaining, but choppier. It is what Peirce called "The Neglected Argument":

"If God Really be, and be benign, then, in view of the generally conceded truth that religion, were it but proved, would be a good outweighing all others, we should naturally expect that there would be some Argument for His Reality that should be obvious to all minds, high and low alike, that should earnestly strive to find the truth of the matter; and further, that this Argument should present its conclusion, not as a proposition of metaphysical theology, but in a form directly applicable to the conduct of life, and full of nutrition for man's highest growth."

This, of course, is North American 19th century verbosity at its most florid: never choose one word when five will do. But just two days before sitting down to plunder Bloch's book, I had written to my ever-patient editor in 21st century North America: 'If God is to be respected, he must be truly universal, truly affecting all forms of life everywhere in this vast cosmos in the same way.'

Do you now understand my relief and pleasure? I am not alone after all.

And I could, of course, also have used this, which some of you will recognize: "Truly, during the days of your existence, inspirations come from God. Do you not want to follow them? Tell unto reasoners that, for the lovers of God, intuition is guide, not discursive thought."

Now I can begin to explain how Science has discovered Heaven.

Best wishes, Colin.

29th November 2012

Science Discovers Heaven

"What can be said at all can be said clearly, and what we cannot talk about [clearly] *we must pass over in silence."* (Ludwig Wittgenstein)

"Natural selection at a higher level of organization may generate mechanisms that suppress the ability of disruptive 'outlaws' to go it alone at lower levels of organisations. Does selection on human groups act so as to limit the ability of individual humans to go it alone? Such questions are complex . . . but some of the most interesting work in cultural evolutionary theory may come from efforts to answer them." (Stanford Encyclopaedia of Philosophy on 'cultural evolution.')

There is no doubt that natural selection acts in higher level organisations to suppress 'disruptive outlaws'. In human groups selection certainly limits the ability of individuals to achieve independence. The white crow is soon pecked to death.

It has always been dangerous to attempt more honesty than a society allows. It is more dangerous in some cultures than in others. Those who attempt it in those cultures are to be greatly respected. It is wrong, however, to believe that western societies are entirely 'free'; that they do not suppress their own social outlaws. Less demonstrative than execution; less damaging than torture; less terrifying than secret prisons, they can produce similar symptoms of depression and despair.

Instead of being offered hemlock, there is indifference; instead of exile, unemployment. Whilst we Westerners have access to vastly more information than ever before, this may only reinforce a sense of helplessness in the face of political elites and elaborately manipulative governments. A new range of drugs has been developed called 'atypical antipsychotics' to suppress anxiety and frustration. They are called 'atypical' because they are intended for people who may appear perfectly normal.

It was once believed that anyone prepared to admit that they might be a little mad must be sane. It is now more likely to be thought that anyone insisting they are normal must be delusional. Forty years ago, when one of my Cambridge University mentors, Margaret Masterman, an early computer theorist, learnt that I was to teach school mathematics, she boomed cheerfully, in her usual manner: *"If you can stand teaching mathematics in a classroom for a few years, no-one will be able to call you crazy!"*

I am now not at all sure that this is entirely true. A few weeks ago in Oxford I felt a distinct chill when the eminent theologian with whom I was exchanging thoughtful views on theology revealed that she is still a clinical psychologist, and that in me she detected 'a struggle to achieve something'. This might be considered a sure sign of potentially dangerous action.

Once declared by a clinical psychologist to be in need of help, various 'treatments' can be applied. The most notorious, of course, is electro-shock. One of its most famous pioneers explained once: *". . . Some of the very best cures that one gets are in those individuals whom one reduces almost to feeble-mindedness."* Electro-shock is still used.

Naturally I thanked my friend for her anxiety. Quite apart from any mental damage, which they may anyway no longer be able to notice in their new state of feeble-mindedness, their social humiliation may cause people to be ever unable to think of themselves as normal. They have been made white crows. This may be considered its most useful consequence.

It is always an error to provoke governments whose rule depends on strength. These will nearly always block further discourse. In order to speak clearly, I suggest we proceed on the basis of four conjectures. These are simple: but, as I think you will find, they are far-reaching.

The first conjecture is that reality can be perceived only as familiar forms. Here we may find it useful to borrow the term 'representamen' from Peirce. It is ugly; but we need it to stand between the deeper reality and our perception. Recently I heard Lord Martin Rees, the Astronomer Royal, declare: *"There is no reason to suppose that the human brain will be able to understand ultimate reality."* An earlier expression of the same kind is: "The universe may be stranger than we can suppose." Even earlier is Plato's figure of the cave.

The second conjecture is that there are two evolutionary processes: not one. There is the familiar entropic process, materially destructive, either holding or degrading order; and there is the anentropic process, building order, especially as thought; and, through one universally present thought (see below), encouraging all life to adapt and survive. Another way of understanding both entropy and anentropy is in terms of quality of information. Entropy is then a measure of definite information which can only become less definite. A rock, for example, may have form, mass, position. All well-defined. With time, however, the rock degrades to dust and all this definite information is lost. Order has become disorder. Anentropy acts in the opposite sense.

The third conjecture is that our thoughts can only be representamens; they are naturally anentropic. The ill-defined becomes more and more definite; the most enduring thoughts (think of mathematics) have the nearest resemblance to their objects but may never **be** those objects.

The fourth conjecture is that the most powerful representamen the human mind can produce is the pure thought: 'I am'. In human lives, this becomes the human impulse to adapt actively to our environment. It becomes the fundamental impulse to be honest, on which all societies must build. In its strongest form it will appear to some human minds in certain circumstances as the perception of a physical being: as the 'representamen' of God. It appeared to Abraham as a terrifying sky-god; to Jesus, as a father figure. It should not surprise us if a soldier feels embraced by a warrior.

This is the context in which Jesus can be understood as far more important in being a man than, as required to be accepted by Christian mythologies, in being God. He was the first amongst the Jews to suggest that an individual may learn to have a private communion with God, and that this requires only confidence, privacy, and humility.

This alone was sufficient for the majority of Jews, that 'stiff-necked race', to hate him. Their rabbis told them that their existence depended—as they say now—on Abraham's God having adopted them as a people; that they had already received all the instruction that God requires them to follow; that all they need ever do is never to doubt or to question, only to obey.

Like this: *"When the LORD your God brings you into the land you are entering to possess and drives out before you many nations, and when the LORD your God has delivered them over to you and you have defeated them, then you must destroy them totally. Show them no mercy."*

(Deuteronomy 7:1-2)

From our point of view, it is interesting to realise that just as the many representamens of God display an evolutionary history, so too has science. Science has the happy distinction of finding a balance between entropy and anentropy: between the need to conserve order with progress. Its first principle is that everyone has a right to ask questions. This is fundamental to democracy. The second is that any authority may be called to account. This is the Rule of Law.

Jesus made himself even more hated by his own people—and more of a nuisance to their Roman overlord—by declaring that, within their own lifetime, they might see the kingdom of God. This, let it be remembered, was in a very minor country on the edge of an empire whose emperor was its god.

"Verily I say unto you, that there be some of them that stand here, which shall not taste of death, till they have seen the kingdom of God come with power." (Mark 9:1)

How could a kingdom of God come about within their lifetime? And why *'with power'*?

Jesus was offering a peaceful way to retrieve political independence. The kingdom of God was democracy. It would come 'with [the] power' of democratic government.

It was a wonderful idea. But from the reports of his turbulent life, it is clear that Jesus was constantly pulled in three directions. In one lay his determination to continue the most fundamental Jewish moral tradition: of treating others, even enemies, as equals (Matthew 7:12; Luke 6:31).

A second was to invite other Jews to understand his representamen, the Father, as equally theirs. (Matthew 6:6)

But he must eventually have concluded, perhaps in despair, that those who wanted him to be their military leader were right, telling them: *"If you don't have a sword, sell your cloak and buy one."* (Luke 22:36) This comedic insurrection failed before it began. No wonder the Jerusalem mob, always ready to jump both ways, shouted their preference for Barabbas.

As a first scientist, Jesus discovered an entirely temporal meaning of the kingdom of God. But could this really be the home of the god of Abraham and Moses? Could this really be the house of his Father? Is there a world beyond this world? If so, who may be invited to enjoy it? Why should others fail?

We have also now a way to understand why some societies try to stand still, but degrade; whilst others progress too fast, and implode. Once again it may be that only women, the neglected half of humankind, can create a balance: in this world, perhaps in a next.

In my next essay, I want to examine these possibilities.

Next: The Idolatry of Identity

Entracte: On Evolution and Fundamentalism

What Ludwig Wittgenstein meant by his famous aphorism: *What we cannot speak about we must pass over in silence,* is that if we wish to convince others to look differently at reality, we must first find words to describe the differences, then use them to show that these differences are real.

I became interested in philosophy only after I qualified as an engineer. I soon discovered that whilst I could follow others' ideas, I was far less able to think originally.

My attempts soon brought a further realization. I could not be sure that what I thought I understood from others was what they intended. It was as if the earth had become empty space.

This was terrifying. It also helped me into the army's psychiatric hospital. I had already annoyed the government by protesting against its using the army to suppress civil unrest, but when the senior medical officer sent to interview me asked me, in the friendliest manner, how I used my spare time, he next inquired: "And what do you find especially interesting in philosophy?" I told him that I was trying to understand how meaning is communicated; that, in all but the simplest circumstances, it appears highly problematic.

From Ludwig, this would have been routine. The brigadier frowned. *"Isn't this a rather unusual interest,"* he paused, *"for an engineer?"*

I almost replied that Jesus was a carpenter. Out of deference to his rank, I only shrugged.

Three days later I was a mental patient. Communication failed!

Wittgenstein, as you may know, was helped to become a member of Trinity College, Cambridge, by Bertrand Russell. Some years later I was helped there by the government's need for mathematics teachers.

Almost immediately I came under the protection of a group of distinguished thinkers: the New Testament scholar John Robinson, then Dean of Chapel, the philosopher Dorothy Emmet, the theologian Donald MacKinnon. It was Donald McKinnon who one day explained why they felt I needed protection: *"There are killers in this university."* I had dinner one evening with Dean Robinson in his lodging, when he also warned me against any attempt to talk with other theologians, explaining: *"They won't like that you know from experience what they only know from their books."*

Later I realised that he meant that the sincerity of theologians' belief in events of thousands of years ago would not necessarily allow them all to believe in similar events in modernity. What he and his group of like-minded scholars—they called themselves The Epiphany Philosophers—did for me was undoubtedly invaluable. But to be treated—if only for one year—as a full member of this immensely famous college was equally important. Simply in crossing Trinity's great inner court one seems to breathe in the molecules of genius: lively, mischievous, inspiring. Its full and proper name is of course a celebration of the doctrine of the Trinity, of God the Father, God the Son, and God the Holy Ghost, all one and indivisible.

In his later years the difficulty of believing this mysterious and deeply illogical statement would later keep Sir Isaac Newton, even then the College's most famous scholar, in some trepidation lest his lost belief in it be discovered. It never was. Perhaps others never asked.

Ludwig Wittgenstein realised, years before I did, that even when the greatest effort is being made to communicate meaning, even when there is the most sincere wish to understand, the result may be imperfect. The pen of the scholar is certainly powerful. But many words have different meanings. The scholar's bane can very easily become a warrior's cause.

I have borrowed the concept of entropy from physics, mathematics, and information theory. It is variously understood to mean a measure of the certainty of information; the direction in which order becomes disordered; a measure of information lost. There may at first be perfect order. Over time it will be lost. Information at first may be certain. In time it will become less certain. Over short intervals, information may transmit without loss. Over longer intervals, loss must occur. Everything, it would seem, depends on time: which makes one wonder, what if there are actions, or interactions, in which time is not a factor?

Actually, none of this is entirely new. Over two millennia ago Heraclitus pointed out: '*You cannot step into the same river twice.*'

This is why no society can be without change. Societies may be caused to believe that the information by which they are defined is perfect and complete. In time, however, opinions will inevitably begin to differ: causing division. Some may eventually decide that nothing is certain; that everything authoritatively defined has been invented to divide societies from other societies, and now divides them internally; that only doubt freely unites; and that they should therefore not believe anything.

There is, however, another aspect of reality that we must notice.

It is that some systems which are originally poorly defined, disordered, and incomplete, become increasingly definite, ordered, and complete. They achieve a period of stable—or at least relatively stable—existence in both space and time.

This process is true of all organic evolution. The acorn becomes an oak. But it is also true of thought. If thinking is only a random process—as is supposed to be true of biological evolution—we would have to wait for sentences to form themselves. Since, clearly, meaning can be constructed, and since, at least approximately, it can be conveyed, it is legitimate to look for the impulse of this process, its direction, even its aim.

I have given this impulse the rather obvious name of *anentropy*. The very great physicist Edwin Schroedinger once suggested *negentropy*. I think anentropy is more elegant, and Schroedinger never suggested that this negentropy is the origin of life, or that it produces the desire to be honest, or that its direction is towards refining the meaning of: 'I am'.

Well, I may have some information about the aim: but its representamen is still something of a mystery to me, and by now I am conscious that I must be near to exhausting your patience. I therefore intend to write only one more essay. It will be on the attempt to ignore Heraclitus with regard to life, on attempting to usurp God's determination of your identity. If the collection is turned into a book, a last final chapter can describe my final mystery. And my work will be done! Please tell me if you think this worth doing!

Despite the seriousness with which I was treated in Cambridge, and later, with even more loyalty, by others, it has always been possible that my experience was simply a delusion.

If so, this would be true of all other experiences of similar nature. Against this hypothesis is that they have all appeared to create a powerful sense of responsibility to turn the experience, not only into useful information, but into a new statement of what is more universally useful.

This is very hard work. It has ruled my life for forty years. I have repeatedly hoped that this responsibility might be taken by another. But this has never happened. So here we are.

These two words now allow us to understand the aim and direction of most societies. A society ruled by the entropic impulse will emphasise stability, conformity, moral and rational certainty. It will insist on total acceptance of these principles. Social mobility will be limited by heredity, class, or political allegiance. The education of children will be given much attention, as will be the obedience of women, especially as mothers.

Paradoxically, however, as in the case of the ultimate warrior state of Sparta, in entropic societies women may exert the most control. A warrior or priestly caste may believe that they are in control, but this is only to provide the stability that women require to rear their children, being assisted by their mothers and by the mothers of their husbands.

I have long admired the poetry of Genesis. Although modern feminists may be outraged, my admiration becomes boundless if the apple given to Adam by Eve is intended to represent the loss of human freedom by the limitations produced by total moral and rational certainty. To communicate such deep meaning for all time to all cultures is genius indeed! Only the anentropic impulse saved humankind from an endless Stone Age.

Eden is behind us. Can anything like that mythical freedom be recovered?

Historically, the anentropic impulse had first had the representamen of a fierce warrior god, urging the destruction of old idols, the abandoning of ancient worship: demanding new ideas, new adventures, a vision of a new future, even demanding war. As I once explained to my royal host in Qatar, to many men war has been a necessary adventure.

Sacred to the anentropic mind is this need and ability to adventure spiritually, rationally, artistically; to refine the old and create new information. But this is why the anentropic impulse can also be dangerous. Remember Enrico Fermi's explanation of why he helped create the first atom bomb: *"It was interesting physics!"*

Or Richard Feynman's more troubled response: *"We just didn't think, okay? We just didn't think!"* Such thinkers may be indifferent to the poverty, the misery, and the want. Many scientists are wholly engaged in their own spiritual adventure. It is their kind of war.

Social stability is at least as important as personal glory. What is required is balance.

I may have surprised many of you by revealing that I have great respect for inspired religions. I can see in them repeated attempts to encourage a new level of honesty, and simplicity, also always of valour.

If the cultures they inspire become entropic, this is understandable. Originally, however, they were always anentropic. *"Hey, wake up at the back there! This concerns you!"* If now the wish of young people is to be more fundamental, they need to recognise that being fundamentalist means becoming anentropic again, and not—a very *big mistake*—more entropic!

Some years ago I heard HRH Prince El Hassan of Jordan declare that the divisions of Islam are *"a disaster for the entire human race!"*

I wrote to him later to say that all divisions are disastrous for the human race. If we know why they occur, we may perhaps be able to heal them. But there will be many whose authority—and status and income—depends not just on maintaining the divisions, but on even deliberating and malevolently increasing them. *'There are few people'*, Lord Russell once remarked, *'whose happiness is not markedly increased by having someone, some nation, or some creed, to hate.'*

In a previous essay I introduced the idea that theologies invariably stagnate, that they evolve from anentropic to entropic.

I have never seen this expressed before; although it seems both obvious and important. Although diversity is important in evolution, and is essential to democracy, it would certainly be an important benefit to the entire human race if the process could be reversed.

But this cannot be achieved by young people who allow themselves to be called 'revolutionaries'. Revolutions invariably end in chaos. Everyone knows this. Everyone of sense fears this. Do not even think of yourselves as revolutionaries. Do not allow others to call you revolutionaries. Others will soon choose to call you 'terrorists'.

This is a very useful way to avoid taking your ideas seriously.

If, however, young people, young priests, young imams, young rabbis, can see a better future in recovering the fundamental impulse of all theologies, to unite, not divide, they can begin to converge. This would soon smoke out those who benefit from keeping societies divided.

Love to you all,

Colin

25ᵗʰ-31ˢᵗ December 2011

The Idolatry of Identity

"What a piece of work is a man! How noble in reason! how infinite in faculty! in form, in moving, how express and admirable! in action how like an angel! in apprehension how like a god! the beauty of the world! the paragon of animals!"

Shakespeare, *Hamlet,* II.2; note 'of animals': in 1599.

"There may be a sense in which the physical, mental, and mathematical worlds merely reflect individually aspects of a deeper truth about a world of which we have little conception at the present time."

Penrose, R., Mathematician, 2004

I imagine that most of us woke up on this Christmas morning warm and secure, looking forward to the pleasures of the day. I wonder how many spared a thought for those who will know nothing like our security, not on this day or any other, because they fear as mothers for their children's future.

And I wonder too: how many of my old friends, who first encouraged me to try to explain why I taught them as I did, are still reading these essays? Three months of thinking, writing, puzzling, abandoning texts, researching, revising, rewriting. It has been a long haul.

Anyone who has ever tried to transform first mental tensions into thoughts, then thoughts into words, then words which may, as one hopes, make sense to others, will know the determination this requires. Also some pain. I may, in the meantime, have lost you all. If so, entirely thanks to you, I understand our world a little better. This is always hard work.

At first I was mainly addressing the girls, many now mothers, whom I once had the privilege to teach. I realize that it must have been distinctly discouraging when I invited you to take part in 'the most dangerous game in the world'.

But this is no exaggeration. Young women have long been treated by men, often by their families, as either tradable goods or a burdensome nuisance. Becoming a mother achieves some security, but the labels of mental and moral instability, traditionally imposed on women, make it nearly impossible for them to prevent men from fomenting, preparing, and making war. Given the number of nations now with nuclear weapons and Stone Age ambitions, given a still spiraling world population, our children's future is more uncertain than at any time in history.

This is our responsibility. We have the tools; we have the voice.

It is a little noticed fact that women achieved national suffrage in the leading industrial countries only after major wars: in Russia, 1917; in Germany, 1918; in the United States, 1920; in Britain, 1928; in France, 1945; in Japan, 1945; in Israel, 1948; in Iran, 1963; and, as useful counterexample, in Switzerland, 1971.

There is also an encouraging precedent in achieving a major change in the way that people understand their spiritual and rational potential: by writing.

When, in 1517, Dr Martin Luther pinned his protests of Papal power to his church's door in Wittenberg, he had no intention of weakening the source of its power: the terror of Hell.

He only questioned the power of the Church to control his punishment.

Today I suppose it is nearly impossible for us to feel the same degree of terror. In Luther's time, the Church depended on it. In return for its protection, it demanded people's loyalty and unquestioning obedience. In return, it gave them their identity. And collected its tithes.

What Luther was challenging was neither the wealth of the Church nor the reality of Hell. It was this idolatry of identity. He declared that God can speak to anyone: directly, regardless of their rank, gender, or social station; and that priests, in particular, were actually unnecessary.

Almost at once peasants everywhere rose up against their serfdom. Palaces were stormed; libraries burnt. Many died before, with Luther's help, their rebellion was cruelly put down.

Although clearly never his intention, the long process of establishing the right of people to decide what to believe independent of authority began with Luther's questions. In my classroom, I now realise, I was simply continuing this tradition. One of my friends recently added thoughtfully: "And maybe it was because you treated your pupils with respect!"

Atheism is an entirely healthy product of this process. I am a friend of atheism: although I am sure, and I am sure that Luther was sure, that atheism is not the most intelligent alternative to idolatry. The most intelligent alternative is more scepticism. With the realisation, if it is not to fall into idolatry itself, that scepticism has also a source. It, too, can speak to people directly, of all ranks and all social stations. They need only to learn to listen intelligently.

As a first step in learning how to listen, I suggested that new mothers begin to tell their children always to know that they have a right to be honest; and always to know that they have the right to ask questions. This would soon produce a generation of young messiahs.

To my surprise, this modest proposal was furiously denounced both by my pious and my atheist friends. They all accused me of their own notion of impiety.

Fortunately, reality can correct such superstitions.

The huge surge of mainly young people's protest against corrupt government and dishonest corporations is happening because they have begun to decide that they have the right to be honest and to ask questions. Even more striking is how many young women are prepared to risk beating, imprisonment, rape, disfigurement, and death in order to take part.

Essentially they are finally challenging the tradition of Eve's wicked deceit.

There are many variations of the story. We will find this fact to be significant. In most cultures it is a kind of Disneyland justification of traditional, but continuing, female debasement.

Of course, you may say, it is entirely natural of primitive societies to divide responsibilities this way. The women then benefit from a society's stability in which to raise children. The men decide how this stability will be sustained. But can the story be read in a different way?

Most recently I showed how we can escape from Wittgenstein's prison: in which we are obliged to remain silent without words to speak.

The two words we need are admittedly a little clumsy; but one gets used to them. 'Entropic' describes the tendency of ordered structures to decay, unless carefully restrained. 'Anentropic' describes the fact that ordered structures can become more ordered, ultimately even conscious.

The appearance of life requires a very special kind of anentropic impulse, prompting life to appear by refining material order until consciousness appears, then allowing it to adapt actively to its environment. The mechanism by which *the environment* selects adaptations is insufficient to explain the vast variety of life. And, further, if such an active impulse acts on Earth, it must act everywhere in the universe. Human exceptionalism is just another idolatry.

By curious incident, when I left the Army, I was offered work by a man who, as I slowly discovered, was a great-grandson of Charles Darwin. He was just as cautious as his great-grandfather had been. Later, when we were friends, and when I might ask him to decide on one truth or another, he would often reply: "Why not a bit of both?"

'A bit of both' produces the best modern consensus of evolution. Instead of Intelligent Design there is the Anentropic impulse.

Similarly, a different way of reading Eve's story requires no perversity of judgment.

Eve might have kept the apple. Instead, she *gave* it to Adam. It was women, in other words, who first decided that men should be responsible for maintaining social stability. Inevitably, the only order they are able to create is entropic. To prevent disorder from appearing, ever more regulations are required. One can see this in the most modern societies.

The rest is history. Having given over social control to men, women were ever more oppressed. Modern attempts to enfranchise women: in Jordan, in 1974; in Qatar, in 1997; in Saudi Arabia, promised—are evidence that they are now needed to save societies from paralytic decay.

Women, as I once told HH Sheikha Mozah of Qatar, cannot prevent wars, but women can help men to find more fruitful spiritual adventures than wars. This is what education can achieve.

But the mystery remains: what does the Garden of Eden represent?

What did our ancestors lose when they left it?

Only Abraham, Jacob, and Jesus are said to have seen God face to face. They felt his physical presence and they heard his voice They spoke of Heaven as a place where God resides. I think it may be understood as a level of consciousness everyone can achieve.

In the last analysis, the basis of this consciousness is nothing supernatural or esoteric. It is simply honesty. The Sufic tradition approaches it very nearly: but without words to speak, the great Sufi teachers have been obliged to be silent.

Science strives to be honest. Accepting that its striving is also spiritual can save it from the ultimate verdict of triviality.

This is the last of my Facebook essays. I will now retire to my cave to turn them into the book that I have promised. In its final chapter I will explain why I think that Heaven—impossibly—may still have a physical, if not a temporal, existence; and why I cannot think otherwise.

Forty years ago I could never have written these essays. It was not that I was frightened. It was not because I was unsure. It was because I would have been treated as a clown.

Now I have served my time. I have also learnt to speak.

But I like to think I am nothing special. We are just pioneers.

Thank you all.

Colin

25ᵗʰ January 2012

Who is God?

Thanks to the magic of the internet, I was recently able to watch the famous discussion between the four distinguished thinkers: Dawkins, Dennett, Harris, and Hitchens, concerning the existence of God.

The most read of their books is almost certainly Richard Dawkins' '*The God Delusion*', closely followed by Sam Harris's '*The End of Faith*'; then Christopher Hitchens' '*god is not Great*'

[sic]; and, finally, by the most professionally qualified as an eminent philosopher, Daniel Dennett's *'Breaking the Spell'*.

They all arrived at the same conclusion: God does not exist.

Individually they offered further opinions: that those who still believe that God exists are weak-minded, deluded, hysterical, or mad; and, if they impress their beliefs onto children, are evil. But they also insisted that they must be *dishonest.*

It was the last that appeared to me most perverse.

What if these extremely confident and competent thinkers forced themselves to *imagine* believing in God? Would they then suppose that they had suddenly become credulous, deluded, hysterical, or mad—or would they try to understand the world more thoughtfully?

Their real problem, of course, is that they do not know what to imagine. They lack any experience of God. Without any experience of God, they cannot understand the concept.

The German philosopher Husserl described the sequence by which knowledge is formed as: experience; followed by concept; followed by name.

When I mentioned this to an even wiser friend, he pointed out that a concept may also be prior to experience. This observation later turned out to be even more important. A simple example: a table may be first experienced as the surface to which a mother calls her family to have dinner. This forms both concept and name. It is then only a step to relate the concept to any similar flat surface: from the microscope's table, to a sheet of paper; even to a flat-topped mountain.

What if the experience of God is unique? What if it is literally incomparable? In King Solomon's 'Song of Songs' it is made akin to sexual ecstasy. If even *this* is inadequate, then those who have no experience of God are not being dishonest in declaring that they do not understand what others mean: but they are still wrong to claim the concept has no content.

Let me introduce Dr Richard Bucke.

For twenty-five years Dr Bucke was superintendent of an asylum for the insane. There he must have had a wide experience of the feeble-minded, hysterical, mad and evil. In 1872, aged 35, he had what he believed was an experience of God.

He seems to have been a solidly sensible man. Nowadays, we would call his experience transcendent. He set out to catalogue similar experiences, publishing them in a book called 'Cosmic Consciousness'. His list contains the usual suspects, with thirty-six more.

What is most interesting to me is his attempt to describe the primary characteristics of the person most likely to experience God. They are men—patience, ladies!—'*between 30 and 40, with good intellect, high morals, a superior physique, and an earnest religious feeling.*'

When I first read this I found it as unsettling as young Gordon Kerr's explanation, years ago, of why he, I, and Andrew Nightingale were different from the hundred other young officers on our Warminster staff course: '*We are killers: they are not. They would hesitate: we would not.*'

This is a detail missing from Bucke's formula. It makes me wish I might meet some intended suicide bombers, for we might be able to talk. On the other hand, I must reject: *"earnest religious feeling"*, unless this includes being earnestly atheist, for this I then was.

The rest fits exactly. I was 29; mentally and physically extremely fit; trained to be calm under stress: trained, above all, to observe and recall accurately. In addition, to excuse that other quality, a certain determination is undoubtedly required to pursue the truth: not for days, not for weeks, or for months, but for years. To catch a glimpse of that young man follow: www. gardenofdemocracy.org/source.html, also archived in The Way Back Machine.

You will find his report unusual in involving both a very powerful movement and a physical encounter. It also left a visual memory, of darkness, as opposed to light, and in the darkness an object and place. It is as if one is being told: *"This* is here." Later I will explain why this may be important scientifically.

Knowledge can be developed in the form of new experiences derived from a concept.

This is clearly how the first tools were made. A rock is used as a hammer. This experience creates the concept 'tool'. But now the concept can inspire new experience: 'blade', 'scraper', 'borer', 'point', 'hook', 'knife', 'spear', and so on.

Science can develop in either direction. The experience 'heat', for example, creates the concept 'action at a distance'. It was the advent of this concept, in explanation of gravity, magnetism, etc., that began the raising of science from the mechanical into the electric age.

Unique personal experiences may also be understood to have a universal significance. This is often how sciences develop. Can consciousness move still higher? Theoretical physicists are just beginning to invent their own metaphysics.

Distinguished scholars of unique transcendent experience have little difficulty in deciding which is authentic, and which not. The problem, however, is not to judge authenticity. It is to know what it means. For a discussion of this, see http://gardenofdemocracy.org/trinity.html.

The gentlemen doubting God in the first debate are all well-intentioned and highly intelligent. It is impossible not to share their anguish, their horror that the concepts of holiness, perfection, and faith have been attached to so many unrelated experiences: from speech to texts, gestures, dress, names, places, land, and, not least, to the people themselves who exalt themselves in this way above others. And this is all called sacred knowledge!

This was far more understandable when stars were holes in the roof of a tent. To believe now—with the knowledge that we have now of the immensity of the universe—that the God whose command directs and guides life throughout this immensity has any interest at all in mankind's notions of the sacred is no longer possible. Such hubris is absurd: and dangerous.

It soon became apparent to me in my own case that conscious experience is not always as simple as we suppose. Minds have to present unfamiliar experiences in familiar forms which consciousness recognises. These are the forms the American philosopher Charles Peirce called 'presentamen'.

This addition to our understanding of knowledge makes it possible to interpret my flight across the universe—a journey which an eminent Oxford theologian, otherwise respectful, gravely informed me was 'physically impossible'—as a presentamen. Perhaps it was meant only to signify the shallowness of our awareness of existence: and not that I discovered WarpDrive.

My real task was to understand the significance of the whole. That God appeared to me as a warrior, young Kerr would have found delightful, and understandable. We humans have long created images of our gods as warriors. Even Pallas Athena was armed. Such presentamen fit the world ruled by Zeus from Mount Olympus. It no longer fits ours.

For years I struggled to understand the concept to be derived from my experience. It had to be respectful of all of those who have made this journey before—and I believe there are many more than Dr Bucke counted—but it had to state God's demand in words that everyone would now understand. There was no longer any question of a chosen people. We are all chosen.

In addition, of course: *Why me?* Out of all the millions so much cleverer, more important or more influential, why choose a young soldier on his first night in a modern lunatic asylum? Why not a pope, or a patriarch, or president? Someone with some power!

The answer that finally restored my balance was to realise it was just an accident.

Circumstances placed me in just the right place, in just the right frame of mind—with, as it turned out, the right support—perfectly tuned to receive a signal tirelessly sweeping through this universe. I was just a good receiver. More circumstance made me a teacher. Then I realised that all the sciences are a product of this signal too.

This is why I taught as I did. It will sound a little dramatic, but I could not allow myself to teach dishonesty. I had to teach you to test truths for yourselves.

"Be honest!" is the message addressed to life throughout the universe. This is far more haphazard than intelligent design. Because few environments welcome life, the command becomes: 'build', 'build', 'adapt', 'adapt'. Any form of life must adapt honestly to

its environment. Any that cannot adapt are destroyed. This is how evolution works. It is a constant fight to stay alive guided by the simple universal message: *"Be honest!"*

The purpose of all religions is to provide comfort, security, identity. Secular societies are not necessarily wiser or happier without religions, but are less likely to be controlled by men.

As I was writing, an Oxford scientist published his conclusion—presumably after many years of research—that most wars are caused by men.

Hmmm.

That's interesting.

There is another possibility, equally well-known.

If the personification of the constructive impulse is imagined by men to be a hugely more powerful version of themselves, much the same has happened to the destructive impulse.

Virtually every culture has imagined it personified as Satan.

In most traditions, Satan finds it much easier to take control of men.

And ironically the most vicious wars are usually caused by men who announce the fact by stating, *"I am certain."*

It's just a trick of English. But this is interesting as well.

My next essay will explain how mothers can teach their children the sense of the goodness of all religions, and of science: and how this may stop the shame and waste of wars.

30ᵗʰ January 2012

Who is Certain?

Most human societies have imagined God to be in human form. Most have agreed to be told how God wants them to behave.

I have proposed that behind all the many forms of social behavior which have emerged in this way is a far more fundamental imperative.

We now know of countless billions of galaxies, of trillions of possible worlds. No matter whether simple or complex, the probability of an organism's survival will depend on its active adaptation to its environment. This active adaptation can be generally described as learning to be honest: not demanding to be accommodated by a changing environment whilst remaining unchanged; constantly exploring the possibilities of a more fitting adaptation.

Whilst this requires only a minor change to the more mechanistic theory of evolution, it requires a very much more drastic reduction of belief in God as an all-knowing, all-powerful father figure; and even more particularly of a God believed to be especially concerned with the survival of only a minority of people.

Many societies imagine that active forms of the discouragement of life may also be material. Demons are held to be responsible for many misfortunes, and the most powerful of these is imagined to have one name. His name is Satan.

In Judaic and other traditions, Satan has actually a special responsibility to God. He is sent by God to try to seduce men and women from remembering their duty.

But what, essentially, is this duty to God?

There is usually little disagreement in a new faith concerning this imperative. Initially, nothing may be required but a simple avowal of belief.

But, as they have matured, the same difficulty has arisen in most. Different interpretations are announced by different scholars and schools of scholars to be more certain than others.

These new certainties will not be accepted by everyone. Some agree. Some disagree. Some are not sure. The most certain faction decides it is most faithful. The less certain are held to be less faithful, even heretical. It becomes important to decide what to do with them.

Written at the beginning of the 18th century, 'Gulliver's Travels' contains a savage parody of how such matters may be resolved:

". . . *the Bulk of the People consist wholly of Discoverers, Witnesses, Informers, Accusers, Prosecutors, Evidences, Swearers . . . It is first agreed, and settled among them, what suspected persons shall be accused of a plot; Then, effectual Care is taken to secure all their Letters and Papers, and put the Owners in Chains. These papers are delivered to a Set of Artists, very dexterous in finding out the mysterious Meanings of Words, Syllables, and Letters . . . Where this Method fails, they have two others more effectual, which the Learned among them call Acrostics and Anagrams. First, they can decipher all initial Letters into political Meanings . . . Secondly, by transposing the Letters of the Alphabet . . . they can lay open the deepest Designs of a suspected Party."*

This may be imagined as how Satan works. A fraction of people of a faith are persuaded that they are more certain than others. All the work that brought them together is destroyed. Soon the same will begin to happen again, and again.

It is not necessary to believe that this is Satan's work. It is caused by being certain.

The day before I decided to attempt this essay, a friend sent me some notes I had made in 2009 in an old house in the Hebrides without telephone or radio, but with a great library of books.

They arrived the day I began. They contain a perfect set of quotations, collected, then forgotten. Neither Jonathan Swift nor my next helper refers to Satan to explain how people within a faith, religious or political, may drive their scholars to define its particulars with ever greater certainty, with the inevitable consequence of creating ever more heresies and heretics, dividing their faith into even more mutually loathing factions.

Three centuries after Swift, Albert Schweitzer, after being awarded the 1952 Nobel Peace Prize, offered this explanation:

"The organised political, social, and religious associations of our time are at work to induce the individual man not to arrive at his convictions by his own thinking but to make his own such convictions as they keep ready-made for him. Any man who thinks for himself and at the same time is spiritually free, is to them something inconvenient and even uncanny. He does not offer sufficient guarantee that he will merge himself in their organization in the way they wish. All corporate bodies look today for their strength not so much in the spiritual worth of the ideas

they represent and to that of the people who belong to them, as to the highest possible degree of unity and exclusiveness. It is in this that they expect to find their strongest power for offense and defense." (in 'My Life and Thought', H. Holt Inc. 1933; Mentor 1953)

The Korean War had begun two years before. The Cold War which followed was to last for thirty years and consume tens of trillions of dollars of essentially useless expenditure both by the West and by the Soviet bloc, whilst making the secrets of nuclear, chemical, and biological weapons ultimately available to every true patriot and any serious crackpot of every nationality.

Yesterday evening I was privileged to hear a lady lecturer of psychology talk about the historic Jewish tradition of the possession of women by spirits: not, please note, by spirits of men, just spirits.

Invited to question at the end of her talk, I asked: *"It is the obvious presumption of modern psychiatry that a minority of people are sick whilst the majority are sane. Has anyone ever considered that the reverse may be true?"*

This is not at all a frivolous question. In mediaeval Christianity, and still in modern Christian dogma, the majority of people are irreversibly damaged morally by Original Sin. Only a few priests are unscathed.

The lady was somewhat bouleversed, as the French might say; but she made a brave attempt to reply. *"How could we know if that is true?"* she asked in return.

Her question was then answered by a tall rabbi, immaculate in black, sitting behind me with his wife and family. *"The majority,"* he suggested, *"would behave pathologically."*

How can we teach our young people not to behave pathologically: to ignore all Satan's tricks and seducements, to regain both the sense of their unique good fortune to be alive on this precious world of ours, in the immensity of its vast universe, and of the intelligence and determination required of them to return to God's path and survive?

The extraordinary diversity of Satan's repertoire of flim-flam is again apparent in the modern perplexity of whether or not anyone, young or old, has actually any ability to choose.

This is no minor problem. To many philosophers, consciousness and free will appear so difficult to define that it is simpler for them to insist that neither exists: rather like God.

Some weeks ago I had an occasion to test this belief when I was trying in an earlier essay to describe the range of human emotions.

I wrote that, of course, at one end of the spectrum there is 'hate', whilst at the other is 'doubt'. No! I didn't mean that. I meant to write 'love'. The opposite extreme to hatred is obviously love. Of course! Whatever did I mean by writing 'doubt'?

By now, as you will realise, two levels of my consciousness are deployed. The one which I intended to write: 'love'. The other: which I wrote differently.

The first level is surprised. The second is waiting.

Curiously, I felt no compulsion to erase this mistake. This was because a still higher level of consciousness, just now engaged, was telling me: *'It's true. Leave it.'*

And so, trusting that final level, and although I did not understand why, I left it.

I had exercised free will.

If any of you have read of my experience already, you may also know that I am possibly possessed by several spirits. One repeatedly annoys me by producing the most splendid support for ideas *after* I have struggled and sweated to outline them.

The example above is unusual. There must have been some reason not to work to rule.

Another spirit guards my door to paradise. Yet another holds the key to all the knowledge that I felt was streamed into my twenty-nine-year-old mind in those few seconds of illumination.

It is not easy to retrieve this kind of knowledge. Plato and his old friend and tutor Socrates believed that much the same store is possessed unknowingly by everyone, and that to help them retrieve it everyone needs a very careful and very patient teacher.

The great obstacle to their being successful is described in Plato's famous parable of the prisoners in the cave. They can see only the shadows thrown on the wall in front of them by the light of reality streaming in from the cave's entrance behind them. They cannot stand up, turn around, or leave their cave to see the reality outside.

To this, Swift and Schweitzer might add: and they dare not.

Shortly after my question, I was joined over the chocolate fudge cake—chocolate fudge cake and intellectual challenge: an unbeatable combination—by a young man, about the age of most of you, with some interesting questions for me.

Whilst we ate fudge cake, I discovered him to be a physicist.

Oxford University's physicists may not be the smartest in the world, but as Yogi Bear might remark: 'They're still smarter than they really need to be.'

"Which is more powerful in science," I asked him finally, *"truth or doubt"?*

Without hesitation, he replied: "Doubt".

Which is why, without knowing why, I wrote: *'doubt'.*

Science has learnt how to avoid Satan's trap. Most other systems of thought have not.

Satan's trap is certainty. To avoid it, all one has to do is to renounce being certain so eagerly. It's not so much more difficult than taking a smaller slice of fudge cake. Try instead to be honest about what you really know: not what you have been told. And keep on asking questions.

Paradise is this way: Hell, is in the other.

5ᵗʰ February 2012

How to Educate Messiahs

All that your children really need to develop their full potential is to learn how to decide what an action *means,* as distinct from what it first *appears* to mean.

This is where doubt is more powerful than belief in getting to truth. A mathematics classroom happens to be a very good place to learn. It is not the only place; but it is the most convenient.

Does this sound difficult? It is not. Look: a sentence in a text-book, any text-book, is the result of an action. *"Please read it aloud,"* I would ask one of my pupils, and then I would ask another: *"What do you think that means?"*

Almost always the first response will be: *"Uh, I don't know."*

"That's okay; that's alright. Just read it again: aloud."

And then I would ask the same, or another: *"What do you think that means?"*

By now there should be at least a first suggestion.

"Okay. Does it mean the same to all of you? Can it mean anything else, anything more?"

Slowly, but surely, everyone will begin to realise: "This is how to learn*!"*

And then they also begin to realise: "But I can do this by myself*!"*

These were the principles of learning that we explored in our classroom after I had realised how easily I could damage both your intelligence and your pleasure in learning by attempting to teach you as if you were just one single undifferentiated brain called 'The Class'.

Ignoring children's differences like this produces emotional, mental, and moral cripples.

Every child is potentially a messiah. It might even be supposed that the aim of most systems of formal education is to ensure that they are as rare as possible. This happens.

And yet, whatever the formal system, some will survive. Some will preserve that modicum of primal innocence in believing that there is always more to discover, more to be learnt.

All religions accept that some messiahs will always be active in the world. In general, the aim of a messiah is to show that everyone shares the responsibility for making peace or making war. Everyone has this choice. We have it now.

Perhaps we can help our young messiahs best by recalling, in a single sentence, what the most outstanding of earlier messiahs said to their contemporaries, and say to us now.

It might be expected that most messiahs will be found in religions. But religions are run by professionals insisting that there is no need to doubt, that their religion is already completely true.

Professionals like these create more divisions than they can heal. And, in addition, they do not welcome unlicensed interference.

This was a problem for Socrates.

And then he refused to apologise. This was a clear challenge to the majority on his jury who were obliged every day to be humble before the rich, the powerful, and the immoral.

"An honest man," Socrates told them, *"is like a child."*

Another insult! What does a child know that a man does not?

As Forrest Gump might say: that's all you need to hear from Socrates.

Unlicensed interference was a problem for Jesus too.

He was clearly a highly charismatic young man, but fatally confused. He could not decide whether to encourage Jews to become a democracy like Athens; or whether to accept the Emperor Augustus as a god; or whether to lead his followers as armed terrorists.

He hesitated too long. The Romans clearly feared him as a potential terrorist. They sent to arrest him a full cohort of soldiers: around 300 heavily armed men. Later, Jerusalem laughed at his indecision. They preferred Pilate to free Barabbas. He might at least begin to fight.

Three centuries later, without any sense of irony, a gaggle of priests decided to increase their own importance by declaring Jesus not only to have been a god, like any Roman emperor—an insult in itself to his courage—but to be The God, eternally, and his Father, and the Spirit of honesty and truth. This clutch of illogical imponderables has been a barrier to peace ever since.

Yet despite the wars that have been fought, and that may yet be fought, in his name, Jesus has been decidedly as important as

Socrates. What then was *his* most important sentence? William Blake, number eleven on Dr Bucke's list, declared it to be: *'Forgive and be forgiven.'*

Interfering with professionals was Muhammad's problem too. The professionals of his time, the pagans, the Jews, and the Christians, at first derided him, then let children pelt him with offal, then threatened him so seriously that he had to leave his home and surround himself with warriors simply in order to survive.

Let us not mistake his purpose. He became a warrior. The men he led slaughtered, plundered, raped, and enslaved. There is a battered old leather quiver, dark with age, in the Topkapi museum in Istanbul. It is said to be have been his.

But to think of him *only* as a warrior is a very serious mistake. He was a brave and thoughtful man who refused, most remarkably, to allow anyone to suggest that he was more than a man. He made peace between the warring tribes. He forgave those who had fought against him and he turned his enemies into friends. And even more than courage, he valued honesty: especially of scholars.

Islam could turn to the same inspiration today.

And all of this is true because, fundamentally, and still most remarkably, Muhammad's sentence is the most powerful of all. Here it is: *'There is one God for everyone.'*

For a time this hugely powerful elementary message raised Muslim mathematics, science, and medicine to historic achievement. If it had been left unchallenged, it might by now have illumined the world; but later arguments divided it, its sense and its meaning, until all its fire was stifled and the tribes that he united divided once again.

His, with these earlier messages, could unite all the faiths we know.

That they have not, I believe, is why many of you call yourselves atheists. You are not atheists. You are the flowers which grow from the prophets' footsteps. You are on the right path.

Messiahs are always in danger from those whose power they seem to threaten. But they know themselves to be in constant danger of being silenced even by those who mean well.

On that evening, forty years ago, I knew at once that I had had a hugely important experience. I did not then expect that it would direct the rest of my life.

The next day, however, after a good night's sleep and a hearty breakfast, as I was preparing to meet my military and medical inquisitors for the first time, I realised that to declare that it had occurred in this place without any support from any modern professionals would be to invite them immediately and unconditionally to judge me mad.

We talked instead of other things: of sedition and of treachery and of offering possible comfort to an enemy. Much later, in my essay 'Trinity', I imagined—it was not very difficult—the real perplexity of professional philosophers and theologians to whom I told my story. (For 'Trinity' see below.)

They were the kindest people imaginable; but they were clearly completely unable to agree what to do. The best advice one of them could give me was: *"Other theologians will not like it that you know, from experience, what they know [only] from their books. Stay away from them."*

So, you see, it is impossible to say how to continue a messiah's education. But at least we now know how to start. In the first of these essays I warned that this is a dangerous game. I hope I may have persuaded you that it is the only game in town.

Either we win this game: or our children may lose everything.

You may have been persuaded by my treatment of the God debate a few pages back that I disagree with the debaters entirely. In fact, I am critical only of their certainty. Their certainty is very close to the certainty that they criticise in others. Certainty starts wars.

By now, as well, if you are a mother, or if you expect to be a mother, I hope I will have persuaded you that your responsibility is to help your young messiahs preserve their innocence.

Telling them that they have always the right to be honest and to ask questions will not just give them a full grade advantage at school, especially if their teachers understand the real value of their questions. It is also the first step of their spiritual training.

My final addition is more than a sentence. It is also from someone you will not know. But he thought long about these questions, and he, finally, is a Jew.

"If we judge the other, if we compare the other to ourselves, if, with whatever worthy motive, we play the schoolmaster or even the loving father and guide, there can be no spiritual meeting: for we have by no means cut our moorings: we have stayed on our own shore, and beckoned the other to us. He will not come." (Victor Gollancz, in '*From Darkness to Light*', p. 317, 1956)

And, finally, try to forgive your mathematics teachers—and your religion teachers.

Their material is difficult. They do their best.

Colin

('Trinity' can be found in http://web.archive.org/web/200609 02011441/http://www.gardenofdemocracy.org/)

5ᵗʰ February 2012

From Saif Albasri

Mr. Colin Hannaford happy seeing you here again. You can post your essay in english. Our house is multilingual . . . If someone raises questions, I will translate. But the majority here speak english.

9ᵗʰ February 2012

Thank you. I am reassured by your cheerful response and kind offer.

I believe that you of Conscience House and I share a common concern.

Billions of young people are locked into systems of political and religious thinking which are so certain of their truth that there is no room for development or compromise.

The danger of attack by one or more on others has become acute.

The involvement of nuclear or biological weapons will make this catastrophic.

The danger is increased as economies contract or collapse from fear.

The question is whether the risk can be reduced.

I think it can, and very simply.

I do not agree that any danger is created by the activity of religions.

I believe that it is created by the inactivity of religions.

Virtually all monotheistic religions declare that they possess definite knowledge of the existence and the nature of the supreme intelligence of our universe, creative and inspirational. The promise of science, if less ambitious, is similar: to reveal the logic of that intelligence.

If any could actually demonstrate and share this knowledge and logic universally, humankind would at last be able to leave tribalism behind and recognise its unity.

This is what religions and science have promised. All have so far failed.

I believe that many young people might achieve this knowledge quite easily.

I therefore propose that everyone reading this might take part in an experiment.

The conditions are unusual, but are easily described. The confidence of young people today in their powers and courage is greater than in my youth. There is no danger except that of disappointment. They will also know that not all experiments succeed at first.

In my earlier essays I have explained how young mothers—and grandmothers—can encourage young children to think independently. There is need for fathers' encouragement too, although there is often the problem—I have known this myself—that fathers may fear the rivalry of their sons. They should think rather of the joy of parenting a new messiah.

This is the first step. The next step requires more adult courage.

It is not to be expected that everyone will succeed. The disappointment for some may be very great. But if only a small fraction of the huge number of young people who may participate report that through their own initiative they have learnt what I achieved by accident forty years ago, more and more will be encouraged.

And this will easily change history.

For Peter O'Broin: who asked: Can you tell us the bus-stop story again?

Sure, Peter. Here it is.

BUS

(A Physics Lesson: aka The Leap of Faith)

No matter how perfectly a lesson is prepared or how perfectly delivered, I had come to realise that no class will learn anything if they are just not ready to learn.

This is the obvious truth most often ignored in education. Thousands of years of 'educational research' can be binned. Education really is this simple. A teacher must know how to get a class to give him, or her, their full attention.

What do you do when a class arrives for your lesson already fed-up, bad-tempered, tired—having been thoroughly mauled by a previous teacher, or thoroughly bored by a previous lesson?

There is absolutely no point in trying to press on with the magic of algebra or the wonders of trigonometry. I am inclined to help them to relax; to give me their attention, and only then to focus on what we have to do. The easiest way to do this is by telling them a story, and one story that has never failed to please is how I once caught a London bus.

I had been staying with friends who live in the centre of London, and one morning I had made up my mind to visit Harrods, in Kensington.

My friends urged me to take an Oxford Street bus, telling me that this is—and it still is—the most convenient way to travel around central London. I was told the number of the bus; and the bus stop at which to stand in order to catch it. Apart from tying a label around my neck with my name and address, and giving me a package of sandwiches, there was nothing more they could do to speed me on my way.

I walked across to Oxford Street—this early in the morning it was surprisingly quiet—and I stood patiently at the bus-stop for fully ten minutes as big red double-decker bus after bus rumbled past. All were the wrong ones. Finally I decided to walk.

I had walked only fifty yards when behind me I heard the unmistakable grumble of yet another bus.

Turning to look, I realised that *this* must be my bus! It was now rather less than fifty yards away, and it was accelerating hard. In the clear morning air with sunlight flooding across Oxford Street from the south, I could see that it was empty.

I could also see the driver, and by the way that he was holding the wheel, it was clear that he would be happy to keep it empty. I might wave at him in vain. The daily life of a London bus-driver, endlessly stopping and starting, is not easy. With an empty bus and an empty road in front of him, he had obviously no intention to stop for one stupid passenger fifty yards past an official stop.

There then flashed into my mind in this moment—in, I suppose, about two seconds—the complete and exact description that I had read just a few months before of the method taught to members of the French Resistance sixty years ago by the Special Operations Executive, the SOE, for catching trains between railway stations. In those days, especially if you were an agent, this was an extremely useful precaution, because all the stations were controlled by the French police and the Gestapo, the German secret police. Either one—or both—would carefully check any traveller's identification papers.

To avoid any inconvenience that might arise from this—like being shot—the agents were taught to wait beside the railway line at night until they heard a train approaching. The method they then used was possible—*is* possible—with any kind of train, either passenger or goods, but a goods train was best because it would be less likely to have guards aboard. Once one got into a goods wagon, one could expect to be relatively safe for many miles, for it would almost always stop in a goods yard: there might be less security there as well.

The agents had to stand with their toes on the edge of the railway sleeper—the ties, Americans call them—so that as the train passed them it would be only inches away from their body and their face. Then they were to bend sideways, in the direction the train was travelling, and hold out their arms above their head— rather like a ballerina in Swan Lake, but with their palms flat as if they were about to pat the side of the train—and then they were to move their hands forward until the projections of the moving train were just brushing their fingers.

The main idea was this. At the front and rear of every carriage, also on almost every wagon, was a vertical metal handle. Below both was a step. To get up into the carriage, or to climb onto the wagon, people would take hold of this handle with one hand, and pull themselves up onto the step. That was what they did when the train was *not* moving.

Standing there in the night, on their toes—with the side of the train roaring and crashing past their faces just inches away, and those great steel wheels hissing and banging below—the agents would incline further and further forward until he, or sometimes she, could feel those vertical handles flicking past under their outstretched fingers; and then, at the very last moment, they would *hook!* their fingers, catch the last of the handles, and the huge momentum of the train would simply pluck them off the sleepers, and they would come down safely—*hoopla!*—onto the step.

Nothing, in principle, could be simpler: *un morceau de gateau!* ('Piece of cake!')

All of this travelled through my mind in a couple of heart-beats. By now I could see the driver's face clearly through his almost vertical window. I could see his arm move. I heard the engine note drop as he moved determinedly up another gear. He was deliberately looking far beyond me. I did not exist for him.

Of course there were no sleepers to stand on here, but I could see that the big tyres of his bus would pass within two feet of the kerb. The bus might have been on rails itself. Stepping down from the kerb, I stood now so that the tyres would just miss my toes, and assumed the precise position required by the Special Operations Executive. (At this point, incidentally, before a fascinated class, I would assume this position. Demonstration is a lesson in itself.)

The front of the bus roared past. The driver's face, flashing by, looked sideways through his little window. He looked amazed. The great smooth flat red side of his bus is now sliding past my fingers. How frightening to have to do this at night, in the dark, when any unexpected unseen projection might kill you at once, throwing you aside like so much rubbish. Horribly injured, or dead. That was courage. The air dragged by the bus is lifting my hair. I can feel the lines of rivets in the red metal panels flicking my fingers.

Now! *Hook on!*

In those days there was a platform at the rear of all London buses for passengers to get on and off. The conductor of the bus—he took the fares and gave out tickets from a little winding machine—would often stand there staring at the traffic. In the middle of this platform's outer edge was a long chrome bar reaching from the floor to the ceiling. (With a young class I would sometimes stop at this point and draw a bus quickly to show them.) This bar was more or less where the handle would have been on a French train, whether passenger or goods. This is what I hooked on to.

An empty London bus has a weight, I should say, of about ten tons. It cannot accelerate all *that* quickly, and even now it was probably travelling at only a bit more than twenty miles an hour. There was a tremendous jerk on my arms, and a very loud *"Twong!"* that echoed through the empty bus like a plucked string on a big bass guitar, and I was suddenly travelling down Oxford Street, horizontally, pulled behind the bus rather like a solid flag. With legs.

The driver was still accelerating hard. He had apparently decided to leave behind the idiot whose toes his tyres had just run over. What he had not yet realised was that I *am* now his only passenger. He cannot see me. I am still airborne, for I have not yet got my feet down on the platform, and I am still hidden from his view by the side of the bus.

I am surprised to find that I am still horizontal, although the reason that I am still horizontal—and if I had only had another second to think about it, I might have expected this before I executed my plan—is simply physics.

I weighed about twelve and a half stone, around one hundred and eighty pounds, or 70 kilos. This mass—that is, me—cannot be accelerated *instantaneously* to the same speed of the bus. Acceleration takes time, however short, in which a force, however large, has to act to give a mass the kinetic energy it requires to move.

That first deep *"Twong!"*—now left behind in our wake—was the sound of this force beginning to act on the mass—that is, me. I am horizontal because my arms are parallel with the ground and that is the direction in which the force is acting. I am alarmed to see that the bar—it is now, of course, above my head—is bending like a bow with the strain. And now, just as if I am on a trapeze, I begin to swing, very rapidly indeed, in behind the bus, and this is how I discover—*only by doing it myself,* you see—why the SOE advised their agents to catch hold only of the very *last* handle on the train. The reason is that then there is nothing more behind the train for them to hit.

The force that has just lifted me off the road is now also causing me to rotate. I am now not only horizontal. I am also now rotating towards the back of the bus because my centre of mass was not directly behind the bar when the force began to act. Now any body, as you know, that is once made to move by some external force in any particular direction, or that is made to turn about its axis, will continue to move or turn in that direction until it is acted upon by some other *external force*. This is Newton's First Law.

On this older type of London buses there was a second bar for the convenience of the passengers. This is shorter, also chromed; but is much sturdier than the one that I am still holding. It is just to the right of the platform, at the rear, and I now collide with this bar with a frightful thump. This is the new external force. It stops me rotating. My horizontal speed is now the same as the horizontal speed of the bus, so that I am also now dropping onto it. I still have the presence of mind to bring my feet down under me, to land on the platform, just as the conductor—he has a black moustache bristling in his white face—comes clattering down the stairs, like a sack of coals, in a dark blue London Transport uniform.

He must have seen everything from the upper deck. Even from that perspective it must have been impressive. First this solitary pedestrian is just ambling along the pavement. Suddenly he turns, looks up, making a sudden, terrible decision and throws himself towards the bus, steps into the road, and disappears under the wheels. A flamin' suicide!

Now, discovering that the flamin' suicide is standing on his platform, alive and well, not left behind in Oxford Street like a squashed tomato—and he *had* looked swiftly behind to make sure there are not *two* maniacs about this morning—he is remarkably unrelieved. He is instead extremely angry.

"What the *fuckinell*—do you think you're ***doin'!*" he yelped, making no attempt to praise my intrepid spirit, still less to give thanks to God. He was holding his ticket machine with one hand, the other was over his leather money bag—as if I might now make a spring for a ticket or his cash. These days, his expression revealed his thoughts: you just never bloody know! (These are colloquial expressions which may, of course, be modified to suit the audience.)

Meanwhile I am acutely embarrassed. Temporarily, I discover, I cannot speak. There is a really terrible pain in my side. Still holding onto my bar for support, I am bent forward from the waist, whooping for breath.

"Unnghh, " I manage finally, and then—and I always think that this is so typically English, "I'm—umm—sorry. I just want a ticket—unnghh—to—'aaarrods. Aarunngh. Please. "

"Well, " said the conductor with great satisfaction, "then you can just gerrorf *this* bus, mate. *We're* goin' to Swiss Cottage!"

And he binged his bell: the bus ground to a halt; I gorroff—just as he had advised; he binged his bell again, and as his bus roared away, he stood on the platform staring back at me; he was shaking his head *un*sympathetically, and making rude gestures with his free hand.

Of course, the SOE also taught its agents how to get *off* a moving train: so that when they arrived, at wherever they happened to be going, they would not have to explain to anyone where they had come from. This is another relatively simple technique. It involves throwing yourself sideways from the train, if possible down an embankment—best of all if it has slowed down on an incline. I didn't think of this at the time—and, anyway, the bus had already stopped to let me off.

Now, if you'll all stop laughing—*when* you have all stopped laughing—we'll get on with some work. One day I must tell you about the Terror Ride of Grafenwoehr. That might be next week.

Now, all of you open your books!

12ᵗʰ February, 2012

Adults Only

"Can atheists achieve union with God?"
I thought about this question whilst making a pot of tea. *"Yes, they can. Actually they have an important advantage."*

"Can you explain this briefly?" You mean now? I can try.

Suppose that we have been sharing a prison cell. You have been told you may soon be released. I will soon be shot. You have learnt to trust me. You asked me these questions.

Here's what you probably already know.

Until recently the sciences were highly materialistic. Now it is becoming apparent that what is most important in any possible universe is the ordering of information. Scientists would like to know what fundamental principle controls this ordering. They are having to guess.

Some ancient religions, especially of India and China, have always claimed that we only perceive an illusion. Beyond the illusion is a void. Within the void is the intelligence that orders and controls the universe. The aim of these religions is to contact this intelligence.

Traditionally this principle, this intelligence, is known as God. You may have talked to it as a child. I have suggested that it may be understood as honesty. It may appear to us as a hugely powerful protective being of our own form and nature. This is also traditional.

And this is what you want to meet. To do so requires a higher level of consciousness. Paradoxically, you may then feel like a child again, with a child's innocence and courage. This will already make it worthwhile. You may also decide that, if it is eternal, so are you. This is a foolish thought, but comforting. It is the basis of most if not all religions. It may be true.

Now we can begin.

All systems of belief are meant to be consistent and coherent.
They are all orderings of information.
Like a phase state.
Phase states are usually stable.
When they become critical, they can change almost instantly into another.
A very cold liquid may be in a critical state.
A tiny crystal has a different order of information.

It is like a contradiction.
It can cause the liquid to change almost instantly into a crystal.
This reacts to light—that is, to information—very differently.

Contradictions always disturb systems of thought.
They can cause whole systems to change instantly.
I had once a total belief in science.
I had begun to realise that I only knew what I had been told.

Then a major contradiction appeared.
Certainty ceased to be certain.
In this instant I realised
That I didn't try to be honest and to ask questions
For myself.
Angrily I demanded: WHO wants this?

I have described elsewhere what happened next.
Now you may be in much the same situation.
You believed in your religion.
It was your system of thought.
You believed what you had been told.
You were not allowed to speak differently,
To think differently.

I want you to go back to your religion.
To enter it uncritically.
To immerse yourself again.
To sing and pray joyfully,
Just as you did when you were satisfied.
You need to do this until you know
That person again.

Uncritical, unquestioning,
Without self,
Believing its contradictions can be explained.
Learn to pray as well alone.
Do this also joyfully,
Without question,
Without doubt.

Learn to be satisfied with this too.
One day:
Be sure this will happen.
It may be in public worship.
It may be in private,
And alone
Something will trigger your need.

Suddenly you will realise
That the system of belief
That you have again learnt to depend on
Is unable to deal with contradictions
Which you cannot accept.
Then, in that instant,
You will know that there is a higher intelligence.

It *expects* you to make this discovery,
It has waited for you to realise that this is why you are alive.
Then you should say, aloud if you like: "I want to know YOU!"
If there is a response,
And there may be, then you can ask:
"Please, fill me with your grace."
And this may happen too.

I wish you the joy of it.
Of course, you may ask,
What if I fail?
And why can millions pray every day
Without making this discovery?
What's missing from this plan of yours?
Nothing.

But they can see no contradictions.
This is why there are so many religions.
They provide comfort to many.
But they also divide.

Some believe that science describes reality.
That science would end wars.

But, pointlessly discovering a pointless universe,
Life without consciousness or free will,
Such science declares that life is pointless too.
Sad people.
Dangerous people.
Their lives have no value or purpose.
Neither, they say, has yours.

They are wrong.
All can decide for themselves
What level of consciousness,
What order of information,
What quality of knowledge,
They want for themselves.

The gate is not always open.
But nor is it locked.
Try.
If you fail, try again.
This is expected of you too.
Everyone has greater resource
Than they suppose.

Athletes train themselves to exceed every previous
performance by imagining themselves exceeding. This has been
an attempt to help you imagine an event which you may have
believed impossible. The event is modelled on my own experience.
It was recognized by scholars as authentic, precisely because
others have made very similar reports.

As far as possible, try to be spontaneous. It is important not to
be anxious. I was not anxious. I was angry not to have recognized
my boss, my overseer, for so long. It was not necessary for me to

meditate for hours or wait for some drug to take effect. I asked for help. The response was instantaneous.

Many have tried and failed. Perhaps they were too anxious. Perhaps they were still trying to prove their own belief. But honesty is ruthless. We live on air, water, food, warmth. Hatred kills. Love must be demanding: on the lover. These beliefs are true.

It is essential to throw off your old beliefs, just as children throw off and trample their clothes in order to feel free.

But it is also essential to know that you are not begging for refuge.

This is your home. It is your right to ask for grace.

In this experiment, you have the advantage of being many, whilst at the same time everyone can remain anonymous. Atheists have a further advantage in being almost free of unnecessary beliefs. It is essential not to pretend. Remember that many are called: few are chosen. You are not trying to prove anything. You are not competing. Dishonesty may impress others, but you must live with it.

If you are able, let us know how you get on.

14ᵗʰ February, 2012

To Jimmy Kilpatrick,
Founder and Editor-in-Chief, EducationNews.org.

Dear Jimmy,

These essays are getting increasingly personal, but I hope you may still be able to publish this. I posted it in 'Children for an Honest, Just, and Fair World' this morning.

These Facebook pages are now being noticed by at least 3500 young people. The most serious seem to be young Muslims, ditto Jews, and even some Egyptian Christians. They all appear to have recognized that their different religions—or rather, the certainty of their priests in their various religions—make any kind of peace impossible between different religious and nonreligious factions, and has the same effect on attempts to achieve democracy.

This is already becoming obvious in Iraq. It may be very soon the cause of another civil war in Afghanistan, Syria, and Pakistan. In fact, the whole rickety religious infrastructure of the Muslim East, in which religion has never been separated from government, as the US founders wisely decided it must be, is ready to collapse.

What I am trying to do here is to suggest to these young people that at least some of them, potentially all of them, but in any case an important fraction, can confirm the existence and nature of God for themselves.

You will see that I have deliberately written as concisely as possible, supposing that this text may be translated into various forms of Arabic—and also in stanzas more like poetry than prose—and in doing so I have found it entirely natural, even necessary, to use some phrases which you will recall the man called Jesus used in attempting to instruct his disciples.

I found this strangely moving. It was not at all premeditated. It just happened that "if you will enter the Kingdom of Heaven, you must throw off your garments, and trample them underfoot, as children do" perfectly describes the necessity to abandon the show of beliefs; that they are actual obstacles to higher consciousness.

Equally, "many are called: few are chosen" is a perfect warning to these youngsters that they may not succeed if, even because, they try too hard. It seems necessary to achieve a state of mind, seemingly very paradoxical to our more cautious Western minds, but very well known to Zen Buddhism. It is the confidence which has no reason to suppose that one's aim will succeed, whilst being perfectly sure that it will: even that it must, having already occurred. Could Jesus have known this first?

Someone said many years ago: Our world is not only stranger than we imagine; it may be stranger than we *can* imagine.

Amen to that.

I have one more essay in mind in which to explore this further: then I shall revert to writing about planting beans early. Or could that be another metaphor?

Whatever you decide, I hope you are well.

Love to all, Colin.
(Actually, of course, there were to be many more!)

On Metaphysics

Dear Friends,

It's time to lighten up a little! About a week or so ago I was invited to a conference in Oxford on metaphysics.

Now I have always understood metaphysics to mean attempting to understand whatever may be known or may be believed about reality that physics is not (yet) able to describe.

Naturally I was delighted to be honoured. Recognition, at last! When asked to submit some material for the conference to discuss, I sent its secretary a copy of 'Source', as an example of metaphysical experience, and 'Trinity', as the imagined debate of a group of eminent theologians and philosophers attempting to decide, forty years ago, how to deal with it.

As you know by now, they, bless their hearts, decide that none of them could. I agreed with them, by the way. What I had reported was clearly way outside their experience, and they made no attempt to hide this. But they did recognize what I told them as important in providing an authentic evidential basis for all those religions whose origins are lost in the mists of time (cue heavy music), and I still think they should have tried.

This, anyway, is why I came to the European School to teach you mathematics, instead of being encouraged to teach what I suppose could now be called 'heuristic theology' in a university. Perhaps we can get someone to endow a professor's chair with that title. This would be fun.

Meanwhile! The Oxford conference is likely to attract a group of equally eminent Oxford scholars. My attempt to offer them the same opportunity as my old Cambridge friends had clearly a very similar effect on their secretary. He replied: *"The pieces you sent are quite broad in subject matter, and do not concentrate on matters of metaphysics as construed in mainstream philosophical writing."*

His rather anguished tone is an indication that he would like to help. But even more important is the indication that he wouldn't wish to be found wandering perilously beyond the limits of 'mainstream philosophical writing.' Anything might happen in those wild and dangerous wastes, full of unphilosophical people. He continued:

"Examples of such themes, that are at the very heart of metaphysics, may be found, for example, in http://plato.stanford.edu/entries/categories/ *and of course there are many more available examples. As you might have inferred, I do not wish to prescribe what metaphysics actually involves, but I do wish to guide the meeting to have a recognizable focus on matters that academic philosophers regard as metaphysics."*

I did not find this entirely unexpected. Actually, I found it hilarious. I replied:

"Thank you for your care. I have looked at this very dense article. It seems that very few of the profound thinkers who have contributed to it have had much to say about metaphysical experience, only about metaphysical theories. But if theories are not grounded in experience, or are at least attempts to explain experience, then philosophers are clearly open to the criticism, as Dr Johnson once said, of being merely fond of their own notions. I will be happy to talk about metaphysical experience. It really isn't very difficult, although I would not expect it to appeal to those who prefer to talk about their notions. It requires rather broader minds, and grit."

Possibly I have been unkind. This was the comment of an independently eminent friend:

"But you *are* unkind. It's as if you were to ask a society of art critics to show their paintings."

Several of you have told me of your happy recollection of the physics lesson I used to give about boarding an Oxford Street bus. I suppose a strict physicist would insist that this is not physics. Where is $f = ma$?

It is a happy memory for me too, but I never tried that trick again. Do not!

Colin.

22nd February, 2012

On Heuristic Theology

'A long tradition maintains that knowledge of God is naturally available to any human being without the aid of special divine grace or revelation. But the universe as scrutinized by an impartial and rational spectator can seem blank or inscrutable, and those who do not see it as the work of a divine creator do not seem guilty of any error of logic or observation . . . . We need a different kind of religious understanding, one that takes account of the special conditions under which God, if he exists, might be expected to manifest himself.'

(Professor J. G. Cottingham, OUCSR seminar on the 23rd February 2012.)

But:

'The four common barriers to inquiry are: first, the assertion of absolute certainty; second, maintaining that something is absolutely unknowable; third, maintaining that something is absolutely inexplicable because absolutely basic, or ultimate;

fourth, holding that perfect exactitude is possible, especially such as to preclude unusual and anomalous phenomena.'

(Charles Peirce.in http://www.sccs.swarthmore.edu.)

These essays are a personal attempt to find safe educational paths through the minefield of sectarianism, atheism, political ideologies, even agnosticism. A straight path for everyone sickened by humanity's stupidity and violence: paths to peace and to God.

Does that appear too grandiose? Perhaps a little cracked? Let me explain.

Minefields are usually laid to leave no such paths. Since the field we need to traverse has been laid out over millennia, since it is now littered with ancient munitions, many capable of exploding at the least tremor, it might seem that our attempt must be hopeless.

The solution is to be guided heuristically.

Most of the major religions claim that they worship the same god. If they did, their adherents would have no reason to kill. They kill to defend their idols.

Heuristic theology means replacing idols by a truly universal impulse: the impulse to be honest and explore or inquire; essentially the guiding principle of life.

This impulse may sometimes appear as a human form.

This is less important than the message.

When my first mentors, especially John Robinson, advised me to find a way to use my new knowledge in my new career, this seemed highly impractical.

The only subject that I am qualified to teach is mathematics.

Who ever found God in mathematics? Soon, miraculously, I began to realise that the whole history of mathematics can be best understood as the consequence of three aspects of the same inspiration: to wonder, to inquire, to be honest.

This I could certainly encourage in my lessons. I did.

But being soon appointed to teach in one of the twelve European Schools of the European Union gave me reason to think even more widely about teaching math as if it were only necessary for children to be told what to do. Surely they should be helped to think?

In 1992 I had become so alarmed by the general absence of concern that I told a conference of educationalists in Bavaria that teaching mathematics in this way helped Hitler to power in Germany and Stalin in Russia. If democracies are to remain healthy, mathematics must be used to help children think critically, logically, and inventively. It cannot be used only to condition them to obey authorities without ever questioning orders.

And since, I argued, virtually everyone in any modern society is still being exposed to this malignancy, it must have serious mental, moral, and social consequences.

Twenty years later the European Union is bankrupt and near collapse. The United States is humbled and in debt. The general cause of both of these enormous disasters is now generally understood. They were caused by unquestioning belief in the certainty of financial authorities, in the truth of elaborate mathematical models, and by widespread political dishonesty.

In short, they were the rotten fruits of misused mathematics education.

Originally all that I ever wanted was to leave my classroom every day feeling that I had done some good. My fifteen year attempt to warn that the misuse of mathematics education is actually killing our societies left me exhausted.

If I had not been rescued by my old students, I might have quietly given up.

Their affection for me made me remember that I have more to say.

The fundamental units of societies are individuals. Individuals need great courage to resist a society's pressure to behave as it expects. As Albert Schweitzer wrote eighty years ago, *"Anyone who is spiritually free is inconvenient [in an organization], even uncanny [disturbing]. Such people do not offer sufficient guarantee that they will merge into organisations as they [the organisations] wish."* (My additions are in brackets.)

Such individuals may be helped by the support of others like themselves. This is how many of you reading these accounts are helping others. But the fundamental spring of courage is the determination to be spiritually free. What does it mean to be spiritually free? Is Schweitzer right? Must it always be this dangerous? As usual, this depends: more numbers, less danger.

Most religions were originally inspired to support this determination. As major associations, they generally fail. They insist too much on everyone doing as they are told.

Systematic theologies to support such mass behavior have been worked out and worked over for millennia until every question, every answer, every gesture, guarantees that the majority of its adherents will merge together as required.

The heuristic theology can work within these systematic theologies, but its purpose is to provide individuals with an individual theology: one that works for them.

The first step is to know that God is your reason for wanting to be honest. The second step is to know that to be honest it is necessary to ask questions; the third, that asking questions is necessary to discover what one does *not* know.

With these three steps we can teach children. The primary aim is that they will know God to be this impulse. The secondary aim is to support a society in which spiritual freedom is normal.

The 'special conditions' under which this can emerge largely require the removal of the barriers described above by C. S. Peirce.

Charles Sanders Peirce, it may be remembered, was so much shunned by his contemporaries that he died penniless, leaving so much original work that Harvard's modern scholars have not yet published half of it. He left also what he called the 'neglected argument' for the existence of God. Here is one of his several explanations:

". . . there is a reason, an interpretation, a logic in the course of scientific advance, and this indisputably proves that man's mind must have been attuned to the truth of things in order to discover what he has discovered. It is the very bedrock of logical truth."

('A Neglected Argument for the Reality of God.'
Peirce, C.S., 1908)

There is a danger, of course, in telling young people that God may appear to them in person. All people are suggestible; the young, most of whom like to believe that they are not, are the most highly suggestible of all.

This is why they all learn to speak alike and wear the same clothes.

But they have also the advantage of courage. They need only to be told a thing is possible to want to try it. They will come to no harm if they are honest.

In her lessons on subjective knowledge, the Oxford philosopher Margaret Yee draws a diagram of three concentric circles to describe what most people believe they can know. In the centre circle is 'common' knowledge, which is possible for all; in the next ring is 'scientific' knowledge, which is possible for some; in the outer ring is 'spiritual' knowledge, which is supposedly open to the rarest minds, and closed to everyone else.

Dr Yee disagrees. She suggests that any knowledge achieved by one mind can be achieved by others.

After first encouraging mothers to bring up their children as the new messiahs, I suggested in my previous essay how young adults may develop their spiritual freedom.

Now I have a further duty in mind.

In most Western countries there are now more older people than young. Some of the former may wish to be included.

I was prompted to think about this when, a year ago, I met an old soldier, Dick Channer, twenty years my senior, decorated for his courage in the crucial battles that finally checked the Japanese advance on India. Once he learnt of my experience, he asked: *"Tell me all you know. I am much nearer needing it than you are!"*

I told him as much as I could. Now I think I can do better.

Many older adults will have enjoyed the comfort their religion has supplied. They will be most unusual, however, if they have not reflected that there are many active religions.

All insisting that they are certain.

They will also have realised that most people's faith is not achieved heuristically. It is the faith of their family, their tribe, their region, sometimes of their nation.

Should the old believe that they may meet God, if at all, only *after* they die?

In an increasingly secular West it is widely supposed that it really doesn't matter what anyone believes. It is common for many to be persuaded that all human life—as I once heard a famous Oxford philosopher declare—is no more than 'an extensive chemical activity'.

I would not call this agnosticism or atheism. I would call it lacking belief in one's own importance: something even soldiers do not do.

But when the lip of death is getting nearer, and as you begin to accept that your 'chemical activity' is not, after all, going to be indefinitely extended, you may need more than stoic resignation, and more than a hasty renewal of faith, to go cheerfully into that dark night.

In my next essay I will share with older readers what may be helpful to them.

Its basis, once again, is very simple.

It is to know that death is a question answered in life.

Colin.

27th February 2012

Dear Friends,

I have recently learned to imitate Descartes, to use the interval between deep sleep and full consciousness to recall my dreams and learn from them. This is often surprising. This morning I remembered dreaming of finding a Neolithic sculpture of a head: just an oval of slate on which had been scratched a mouth, eyes, nose.

I also realized that whilst we have progressed sufficiently to try to understand metaphysics, the structure behind material reality, the next step is to understand metanoia, the structure of understanding itself. The principle on which it is built I have called the impulse of honesty; mathematicians call it elegance, and artists call it beauty; it is the principle on which the universe is built. Perhaps that is the message my Neolithic artist was trying to leave for us to see. Later cultures, and our own, call it God.

29ᵗʰ February 2012

Oxford High Jinks

Jink v. 1. intr. Move elusively; dodge. 2. tr. Elude by dodging. 3. n. Act of dodging or eluding. [OED]

If you had been in Oxford last week, you might have enjoyed sitting in the magnificent rotunda of the Sheldonian Theatre to witness Dr Richard Dawkins, currently known as Darwin's Rottweiler, in debate with the Archbishop of Canterbury, Dr Rowan Williams, who should be known as the Welsh Hammer, discussing the existence of God and his work.

Its University organisers obviously hoped this would mirror the famous clash of 1860 between Thomas Huxley, then known as Darwin's Bulldog, and the Bishop of Oxford, Samuel Wilberforce, known privately as 'Soapy Sam'.

At that meeting strong men trembled and women fainted. Its reprise was refereed—if this is not too sporting a term—by a previous Pro-Vice-Chancellor of the University, Sir Anthony Kenny, himself a philosopher of great eminence, once an ordained Catholic priest, now agnostic.

I still feel indebted to Dr Kenny for having refused to let me become a philosopher.

This was in about 1968. By then he had abandoned Catholicism and was teaching philosophy in Balliol College, reputedly Oxford's foremost intellectual. I had recently been told by the Army medics that I would be totally deaf by the time I was 30. They advised me to start a new career, "in which, by then, you will not need to discuss anything with anyone."

Philosophy seemed the obvious choice. Balliol responded to my request by arranging an interview with Dr Kenny. After the usual preliminaries, when he asked me what I expected to gain from it, I replied: *"I hope it will help me to understand the world a little better."*

There was a thoughtful pause. Then he responded with a deep but kindly chuckle: *"Oh no. I don't think it will do that!"*

Even then, I was not entirely dissuaded. I took my request to Cambridge. There I was interviewed by a member of the philosophy faculty. He was also polite; but he made much the same remarks. Finally, in desperation, I asked him: *"So, if you think philosophy is no good for anything, why do you do it?"*

He pushed back his chair, lifted his feet to his desk, clasped his hands behind his head, and declared: *"Because this is the best job in the world: and I've got it!"*

I am sure now that they both did me a great kindness. I know now that few philosophers have any great interest of doing much more than describe the world: only the most dangerous, or the most careful, will attempt to change it.

Certainly no danger of any change emerged from the Sheldonian last week.

It was all very polite.

It reminded me of the contests organized between two small boys at my prep school, who were first equipped with absurdly large gloves, then encouraged to whop each other about the head, doing no great harm to each other but 'building character'.

Dr Dawkins, in my opinion, has enough character already and, in my experience, is uncommonly polite. As befits the highest Anglican prelate in the land, His Grace, the Archbishop, never raised his voice. As if occasionally warning against holding or low blows, Dr Kenny would dart in between them from time to time to explain a point of philosophy, but the final result was a draw.

Nothing at all was achieved to increase anyone's understanding. Where it began, it ended.

A few hours later I was attending a seminar organized by Oxford University's Ian Ramsey Centre for Science and Religion in Trinity College and generously supported by the Templeton Foundation.

It was addressed by Professor J. G. Cottingham, whose précis I used last week. In it, he declared that *"we need a different kind of religious understanding, one that takes account of the special conditions under which God, if he exists, might be expected to manifest himself."*

I had high hopes that this *'different kind of understanding'*—actually he called it, as scholars do: *'a different kind of epistemology'*—is what I would hear. I hoped he would finally have the courage to abandon the endlessly compromised and hopelessly entangled articles of reason and of faith which the meeting in the Sheldonian had just failed again to resolve, and save me from the responsibility of doing it myself. I was seriously disappointed.

I pulled a hamstring last week, and could not cycle.

I drove home in *such* a bad temper.

On the way, I was composing a variety of explanations for my disappointment. One revolved around a lengthy dissertation on the inability to see a forest for the trees.

"It is of course necessary to accept that, whilst there is no certain VERIDICAL evidence for the existence of an ACTUAL forest, if indeed SUCH can exist at all, it seems to me that if we ACCEPT the truthful INTENTION of those who declare they have seen A TREE, and even many trees, often all together and at the same time, that we may INFER that the existence is at least plausible of what may be supposed to be A FOREST. If, that is, there are ENOUGH trees."

Half a mile later, after the station, I was remembering Charles Darwin's musing, in a letter, that life must have first struggled into existence from some 'warm brackish pond'.

"It's still struggling, Charlie," I muttered. *"Down here, in this warm brackish pond, in Oxford, it's still struggling."*

Believe me, dear readers, I am a modest man. I was brought up modest, to dislike braggarts, and never to think too highly of myself. On the way home that night, however, I found myself thinking: "Well, chum, you had better face it. You know more than Professor Dawkins, His Grace the Archbishop of Canterbury, the Pro-Vice-Chancellor, and Professor Cottingham."

BUT I DIDN'T LIKE IT!

With friends like these, God needs no enemies.

After I calmed down, I wrote to Dr Kenny to recall my gratitude; but also to declare my disappointment that a debate involving three of the most distinguished scholars in Britain, as distinguished as any in the world, had failed to produce a mutually acceptable description of God that might be understandable to, say, a ten-year-old.

I offered a description, which, I said, will pass all Dr Dawkins' tests; will pass his own as an agnostic; and will help His Grace to understand that God is even more universally active and powerful than is commonly imagined.

My description requires three words; they can be translated into any language; their obvious truth can help billions of young people everywhere to achieve greater peace, justice, and safety.

I am still hoping for a reply from Sir Anthony, but Major Channer MC, whom I mentioned last week, has already replied: "I like your words: 'The first step is to know that God is your reason to be honest.'"

That's fourteen. They can be reduced, of course, to three: God is honesty.

Only let it be understood that 'honesty' must not be static, lest it become certain.

It must be understood as a direction: like justice—and fairness.

3rd March 2012

Metanoia

I was not much concerned when the Oxford Philosophical Society explained that my notion of metaphysics is not that 'of most mainstream philosophers': or, indeed, as we saw last week, of His Grace, the Archbishop of Canterbury.

I was concerned that I promised to explain how your parents, grandparents, even your great-grandparents, might achieve union with God.

Most religions promise to do this. It is not at all unusual. They have the advantage of the dispatcher who pats parachutists as they step out of the plane. They never come back.

Our sky-divers are still with us.

But this is really just an extension of what we have achieved already.

Last week, for example, I met the President of the United Nations 66th General Assembly, H.E. Mr Nassir Abdulaziz Al-Nasser.

His Excellency explained in his lecture to the University that the United Nations depends primarily on its moral authority. I told him afterwards that its moral authority would be greatly increased for four billion young people if the United Nations added to its Universal Declaration of Human Rights of 1948 that children everywhere have the right to be honest and the right to ask questions.

This, I explained, would improve societies from the bottom: far better than trying to persuade 193 national leaders to do this from the top. I gave him a copy of my report of the conference I organized in Windsor Castle for the Qatar Foundation explaining how to use school mathematics lessons to do this.

He promised that his office would respond. He seems a good man. We shall see.

As for this challenge, at first sight the demographics of Facebook are discouraging.

It has six hundred million users. Over seventy percent are not thirty. Only five percent are over seventy. On the one hand, this is thirty million: quite an audience!

We will promise only to help them to see what is in their way.

My own experience of meeting with God was intensely physical, highly complex—and very brief—but it has directed my life ever since. I prefer to think of it now as an instance of what the American philosopher C. S. Peirce called a 'presentamen'. Similar experiences have been reported as a whisper in a storm, a voice from a bush, a violent embrace. Their essence is that they combine reassurance with useful commands. They never urge violence, or incite crime.

They can be doubted: except by those who receive them. Even if they are now denied, traduced, or ridiculed, they cannot be ignored. They are history's punctuation marks. They define and separate entire episodes. The hard part is to understand the whole.

Hard too is to know how to communicate its essence: without the experience?

I spent several mornings imitating Descartes, hoping to find an explanation, as I demanded previously in my High Jinks, that even a ten-year-old can understand.

It seemed impossible.

If metaphysics is behind physics, I wanted to describe what lies behind understanding.

Almost at once a word occurred to me: 'metanoia'.

I soon discovered that this word has a long history. For theologians it means 'a turning about' or 'conversion'. I am told that it appears ten times in the New Testament. Perhaps it was not used there as I will use it here.

C. J. Jung, the creator with Sigmund Freud of modern psychiatry, found that many of their patients suffered from a complex of contradictory beliefs. These complexes they named psychoses. Their patients' anguish was caused by their inability to recognise the contradictions. They adopted 'metanoia' to mean the insight which resolved their psychosis.

A psychosis can affect an entire nation. Politicians may deliberately obstruct each other's actions 'in the nation's interest' so that vitally necessary action is impossible.

Interesting. I was still perplexed. Until one morning.

Remember pop-up books? As children our pleasure was to open them just a crack to see a tangle of coloured cards, then to open them fully to reveal an entire tableau.

I was suddenly wide awake. It was three seventeen a.m.

In a sequence almost too fast to register, I was being shown that 'metanoia' can also be used to understand that behind the physical universe there is another of pure knowledge.

A powerful insight is required to see that this must be true. Out of this deeper universe our minds create what we perceive. Our minds are wonderful, but not perfect. Common sense is the best survival option: but, as science has discovered, what we perceive is another presentamen.

Your social identity is another. As soon as it is pointed out to you, you know it is not who you really are. What can anyone do to prove the identity you now feel?

The answer is surprisingly simple.

Social identities are created by societies. They are firmly attached to a society's beliefs, and therefore to its contradictions. From an early age most societies create a fear in individuals of appearing exceptional, of not merging into organisations, of being spiritually free.

Their typical contradiction is to maintain that their beliefs are obviously true, whilst imposing them through education and maintaining them through fear.

Typical too is that laughter is not permitted. They find humour deadly.

To find one's spiritual identity it is therefore necessary to learn to laugh: especially to laugh about dying, which is when the social identity supported by these contradictions is supposed to end.

This much I know. After this, I can only conjecture.

Our understanding of our existence is relatively young. The void that Buddhism calls the ground of being lies between the physical and the metanoiac universe. Pure intention survives there.

The Hindu religions offer many god-forms: many presentamen. The greatest Hindu god is Indra, presiding over social duties, social simplicity, social honesty.

Personal honesty is particularly required in the Mosaic laws, in Christianity, and in Islam.

Throughout this evolution of human understanding are frequent reports of spiritual companions. Most familiar historically is the companion Socrates called his *daemon*. Least recognised is that of Abraham and Moses, and the *daemon* Jesus called his Father.

This is shocking only when we do not recognise how common it is. Many families will know a relative with such a companion. Small children have them. Anyone who does not merge easily into organisations may be supported by their *daemon*. They used to be called angels.

Once your loved ones realise that dying will finally release them from their social identity, you should encourage them to make contact with their angel. It should be explained that if they have learnt sufficient honesty, their angel will merge with them. This is an earlier sense of metanoia. Of course, it threatens the control of organisations. Of course it is suppressed.

At an education conference many years ago I once mused that youngsters should be encouraged to contact their spiritual companions (who used to be called angels) to help them through their adolescence. A lady surged to her feet, trembling with anxiety: *"They will become schizophrenic!"*

Nonsense. Schizophrenia destroys identity. It is a terrifying disease. It cannot be created by trusting one's identity. But small wonder that Dr Dawkins sells so many books.

Here then is a simple spiritual training routine for your loved ones to follow: simple but also demanding. If they balk at it, pat them on the shoulder and wish them luck.

The aim is to develop a new sense of humour, and an unfashionable belief in angels. The next step is to decide that if heaven is full of laughter, it is the natural place for them to be.

I have a surprising reason for supposing that our universe has many heavens, but here I am out of space. It remains for me to point out that this spiritual universe is only likely to appear unfamiliar because I have given it a new name. It has also a very old name. Its existence was first proposed by Socrates' pupil Plato at the beginning of modern history.

It is commonly known, especially to mathematicians, as the Platonic universe.

It has been recognised as the inspiration of scientists, composers, and poets. They speak of it through their discoveries, their music, their magic.

It is not usually recommended to common folk like you and me. I think it should be.

Roger Penrose is one of the world's most celebrated, and iconoclastic, mathematicians. He is convinced that the Platonic world is the foundation of his reality.

'One of the remarkable things about the behaviour of the world is how it seems to be grounded in mathematics to a quite extraordinary degree of accuracy.'

('*The Large, the Small, and the Human Mind'*,
Penrose, R. 1997.)

Again: '*Platonic existence, as I see it, refers to the existence of an objective external standard that is not dependent upon our individual opinions nor upon our particular culture. Such existence could refer to things other than mathematics, such as to morality or aesthetics, but I am concerned here just with mathematical objectivity, which seems to me the clearer issue.*'

('*The Complete Guide to the Laws of the Universe*,
Penrose, R. 2004.)

For '*mathematical objectivity'*, I suggest we read '*honesty'*, and for '*honesty'*, read '*God.*' Most guides to death set out a gloomy list of sins to be renounced: then of the grief and fear to be overcome. Humour makes this unnecessary: and there is still time to be generous.

In my next essay—which I hope may be my last: for this is tiring—I will explain why I believe that this training is not just to make dying, as it can be, a happy adventure, to be celebrated, never feared; but why there may indeed be a God in Heaven whom billions of people have been and will be prevented from ever meeting by clinging to deliberately exclusive divisive ideas.

First, truth is ridiculed, then violently opposed, then accepted as self-evident.

6th-23rd **March 2012**
France/Oxford

Between A Rock and A Hard Place

Dear Class,

I have been in France for almost two weeks—with total writers' block.

I had thought this happened only to nerdy neurasthenics, not to muscular physical types (ahem) like me. Now I know better.

Together with the mental paralysis has been a terrible confusion of ideas, although this confusion has at least helped me to understand a little better the debacle which disappointed me so much and which I reported in my essay 'High Jinks'.

Please watch it in http://www.anglicansamizdat.net, and tell me if I have been unfair.

Perhaps I should add here—asseverate, a noble word, and most suitable!—that the announcement yesterday of the early resignation of His Grace, the Archbishop of Canterbury, cannot be due to me.

If in future, however, he abstains from any more theology until he can first explain who, or what, he means by God, I am sure his retirement will be much happier.

In the meantime it is becoming clear that we are part of a growing worldwide realisation with some resemblance to the 'liberation theology' which was developed within the Catholic church in the 1980s in South America.

Many of its priests were concerned that the Church appeared more often to be on the side of the exploiters of the dispossessed and poor rather than demanding greater equality, honesty, and justice. We might say that they were attempting to find the God I have described to you who demands honesty first.

Their ideas were condemned by the then Cardinal Ratzinger, who held that '*it was wrong to apply Christ's teachings in the Sermon on the Mount regarding the poor to present social situations. Christ's teaching means that we will be judged when we die, with particular attention to how we personally have treated the poor.'* (http://en.wikipedia.org/wiki/Liberation_theology)

This, I am sure, was a comfort to all concerned.

A similar idea, popular amongst modern social revolutionaries, is that the current worldwide financial catastrophe is entirely due to an international cabal of bankers and industrialists. A gloriously improbable addition for those to whom nothing is so improbable that it needs the support of any real evidence is that they are controlled in turn by a further international conspiracy, this time of shape-shifting alien lizards, headed by the British Royal Family.

Empowered by all this privileged knowledge, an elite team of kick-ass good guys may soon be able to take control of the whole conspiracy, putting, presumably, the lizards in the London zoo, and bring happiness and prosperity to the entire world.

I feel pretty sure Cardinal Ratzinger would nix this plan as well.

Not, however, because he knows there are no cabals of bankers and industrialists. Omitting the lizards, I am sure he knows there are. It will be rather because he understands what George Orwell explained in his famous treatise of political reality:

"The Nazis and Communists pretended that round the corner is a paradise where human beings will be free and equal. We know that no one ever gains power to relinquish it. The object of persecution is persecution; of torture, torture; of power, power." (*1984*, George Orwell, 1949—slightly edited.)

The dishonesty and injustice, unfairness, cruelty and waste, will continue, whoever is in control, because people everywhere have the wrong notion of the nature of power. They believe that controlling power will produce security for them and their followers: but always, necessarily, on a steeply falling scale.

This is why hierarchies reproduce themselves. Ask the Rothschilds; ask Fidel Castro; and ask Cardinal Ratzinger, now no longer His Holiness Benedict XVI.

Whilst I have offered my own criticism of Jesus, I do not believe his great sermon is in support of hierarchies. It seems to me to propose the same power to everyone, even beyond their lives. The question is: what power?

I am not so critical of Dr Dawkins. Indeed, I am rather fond of Dr Dawkins. He has style. But he too should understand, as my past employer, a great-grandson of Darwin, often used to tell me: *"If it isn't provisional, it isn't science."*

Scientists must not aspire to truth. Their job is to produce explanations; and the test of an explanation is that it should best connect the known evidence—which is all that Darwin claimed—and may predict what has yet to be discovered.

I have suggested that the organisms may not simply wait for a chance mutation to be selected by their environment. They may attempt to adapt actively.

Why not—as my old friend also used to say—a bit of both? Why should evolution be a process of both selection and active adaptation? Recent research that I have seen seems to support this possibility.

This is therefore an adequate explanation of evolution all the way up to 'the most complex and intelligent organism in our Universe: namely, *homo sapiens.*'

We are apparently determined to prove this rule untrue: to prove, to the contrary, that we have no need to adapt to our environment, that it must instead adapt to us.

This is called a Popperian affirmation: also called suicide.

But setting ourselves apart as the exception, our rule answers the question whether life evolves autonomously or by intelligent design.

It evolves autonomously, guided by this impulse. To be, just for a moment, fanciful: imagine a planet so hot that its metals melt on its surface. Guided by this same impulse—crystals being the earliest forms of self-replicating structures—fields of metal crystals would naturally evolve: like flowers, turning to follow their sun.

Such fancies are fun. The next challenge is harder.

Virtually all the religions in the world claim possession of the ultimate truth. Not all despise all the others; but the most closely related usually do, and with the most diligence. They are killing each other now.

If all the later religions began with an experience like mine, why is there so much hate?

What happened to the honesty?

What happened to the joyful embrace: *"But you are of me!"*

It is almost fatally depressing. But this was not the worst of my paralysis. There was also a sense of failure; of not being clever enough; not brave enough; not ruthless enough; and most painful of all, of being too late.

For years I have visited the centres of religious study in Oxford, hoping to find some common ground. Islam I find the most intelligent. Its origin is obviously the most familiar.

All began with this inspiration. Over time the demands of power ravaged their simplicity. To say today: *'I am a Muslim'* is as meaningless as to say: *'I am a Christian'* or *'I am a Jew.'*

Do you mean one of your own kind? Or do you mean one of those stupid, cruel, lying, thieving, superstitious, selfish bastards of the other kind?

In this state of mind I visited the Pyrenean city of Pau. Once the stronghold of the Protestant kings of Navarre who fought the Catholic French for years, massacring each other's people and razing their towns, in 1598 its young King Henry was offered the French crown, provided he become a Catholic.

He accepted, with the famous words: *"Paris is worth a Mass."*

As Henry IV of France, he then ended this ferocious religious war with a truly astonishing feat of imagination. In his Edict of Nantes, he declared:

"We have established and proclaimed, and do establish and proclaim: that the recollection of everything done by one party or the other between March, 1585, and our accession to the crown, and during all the preceding period of troubles, remain obliterated and forgotten, as if no such things had ever happened."

Could any modern statesman achieve this today?

It added to depression. I had been sleeping badly. Two children are laughing at me. A girl and a boy, both beautiful six- or seven-year-olds.

I begin to explain. *"No, no!"* the girl protests. *"We're only little! Tell us so's we can understand!"*

The boy squirms and nods in support.

"Did you die and go to heaven and meet God who gave you a message?"

If this is the simplest these dear little daisies can understand, I must say 'yes.'

"Yes," I replied. In King Henry's time I would have burnt for this alone.

"What about us?" she asked. *"Will we be honest enough to go to heaven?"*

She was angry now. Grown-ups should have answers.

"Look," I said. *"It may be more difficult than you think."*

I wanted to add: *'It may be more difficult than anyone can think.'*

I woke up again, yet more depressed. I should have told them how to begin finding their angels. I was again too late.

There is a fine tall clock in the big living room. Made by McMaster and Son, Dublin, it counts off the hours in deep sonorous notes: BOOM . . . . BOOM . . . . BOOM . . . .

One hears it even half asleep.

Two nights later I woke up shortly after one o'clock, knowing that I knew perfectly well what to write.

But I was afraid.

The cause of my paralysis was fear.

It is easy enough to invent nonsense conspiracies. I was afraid that telling my final secret: soberly, as a scientist, could wreck everything. It must wreck the rule book by which science is currently judged, and this might be seen as mere reckless vandalism, on a par with shape-shifting lizards.

Was this really necessary? Apart from my claim that creation is guided by the impulse to be honest—and this impulse is God—everything has been explained before in different ways, at different times, to different people.

Of course this has caused different people to suppose they are unique: and then to despise, fear, hate others who disbelieve them.

What is missing here?

BOOM . . . . BOOM . . . . BOOM . . . . BOOM . . . .

It took me until after four to defeat my fear: not through reason, more through contempt at my lack of spirit, but still a victory: I was ready to turn the last card.

Then, like Gautama under his Bo tree, there came enlightenment.

Science can support religious belief with evidence that science alone can provide.

Then religions, in return, must accept the instruction of science.

Expect to be disturbed. Reality has this effect.

In Oxford, date lost.

Imagine

It is clearly only an accident that the sounds of 'certain' and 'Satan' are similar in English. The OED makes nothing of it. It is not devilish.

Even so, religions and science disagree mainly because they are certain of very different fundamentals: for religions, it is the existence of the supernatural force which inspires them; for science, that reality must be explored and explained by reason alone.

Revelation is abhorred: unless scientific!

Science attempts to be both simple and consistent. Given two or more possibilities consistent with the evidence, the simplest must be chosen.

This rule was first defined by a heretical 14th century Oxford monk, William of Ockham. It was directed against papal arrogance. He was excommunicated.

If he had been a success, these essays might not be needed.

In contrast, in 1919 the English physicist Arthur Eddington was the first to understand Einstein's theory of relativity. He would not support him, however, until an expedition he led to the island of Principe, near Africa, proved Einstein's prediction that light would bend in the sun's gravitational field. Eddington recorded that the stars close to the edge of an eclipse of the sun appeared to move. Either they moved, or their light had been bent. Eddington chose the latter.

Ordinary people did not need to understand Einstein's relativity; but for much of human history the 'straightness' of light described the shortest distance between two points, the inerrancy of logic, even the flight of Cupid's arrows. Now light could bend.

It was Eddington who made Einstein famous.

He later explained:

'[In science] observation is the supreme court of appeal. Every item of physical knowledge must be an assertion of what has been or would be the result of carrying out a specified observational procedure.'

(*Philosophy of Physical Science,* Eddington, A., 1934)

True to this principle, Eddington later refused to believe the young Subrahmanyan Chandrasekhar, then a student at Cambridge, whose mathematics predicted the existence of black holes. At that time there was no observational evidence.

Still later, rather more surprisingly, he declared:

'The universe is of the nature of a thought or sensation in a universal Mind. To put the conclusion crudely: the stuff of the world is mind-stuff.'

It is hard to participate with our own mind-stuff in the world's mind-stuff.

And it gets worse.

In my research in Oxford I have found an often astonishing contradiction between the public belief of a religion and the private belief of its scholars.

This morning, for example, I read a moving description by the Chief Rabbi of the United Hebrew Congregations of the British Commonwealth concerning the absolute centrality to the Jewish identify of their ancestors' exodus from Egypt; together with a plea that children everywhere should be encouraged to ask questions. (*Credo,* The Times, 24th March, 2012)

I am, of course, delighted with the last. But surely any rabbi must know that Israeli archaeologists have searched, with others, for over fifty years for evidence that over two million people left Egypt at any time to spend forty years wandering in the desert. (As related in Exodus 12: 37-38; Numbers 1:46)

Their conclusion is that there is no sign, no record, no possibility that it could have happened. At the time it is supposed to have happened, the population of Egypt could not have been more than four million.

The two million leaving, even without *"a large number of other people, and many sheep, goats, and cattle,"* would have formed, ten abreast, a column nearly two hundred miles long.

The invention of the myth of the Jewish exodus from Egypt is one of the most damaging in history. It is damaging people still.

But, again, when we read that Jesus, whom Pilate called the king of the Jews, was crucified, died, lived again 'and ascended into heaven', we should also be aware that Jews in his time had no concept of heaven. They focused their attention instead on improving the world around them: or, more accurately, on their conception of improving their world for themselves.

But now comes the killer question.

Have I been too certain? Have I fallen into the same devilish trap?

The American philosopher Willard V. Quine has pointed out, in a mild reproof of Ockham, that any set of facts may have many valid explanations. The most fruitful is not always consistent with other explanations, nor need it be the simplest.

This was the discovery that physicists made in stumbling over quantum theory.

The best explanation does not only explain what is known: it reveals what is not known.

Darwin, for instance, believed all his life that animals pass the characteristics to their offspring that they have acquired in their lifetimes. He had no notion of the role of DNA in communicating forms of life through generations.

His theory allows *only* the environment to decide which survive. The role of DNA is still being explored. Its potential is still unknown.

I have certainly introduced a supernatural element: but not more supernatural than Eddington's mind-stuff; nor, indeed, than Erwin Schroedinger's insistence that *'what we observe as material bodies and forces are nothing but shapes and variations in the structure of space.'*

My suggestion is that life is prompted to adapt *actively*; that this impulse is produced by the universe; that it guides evolution; that this is what previous cultures have called God.

A heresy for religions and science.

Eddington would demand to see some evidence in human behaviour. I have suggested it is the impulse to be honest: that this impulse has repeatedly refashioned religions, and is the constant inspiration of science.

But what if it is wrong?

I described my near panic on realising, in France, that it would be more consistent with the truth to present an altogether different explanation.

This would mean abandoning being just an ordinary kind of a guy who got all excited about teaching children to ask questions in school mathematics.

Instead I would have to admit the possibility that I am very odd indeed.

No-one likes to think oneself a Freak.

Imagine my pleasure on returning to Oxford to find that the week's New Scientist is titled: 'The God Issue', and promises to explain *'why religion may outlast science'*.

I have a soft spot for New Scientist. In 1999 it was the first major scientific journal to support my proposal that school mathematics is teaching the majority of pupils—and therefore the majority of people—to incline to be dishonest.

The NS editors commented in support: *'Mathematics teaching can hardly be said [any more] to be politically neutral.'* (New Scientist, 28 August 1999, No. 2201)

But publication by Britain's leading scientific journal had no effect on the vanity, stupidity, and cowardice of Britain's educational academics, or the authorities they advise.

When an eminent British professor asked to be invited to a conference I had organized for the Qatar Foundation, I and my supporters, all university professors from Hungary, Germany, France, and the United States, were delighted.

To our amazement—more precisely: to my dismay and to the absolute astonishment of my international colleagues—my invited British professor proceeded to trash our efforts. Rather than learn from a mere teacher, or from his supporters, several of whom were of higher status, the Qataris listened to this professor telling them that our proposals were not supported by the British academic community. They were therefore of no value to children anywhere, and there was, therefore, no reason to change anything in Qatar.

The Qatari teachers were visibly relieved. We heard no more from Qatar Foundation.

Remembering that awful time: first my friends' disbelief, then their disappointment, I feel exhausted all over again. I heard no more from the British professor. How could I have been so stupid as to suppose that a university professor would want to support me?

I confess that my heart therefore leapt at the prospect of others taking the bullet: that the 'God Issue' would reconcile religions and science without depending on me.

I have met Dr Dawkins twice. He is uncommonly polite. On the second occasion I told him that his understanding of human evolution would always be deficient if he did not acknowledge the importance of theophanies.

"What are they?"

"Appearances of God to man."

"Poof!" he responded: and if anyone can say 'Poof' politely, Dr Dawkins can: *"They're all fairy stories."*

The contributors to the 'God Issue' (New Scientist, 28 August, 1999), seem to agree with Dr Dawkins. Justin Barrett, Director of the Fuller Theological Seminary, believes that children:

'are naturally receptive to the idea that there may be one or more gods which helps account for the world around them'. (Ibid. p. 410)

Ara Norenzayan, of British Columbia, presents:

'a growing view that religious beliefs and ritual arose as an evolutionary by-product of ordinary cognitive functions'. (Ibid, p. 43)

Robert McCauley, Director of the Center for Mind, Brain and Culture of Emory University, Atlanta, Georgia, suggests that:

'religious ideas and actions spontaneously and inevitably arise in human populations'. (Ibid, p. 46)

Victor Stenger, of the Universities of Hawaii and Colorado, declares:

'If a properly controlled experiment were to come up with an observation that cannot be explained by natural means, then science would have to take seriously the possibility of a world beyond matter.' (Ibid, p. 46)

Now, let us imagine accepting this challenge. Imagine that there really is a fairy-story god: a really physical, affectionate, violent, rambunctious God, who drops in on our modest little home (our universe) every thousand years or so to see how his kids (we) are getting along.

Suppose he has found that the majority of us are tearing up the place; cutting down the trees; pissing in the oceans; multiplying like rabbits; and that all the cleverest kids have let him down. They were supposed to keep us out of the hands of that persuasive little bugger, Satan.

Now, sure enough, Satan has got us so riled up that all we can think about is how to shit on each other: which really means how to shit on ourselves.

Sorry for the patois. I get excited.

Oxford, 1ˢᵗ April 2012

Entracte

Every child fears being called a Freak. Like this:

Every child hopes to be loved and respected by everyone, but most of all by those who matter most.

But the fear does not go away. It is still there in teenagers, still there in young adults, still there in old adults. This fear is as old as humankind.

If we could go back to the early Bronze Age, we would see that the needs of the leaders of organisations for conformity were much the same as today.

To ensure their conformity people were told that an all-seeing, all-powerful god was watching them to make sure that no-one did, thought, or imagined anything other than what his faithful servants prescribed. Their duties were so exhausting that they could do no other work. They needed to be provided for. Their business sense being much the same as now, they made sure that they kept their business in the family.

To imagine being back then, it may be useful to remember playing with our pals aged five or six. At that age, knowing nothing of Galileo's discoveries, Isaac Newton's physics, or, for that matter, the Second Law of Thermodynamics, we could invent any reality we liked. It was a wonderful time.

We might imagine, for example, that we have an immensely powerful magical friend who will do anything we wish.

Suppose, for instance, that we imagined that we have escaped from a cruel king, but were now safe in a magical land which our powerful friend had provided for us.

Of course we have fought many battles; but naturally we have won them all, and now this magical land is all ours.

"But, wait a minute," says the Freak, who is always finding fault. *"So we are safe now because you said the bad king is on the other side of the sea, so he can't get at us anymore. But if that's so difficult, how did we cross the sea?"*

This is typical. But the answer is obvious.

"That was easy," you answered triumphantly. *"I held out my hands over the sea, like this; then I swept them aside, like this; and our magical friend split the sea down the middle like a zipper, and we just walked across as if it was dry land. HaHa! Then the sea came back just as the bad guys the king had sent after us were trying to follow, and they all died."*

"Crikey!" said the others, imagining the whole thing too, and laughing as well. *"Yes, we remember! That's just how it was!"*

"But," said the Freak, *"it would be all muddy at the bottom of the sea. My mom would be ever so cross!"*

Freaks are never satisfied. *"If you don't remember what we remember,"* you say, *"you can't play with us anymore!"*

You shout at him angrily: he could spoil all these games. *"You're just a Freak!"*

Then the others begin to shout as well: *"FREAK! FREAK! FREAK!"*

And he isn't allowed to play anymore.

From then on it became a rule: anyone who disagreed with whatever everyone else agreed was true is a Freak and isn't allowed to play anymore.

*

All teachers know this nightmare. This is supposed to be a quiet lesson, and the whole class has gone berserk, fighting, tearing each other's work . . . then the classroom door begins to open.

You open your eyes. Aah! It's just a dream, not real.

But we cannot make our nightmare disappear. It is our world.

In previous essays I have insisted that there is no need to imagine a God who is a companion and teacher; or that we are modelled on his kind; or that our ambitions are his ambitions.

All these beliefs are very ancient. They have caused many societies to suppose that they are fulfilling God's ambition in dividing, excluding, and destroying other people, whilst making them the scapegoat of their sins.

These beliefs are still common in many countries: look behind you.

Which is why I am about to turn an intellectual somersault.

Very rarely elegant, this manoeuvre is sometimes necessary.

In my case it is necessary for a deeper reason.

I hope you will forgive me for withholding this from you: but I know that God exists. I know that he tries to teach us: his endlessly unruly children; I know he must be appalled that we have still not decided on an ambition that we can share; that instead we are still squabbling over which of our ambitions is his.

The paradox is that today virtually no-one actually believes in God. Whilst science denies his existence, his function has been taken over by an enormous industry whose millions of workers declare that they are the proof of God's existence, for they know his thoughts, his dislikes and desires, and, of course, his ambitions. Our religions are perpetually at war over these.

And yet for all thoughtful persons, questions remain.

What if God exists, quite apart from any religious beliefs?

What if he has looked in on our world and was appalled?

What if this God decided to show us that he is active?

What if he is sufficiently like us to have a sense of humour?

Obviously he will need to demonstrate all this.

Since scientists believe that they can best distinguish natural from supernatural, it would be amusing to reveal some new knowledge supernaturally: not anything that might be hijacked to prove one nation's superiority: just something that science thinks impossible to prove.

He will need a witness: a natural sceptic: fit; thoughtful; trained to observe and report; moderately courageous; stubborn; and, of course, young, for it may be decades before it is safe for his report.

There must be no violence; but, since modern scientists can equal Inquisitors in their zeal in consigning frail bodies to the flames, and since they rarely reflect that science would not exist without previous 'supernatural discoveries', it will be best to make the demonstration in such a setting that the witness cannot be declared insane—as poor George Cantor was, for example, for daring to explore infinities—a modern psychiatric hospital should serve very well.

Then there must be a reason to make him ready for the demonstration.

I always felt that my situation was highly artificial.

Eventually the hospital's military director told me what had happened, that a very famous journalist to whom I had sent my Northern Ireland essay had taken it to a senior government member of his London club and had advised his government to 'fix' me.

Did he know that I had annoyed the government? He had become famous for campaigning against the use of psychiatric medicine to silence political dissidents in Russia. It seemed unlikely that he would want the same for me. He was also famous for annoying the government himself. This was why I had sought his support.

Meanwhile, the hospital's directors had received their orders, but were puzzled.

Most fortunate of all for me, the military director—this was Colonel Ferguson—did not like being used to fix the government's problems. He told me in our final interview that his orders had been to begin treating me, very dangerously, as soon as I arrived. *"Without clinical notes! As soon as I met you I could see some bloody fool had made a mistake."*

Perhaps I was someone's scapegoat: *"Here's a Freak who disagrees with us."*

In the first week, I was tested every day.

What had happened on the evening of the first day had already changed my life. I never doubted my sanity. Now I could relax as modern medicine agreed with me.

But on my first free afternoon, sitting alone in the hospital gardens overlooking the sea, I puzzled too. What exactly had I seen?

I still felt that violent embrace—I can feel it now—but I could not remember *seeing*.

At first there had been deep black space in front of me.

Then that huge dark presence rushed towards me, growing ever larger.

But from where?

No, wait! I *had* seen . . . .

No, no: impossible.

But there it was.

This vast spirit which embraced me had come from a perfectly black sphere faintly glimmering against the deep black of space.

I shook my head. It made no sense: none at all.

But it remained. This was what I had seen.

By the fourth day the tests were becoming tedious.

Then there was a long wait. On the sixteenth, I was discharged. The director wrote in his report: '*This young man, of high intelligence, is not a psychiatric patient.*'

This was in 1972. Most of you know the rest of the story. I qualified as a mathematics teacher. I became aware that honesty is essential to understanding mathematics, and other sciences, that it is essential to understand ourselves spiritually as well as intellectually: that modern teaching is killing honesty.

Teaching is engrossing, rewarding, exhausting. Years went by. I learnt to pray properly, a great relief. From time to time I recalled the mystery. I had seen: what?

A totally black sphere in totally black space?

Still impossible.

But it was all impossible.

Could the intelligence that had received me short-circuit space-time; could it take human form; could its home be beyond our reality; could it be *amused*?

In 1930 Subrahmanyan Chandrasekhar, a young doctoral student at Cambridge, predicted the existence of stars which collapse under their own gravity. His theory was rejected by Arthur Eddington, whose evidence had made Einstein famous.

By the 1950s the scientific community had accepted Chandrasekhar's mathematics—proving that not even light could escape from these stars. They must be invisible.

In 1967, James Wheeler, one of the best minds trying to understand their physical structure, was the first to name them 'black holes'.

Sci-fi movies were soon showing vast swirling vortices, swallowing everything in range of their gravity, crumpling everything, in Wheeler's words: *'into an infinitesimal dot, extinguishing space and time like a blown-out flame.'* (*A Life in Physics,* Wheeler, J.A., 1999)

The movies made it look as if everything around a black hole was being sucked down into a cosmic plughole to disappear like bathwater. To where? No-one knows.

These pictured holes were visible. They could swallow anything. They must even swallow physics. No-one could work out what happens inside them. Perhaps time disappeared as well.

This was how it was told on Star Trek. This was good enough for me.

But about ten years later I was listening to James Wheeler being interviewed on the radio, when I heard him declare very impatiently: *"And a black hole isn't a hole, it's A SPHERE!"*

Revelation!

But still only a revelation.

Black holes are now spheres, but are still invisible.

When I saw what I saw, I had been angry, but not frightened.

This was also a fairly critical moment in my life.

It is also true that I am very stubborn.

In 1976 I wrote the basis of 'Source' for the Epiphany Philosophers in Cambridge. They published my account in their journal (*Theoria to Theory,* Journal of the Epiphany Philosophers, Cambridge). Its editor, Margaret Masterman, placed a copy in the British Library, telling me: *"One day theology students will be citing you in their theses."*

I think this highly unlikely. Religions do not favour fact.

In 1973 two Russian physicists, Zeldovich and Starobinsky, told the British cosmologist Stephen Hawking that black holes might emit particles.

In 1974 Hawking theorized that pairs of protons might be created close enough to the event horizon for one to be gobbled up, whilst the other might radiate outwards.

A black hole would then produce a faint glimmer of light.

It would be just visible against the deeper black of the space around it.

It would look rather like a sphere of polished black quartz on black felt.

Scientific theories must be supported by observation. This observation is impossible to make naturally. Perhaps it could be made supernaturally.

But this is also impossible.

Where does this leave us?

It certainly seems impossible that we share our reality with an intelligence which can set and reset space and time; which can take human form; which appears to enter our reality, and possibly leave, through something resembling a black hole.

Cosmologists now believe that black holes may exist at all galactic centres.

There would be, therefore, many entrances and exits.

But all of this is impossible. This whole 'demonstration' can be dismissed. Who cares whether something impossible to see was ever seen, however it was seen, or that it took forty years to report it! *Poof!*

The truth is that none of this matters. I might also be another shameless fraud like so many previous gurus, with a real appetite for blondes, jets, and Swiss bank accounts.

I leave you to decide what to believe.

For me the demonstration lasted for years.

It was my experience in teaching many of you which convinced me that all children have the right to be brought up as young messiahs: knowing that they always have the right to be honest and that they always have the right to ask questions. This is what I learnt.

We need these young messiahs. We need their innocence and energy.

The fact is that we are killing our young messiahs like the angel of death over Egypt.

Help put an end to this desecration.

Start today. Tell your child that you love honesty.

Explain that science is the art of honesty.

Explain that we only truly worship God through honesty.

Explain that *"the rest,"* as the great Hillel once remarked, *"is commentary."*

Oxford, 11th May 2012

Postscript:

First published in EducationNews.org as 'Insights into Religion, Spirituality, and Global Governance'.

Part I.

Last week I attended a major conference in Oxford on 'Religion, Spirituality, and Global Governance'. The conference was convened by the Academic Council of the United Nations System (ACUNS), the Centre for International Studies (CIS) of the University of Oxford, and the Center for Sustainable Development & International Peace (SDIP) of the Korbel School of the University of Denver.

Its title may persuade those already convinced that secret groups are planning total global dominance, together with a new global religion, and that these were its aims.

I wish they were. But I saw no sign of either. It was simply a meeting of international scholars wishing to improve the future of the world. With great patience and remarkable kindness they allowed me to address them, even when my questions became increasingly outrageous.

I hope I planted a few useful ideas. This is hard to do in modern academia.

One of the paths leading from Oxford's centre to the quiet corner in which their meeting took place is called Jowett's Walk. It commemorates a famous theologian of the 19th century.

Much loved by his students, they teased him with this poem. *'Here come I. My name is Jowett. All there is to know, I know it. I am Master of this College. What I don't know isn't knowledge!'*

Dr Benjamin Jowett was the Master of Balliol, still reputedly the most cerebral Oxford college. He would have had very little patience with the endless preoccupation of modern scholars to find more money from somewhere for more of their research.

"Research!" he thundered: *"a mere excuse for idleness. It has never achieved, and will never achieve, any results of the slightest value."*

Modern scholars have succeeded in turning his censure around. Despite the collapse of educational standards in schools in the US and the UK: a collapse which has become a serious threat to their social cohesion and to their international authority, I have found that many senior educational academics, especially in the UK, view any proposal based on actual teaching experience as entirely valueless. They value only their own and their students' own research, managing in this way not only to flout Jowett's opinion but to reverse David Hume's even more famous dictum: *'Does it contain any abstract reasoning concerning quantity or number? No. Does it contain any experimental reasoning concerning matter of fact and existence? No. Commit it then to the flames, for it can contain nothing but sophistry and illusion.'* (in 'An Inquiry Concerning Human Understanding', Hume, D. 1758.)

'A mere excuse for idleness, sophistry, and illusion.'

These are also the reasons for my slowly learning to be cautious of modern academics. It is always something of a shock to discover that the fact of having spent many years actually teaching real children in real schools is clear evidence to many of possessing inferior intelligence to theirs, likewise of ambition, and to be certainly of low self-esteem.

This is very like being regarded practically as sub-human, which is decidedly unpleasant. The university tenured professor who is capable of listening with intelligent attention to a rank outsider is unfortunately very rare indeed: The odds against it are multiplied many times if the actual experience of the rank outsider contradicts the professor's carefully tailored research.

And this is why I creep into academic conferences like a sniper, close to the ground.

A third reason is one of the first rules I learnt as a teacher: never to think myself as being more intelligent than my pupils. I *should* be more experienced. I *could* be more knowledgeable. But I must *never* think of myself as more intelligent.

This has often saved me from making an ass of myself. Far more important, it has allowed me occasionally to experience one of teaching's truly great joys: of learning from my pupils.

This may be understandably harder for someone lecturing year after year to young students who dare not interrupt or question. But a consequence of a lack of honest and direct rapport can be that some eminent scholars become monstrously self-absorbed, clearly expecting their listeners only to admire and applaud, delivering their wisdom like a drug-addled oracle in the depths of a cave.

Anatomists tell us that deep inside our brain is the brain of an ape, and underneath it is that of a reptile. Only a very thin layer, enclosing them both, is wholly human.

Mine must be even more divided.

The reptile's brain was useful in training to be a sniper: in simply staying still.

The ape's fear of leopards translates into my fear of holding onto any idea too long.

The thin human layer became a teacher. After a few hours, since I am a teacher, I began to assess the ability of the speakers. This depended on how well they spoke: on whether what was said appeared significant; whether their listeners enjoyed what they heard; whether it sent them to sleep.

It may be interesting to readers to know the marks I awarded. I gave one 10 out of 10. He was excellent! I gave two others 9; two 8; one 7; one 6; one 2. The rest got zero.

Zero is really very, very bad. You may know that this mark was yours. Do not throw yourself into the river. Decide to do better. Your listeners may be more intelligent than you are.

The usual procedure in a conference like this is for a panel of scholars to deliver their opinions on a previously chosen topic, for a moderator to invite questions from the audience, for the panel then to respond to these questions.

Since the CIS will produce a formal report, there is no need for me to do the same. What my readers will want to know is what their own correspondent succeeded in contributing.

I must warn that their own correspondent became increasingly emotional and excited, that eventually he abandoned his—or the reptile's or the ape's—natural caution altogether.

Almost all the first day was given to discussing the historical justification of many conflicts; whether conflicts of any kind could be prevented, and how; how societies might be reconstructed after a conflict has ended; what the survivors might hope for in their future.

After the panellists have spoken, the proper form is to ask them questions.

"Can you imagine solutions to these problems," I asked, *"without reference to history?"*

The panel looked polite and puzzled. I hastened to explain.

"Many conflicts are justified historically. But if history is taken away—for example, from the Jews, Christians, Muslims—what would they argue about then?"

There was no enthusiasm for this comical idea. Without history what would anyone argue about! A tart comment was made that Communists always wanted to abandon history.

Not so, I responded. They always identified their enemies historically: then killed them.

Still on my feet, I told of my experience in Northern Ireland: when I had argued with the government that using violence against violence would create only more violence, and of my reward of three weeks in a military psychiatric hospital ordered to treat me as mad.

History was certainly used in Ireland to justify killing. But, I again pointed out: *"Killing doesn't really need justification. Killing is the ultimate thrill, the ultimate pleasure."* Whilst politicians claimed that they had negotiated the peace: *"In the end the pain became greater than the pleasure. The violence just burnt itself out."*

Such conflicts can also end when history becomes irrelevant.

On the second day a different panel was being moderated by a very distinguished scholar of international relations. I asked if I might question them before they began.

"Yesterday," I explained, *"I tried to remove history from your solutions. Now I want to ask you to do without the future."*

This produced a slight smile from their moderator. His panellists were even more puzzled by this second question than they had been by the first. One of the panellists had also been a diplomat. *"No! No! No!"* he shouted. Nothing could be more absurd.

Another had earlier described the enormous difficulty of persuading the UN to agree on anything, when at every level of every dispute everyone could be expected to lie. For him the future would always be needed, simply in order—eventually—to decide the truth.

I still wanted them to realise for themselves that history and the future do not matter as much to everyone else. I asked them to notice a comment of Einstein, that problems cannot be solved at the level of consciousness which has created them.

"What is the largest group in any society," I asked them and the audience, *"with no real interest in the history of their society, nor much in its future?"*

There was silence, until a voice from the audience answered, *"Children."*

Correct. This was a useful advance. Could I build on it?

The final session, on the afternoon of the second day, was given over, as is usual, to summarizing what the conference had agreed.

It did not seem that much had been agreed. It had been proposed that if enough adults learnt inner peace and spiritual wholeness, they would bring peace to the world.

This seems true to me. Peace needs every bit of help it can get.

By now we were all tired. Everyone was slowing down. Three were asleep. The moderator signalled, rather reluctantly, that I might speak. This would be for the last time.

"Last week," I told everyone, *"I had a meeting with my spiritual director, who told me: 'Colin, try to be KIND to everyone!'"*

This was already outrageous. It got worse.

I continued. *"I hope you have all noticed how kind I have been. But now I want to repeat the question that Cromwell once addressed to the presbyters of Scotland when they were in dispute. 'I beg you to consider whether **in the bowels of Christ** you may be wrong!'"* (Actually he wrote: *"I beseech you, in the bowels of Christ, think it possible that you may be mistaken."*)

I should have been more direct.

I wanted them to understand that conflicts are not likely to be resolved by trying to interpret history so that different societies will agree. They won't.

It is children without knowledge of history, or concern for the future, who will have the different consciousness that is needed. They can be qualitatively different from any children who have ever lived before.

They only need to be taught that they have always a right to be honest, and that they always have a right to ask questions. They will never allow themselves to be misinformed into war, or misdirected into war, or lied into war.

This is what I should have said. Instead, I blew it.

Part II.

The story so far: Attending a conference in Oxford on 'Religion, Spirituality, and Global Governance' I hoped to explain that religions, the sciences, and mathematics are all the creation of a far older and more fundamental spiritual inspiration. Knowing this might help people to realise that they are united by religions and science more than they are divided.

I tried to get them all to discover it themselves. I asked everyone, panel and audience: *"Since this is a conference on religion and spirituality before it is about global governance, and since most of us here will have some belief in God or in spirituality, can you tell me: How is God inspiring all people* ***now?***"

One of the panellists at once began to describe how many people were differently inspired: how many were not inspired at all; how others . . .

My question was swamped by this deluge of unfortunate desires. Time was called. I had missed my chance.

Ten minutes later I was standing with a paper cup of coffee in my hand with many of the others at the reception to mark the conference's end when I became aware of a young girl on my left and a young man on my right, and that the young girl was asking: *"What is it?"*

"Pardon?"

"Your answer. How is God inspiring everyone now?"

"Oh, how kind of you," I responded feebly. *"I was so dejected. Well, it's a big question. And the answer's very simple. But it took me thirty years to figure it out."*

"Yes, yes. Well, so, what is it?"

"Honesty."

"What?!"

"It's honesty. God inspires human beings, has inspired them historically, inspires us now, to be increasingly honest. But this is more than universal. It is cosmic. Evolution is not only advanced by the environment selecting what can best survive. Organisms

vary themselves to attempt to fit their environment: neither, in a sense, attempting to cheat it nor delude themselves. In this sense they are also being honest."

They both seemed impressed, but she wasn't sure. *"That's alright,"* I told her. *"Just write me a thirty-line rebuttal, and we'll discuss it."*

But she still hadn't finished. *"And what else did you learn in that hospital? You said something about being inspired there."*

Did I? Oh dear. I said nothing. This was hardly a good time for revelations.

"Oh, no; not another cliff-hanger! Just tell us!"

What red-blooded male can resist a passionate young girl?

I will call her Alice, since we are in Oxford; and the young man, Christian.

"Right," I said. *"Hold his coffee, and hold his plate."*

Surrounded then by others drinking coffee, eating sandwiches, I proceeded to give young Christian a demonstration of theophany. He seemed about the right age. To make it as realistic and authentic as possible, not so easy in these circumstances, I embraced him very hard, as violently as I could. This was also rather comic— since he was taller by half a foot—but I told him as I did so of that wonderful declaration: *"How can you be afraid? You are of me!"*

"Was it a Christian god?" asked Alice.

"It was a warrior. I was a soldier."

"Was it so physical?" asked Christian. In answer I thumped him again on the chest, very hard; he is a very solid young man. *"Yes, very."*

I told him that Bishop Robinson, whom they knew by reputation, had been the third person I had told thirty-seven years ago in Cambridge; that they might be the twentieth and twenty-first.

I told them that I had long mistaken a cosmic instruction for a personal one.

I had thought "Be honest" referred only to me. It is actually the song that the cosmos sings to all life everywhere. It is the law of its laws.

Then Alice said something that she need not have said.

"You must feel enormously privileged."

Then I said what I should not have said. *"Yes, it is an enormous privilege and an enormous responsibility. In the worst analysis it's possible that not more than four or five others have known it in the whole of human history. It's possible too that hundreds of thousands have known it, but that it has been just too terrifying, too dangerous, too difficult to talk about it. On all those counts I have been more fortunate."*

And in this moment I know that all this was true. Enormously privileged: enormously responsible: enormously fortunate: and I have kicked continually against the goad.

The title I intended to give to my postscript of the essays that I have been writing for my Facebook friends was 'Quo vadis?' All the previous essays have also appeared here.

I thought that it meant: "Where now?" On checking I found a very different explanation.

Saint Peter was leaving Rome to escape execution when he met Jesus. *'Quo vadis?'* was the question he asked Jesus, who replied: *"I am going to Rome, to be crucified again".*

Peter was so ashamed by this that he turned back, was arrested, and was crucified.

The truth is that I do not believe these stories. They are myths, and we should not need myths either to understand the obvious.

Humankind has always needed Freaks to teach it honesty.

The Buddha, to tell it that reality is a creation of the mind, changing as a mind changes; the Vedic messiahs, to describe the form of many gods, both creating and destroying, just as honesty can create and destroy; the Jewish prophets, settling on the existence of one god; Muhammad, the last of his line, calling everyone the children of that One.

I have always hated to be thought a messiah. To be called the messiah is not only a weakness of others, it is an invitation to be crucified all over again.

What the world needs now, as I have said already, is generations of children, a generation of messiahs, who know naturally all the tools of peace and who know how to use them.

They need to be told that they have the right to be honest and that they have the right to ask questions. They need to know history, but they must not be persuaded that any part of it is their history. They should not worry about the future. They will create their future.

As their mind and their reality changes, so will their understanding of honesty, and of what questions they need to ask. They will lose their innocence as they become individual.

The innocence of a child is a state of mind in which anything is permissible in order for it to get what it wants. In an adult, the same state of mind is that of the psychopath.

Another kind of innocence is created by submission to the will of God to achieve social identification. In this state of collective innocence nothing is permissible within society that has not been formerly prescribed, whilst anything is permissible outside it to assert its prescriptions. Killing is certainly permissible, both individually and collectively.

The different forms of submission are the reasons why religions form. They are also the reason why they divide and will fight each other with merciless ferocity.

Much the same is true of nations identified as doing God's will. It is generally forgotten that this is how Hitler persuaded his countrymen that they could not fail; how Stalin made the defence of his own ruthless regime into a defence of holy Mother Russia.

Since the identity of their religion or the nation has become the identity of every individual, any perceived slight to either the religion or the nation will be felt as a personal hurt.

All will react. Some will react individually. Some will react collectively.

Some will react like a child in a tantrum hurling its plate at the wall. This may kill us all.

This was a conference on 'Religion, Spirituality, and Global Governance'. Its main concern was to understand how social conflicts arise; to learn how to reduce their ferocity; and to learn how to help societies to repair the damage they do.

My hope was to explain that their principal cause is obsessive identification by groups with their history, and another is an equally obsessive determination—to some extent actually shown by the conference itself—to determine the future.

I tried to offer an alternative within the conference itself.

Perhaps this report will succeed where I failed.

Being aware of God's will as a personal inspiration is entirely different from submitting to any prescription of it. It makes no claim on the future. It is instead an adventure: of the heart, of the mind, and, essentially, of the soul.

It is an adventure that takes many forms.

One of them, much bewildered by its own rhetoricians, is science.

All require free will.

Beware of those who tell you that yours does not exist.

They have not found theirs.

On being compared with Socrates

My most recent report concerned the strength and weaknesses of the recent conference in Oxford on: *'Religion, Spirituality, and Global Governance'*.

I had hoped to explain that religion and spirituality and global governance could all be furthered by informing the several billion children in the world today that they are so numerous now that they are capable of ending tyranny and corruption simply by declaring that God inspires them irresistibly to be honest, and refusing to accept any more shabby lies.

This, of course, is how the Arab Spring began. It is how the 99 percent mobilised. Both are mainly expressions of young people's disgust with governmental chicanery.

I also implied that the response of many academics to a new idea is like that of a herd of yaks. If they cannot frighten a new idea away, they may try to trample it to death.

This must be endured. Now please read on.

Dear Colleague,

I am sorry that you find my report of your conference disappointing. I hope I may be allowed to explain why I found the conference disappointing. I hope that you will recognise that every criticism, however apparently unkind, will always contain some truth; and that you may allow me to suggest how future events could be improved.

It is always hard to write a constructive report if a conference has no clearly defined and declared aim; if the various speakers then do not need to explain how they believe they are contributing to that aim; and if, finally, the plenary meeting describes no conclusions.

You brought together, and marshalled most impressively, nearly two dozen speakers from several countries. Over the two days of the conference they spoke a million words.

They did so, however—so far as I could ascertain—without any well-defined aim. The speakers' contributions lacked structure. The quality of their speeches was surprisingly varied. Some were excellent. Others were astonishingly lazy, prolix, and self-absorbed. There was, finally, no agreed upon conclusion.

One of the most significant remarks—made early on—was that *'people's assumptions generally determine their conclusions'.*

My questions were an attempt to help your speakers recognise their assumptions and to set them aside.

On the first occasion, I asked the panellists whether they could imagine solutions to the problems they were discussing without referring to history. On the second, I asked them if they would try to do the same without referring to the future.

Both suggestions were summarily rejected as either foolish or banal.

But they were neither. The two assumptions that they could not imagine doing without were that their solutions must refer to history and must refer to the future. These assumptions would then greatly determine their conclusions.

They remained still unmoved when I further pointed out that any solution they arrived at must affect millions and even billions of children; that children have very little regard for history; that they are generally concerned only about the immediate future; and that, since their lives will be sooner or later affected by any decisions this conference or any other of equal importance might make, they deserve to be informed and engaged.

But how can they be informed? In what possible way can they help?

This was the reason for my third and, I think, most important question. *"In what way is God inspiring people everywhere now?"*

I had really expected someone to attempt to reply, even if with some sweeping generalization: for, as you know, some generalisations are sometimes useful, even true.

The silence of the entire room was actually very surprising.

To my further surprise—although it is never entirely unexpected—I was not asked by the chairperson to suggest an answer myself, but instead was brusquely cut short. The conference ended right there.

Had it not been for the unexpected intervention of those two thoughtful and inquiring young people, Alice and Christian, in the reception afterwards—and I hope you will recognise that this was an actual miracle—I would never have been able to reply truthfully as I did in my report.

"It's honesty. God inspires human beings, has inspired them historically, inspires us now, to be increasingly honest. But this is more than universal. It is cosmic. Evolution is not only advanced by the environment selecting what can best survive. Organisms vary themselves to attempt to fit their environment: neither, in a sense, attempting to cheat it nor delude themselves. In this sense they are also being honest."

Since I included it in my report to you, I had hoped that this observation might be circulated to everyone who attended the conference. It may not be especially novel: although I have just written to a distinguished Cambridge paleobiologist who I learnt is puzzling over the deficiencies of Darwin's theory to ask if it may fill the gap; but I believe it can help everyone to look at the world with, as you say, 'a beginner's mind': that is with less fear, with less confusion, and with more honesty.

I was happily impressed by your stern warning in reply that I might be leading astray 'the thousands of young people' who read my thoughts and trust me. This is wonderfully similar to that fatal accusation made of a great hero of mine: of 'corrupting the youths of the city and introducing them', if my memory is right, 'to strange gods'.

Actually most of my readers are now in their 30s, even 40s. Many have children of their own. They can assuredly see beyond any stereotypes and prejudice of mine to glimpse the necessary truths, whilst behind them stand silent billions waiting for the most favoured, privileged, and important people in the world—that is, us—to find solutions to our world's problems which do not require agreement about history or the future which will never be achieved, but which can be announced and applied now.

This was my contribution to your conference. Will it be recorded? Will it be noticed? Will it be acted on? If not, what objections to it are there? How are they supported? Who makes them?

Is there any reason why children should not be told that they have the ability to be honest and that this ability is more powerful than any government, simply because they outnumber any government? Here is the most powerful weapon of nonviolence: the refusal to continue to accept shabby lies as certain truths. This is surely why my young Arab writers are reading me.

But I am happy as well to report that I have since been thanked by one of the young people who was present, who wrote to me recently: *'As a young academic I appreciated the way you deliberately challenged the norms of what are generally considered appropriate questions in conference contexts.'*

Others who were present have also told me that they were grateful for my efforts to challenge old assumptions and propose a new approach, whilst I have been recently moved nearly to tears by a young mother whom I knew as a young girl who wrote of my first report: *"I think I speak for at least a healthy majority when I say thank you for your efforts, Colin! Even if people do not always answer, or comment (myself being one of those), we are all still here and reading when we get the time! Thank you☺. Love to you too, as always!"*

I presume that there will be a formal report. If so, I look forward to it. I am sure my editors would welcome the opportunity to publish it, together with your comments. They will be even more impressed if my suggestions are included.

Best wishes,
Colin.

A First Religion

Dear Friends,

I begin this today, on the 3rd of June, my birthday. So many of you have responded that it is impossible to reply to you all. Instead I will follow the suggestion of a favourite philosopher of mine, Baggins by name, that one's birthday is the best time to send presents to one's friends.

We have together created a wonderful present for the world: a conception of an invisible, incorruptible, irresistible God who is also the inspiration of science.

Some of you will have discovered that my life has been a love story. As a penniless young soldier, I fell in love with, of course, a very beautiful girl. As girls must, she decided to marry her own choice. I decided I must still prove my worth. I had first to learn to think again. This brought me, in time, to receive my epiphany.

Nearly twenty years passed before we met again. To my mingled joy and terror, I found that I loved her still. By this time I had been warned that virtually no-one actually believes that mankind is guided by God. If we were, humankind could not possibly be in such a mess. But when I asked her what she wanted most, she replied: *"I wish I could explain the world a little better to the children."* *"Oh,"* I replied rashly. *"I can do that."*

And I started again.

The fact of the First Religion was implicit in my revelation. Some presentamen of it has occurred over millennia to inspire successive religions.

But I was still then thinking as a soldier: all decision and action. To know how to explain it, I had to learn to think as a teacher: to respect you, my pupils. Then, with your help, this is the understanding we have achieved.

The First Religion is simply a deeper theory of evolution.
It suggests there is an impulse of order acting throughout the cosmos.
In the beginning it balanced the early energies.
It created matter for energy.
It organized matter into atoms and molecules.
It enabled molecules to build organisms.
It guided organisms to adapt actively with their environments.
In some, self-awareness became self-consciousness.
Adapting to the seasons produced the early cultures.
As societies increased, other cultures evolved.
Weaker societies were assimilated or annihilated.
First Religion guided social consciousness from idols to abstractions.
The earliest of its guides speak plainly,
Dress plainly, live plainly, need no palaces.
But as societies become more powerful,
Governments become more rigid and elaborate.
Divisions and suspicions appear.
To feel more secure they buy more arms.
Most of our societies are at this stage now.
Our poor become poorer. Our children lack care.
The modern religions are highly ordered.
Followed by billions.
They employ millions of workers.
Many are highly influential in their societies.
Even the United States is polarized by religions. (See Pew Forum Research, April 2012)

One quarter of these workers will be purely exploitative;
Another quarter will be legalistic;
Another is angry that the rest of the world remains unconvinced;
A final quarter despairs that their faith has become too elaborate for this ever to happen.
The followers of most religions are actually divided in much the same way.
Fully half can therefore be invited to join First Religion.

The first advantage of First Religion is to offer an understanding of the world that does not rest on history and with which children can decide their own future. I might explain more here and now, but I intended this to return your good wishes in good time.

Let me first show you how closely First Religion follows the instinct and reasoning of some famous thinkers of the far distant and recent past. You will know most by name.

In that very distant past, when descriptions and objects were first being understood as snares for the mind, Buddhist philosophers conjectured that all perceptions are created by individual minds from a universe of possibilities. We see what is wished to be seen.

A pregnant thought! Indeed.

In 1923 John von Neumann explained how numbers, supposed by every previous thinker to be the bedrock of reality, can themselves be conjured by the mind from nothing.

Von Neumann was a truly great mathematician. His explanation goes something like this. The concept of nothing is itself not nothing. It is a description of something. Count 'one'. Now there are two ideas in our mind: nothing and the concept of nothing. Count 'two'. Next identify 'three': and so on

This is a little laboured. But the intention is much the same: to conceive of order appearing from the interaction of nothing and a mind.

In the 1950s the physicist Eugene Wigner, who helped create nuclear bombs, was asking: *'How is it possible that the process alone of Darwin's natural selection has brought our reasoning powers to the unreasonable effectiveness of mathematics in describing our universe?'*

An answer had to wait until 2006, when our old friend James Theobald Wheeler published his grandly named (by him): *'Participatory Anthropic Principle'.*

Leaning heavily on the theory of quantum electro-dynamics, the most accurately tested theory in science, he proposed: *'We are the descendents of the biological participators who created not only the near and here, but the far away and long ago. Their perceptions created the universe; our perceptions sustain it.'* (I have taken some liberties in paraphrasing Dr Wigner and Dr Wheeler. Their meaning is unchanged.)

Some may hold, perhaps along with Stephen Hawking, that this was the moment our universe appeared; and that *that* observation was made in the mind of God.

Science appears to have come full circle. It is back with the rejection of idolatry, of objects being held to be holy, of places being sacred. Instead it says that *we* are sacred.

According to the ancient Vedic Upanishads, which guide seekers of knowledge to accept reality as it is, it is only necessary to understand: *'tat tuam asi'.*

There are several translations. One most respected is: *'You are that which creates'.*

Back to the myth of the killer Moses, asking how to tell his people of his experience in being spoken to by God, and being told: *"Tell them 'Ehyeh-Asher-Ehyeh'."*

It was another old friend, my tutor Bertrand Russell, who first identified the difference between similar syntactical forms. The first of these alternatives he would have called a declaration; the second an instruction. They look identical. They may sound identical.

How much confusion can be created from misunderstanding three words!

I will finish my first thanks with another of Russell's comments. He is sitting beside me now, in the shape of a battered old copy of his 'Basic Writings', which I find I purchased on May 9th, 1968, in Bristol.

In September that year I went to Ireland as a not very effective intelligence officer in a society polarised by religion for over four hundred years. In Russell's book I find a flimsy folded paper being used as a bookmark. It is a receipt from Morrison's Beach Hotel, Killadoon, County Mayo, and records two persons staying for two nights, June 20th-21st, 1970.

The cost, with dinner, wine, and breakfast is written on it: Seven pounds five shillings and eleven pence. I must have read the following comment that the bill bookmarked. Yesterday afternoon I found it again.

Here is Russell writing three years after what he called 'the cruellest war ever waged': *'Daily joys, times of liberation from care, adventure, creative activities, are at least as important as justice in bringing about a life that men can feel to be worth living. Monotony may be more deadening than an alternation of delight and agony . . . . Love of power still leads to vast tyrannies . . . . Fear, deep, scarcely conscious fear, is still the dominant motive in very many lives.'* (*Authority and the Individual*, Russell, B., 1949)

In an earlier essay, in which I noticed Eve's surprising generosity—in giving control of justice to Adam, rather than keeping it for herself—I noted that there is a curious incongruence.

This does not fit human nature. But human nature can be made to fit it.

Whilst the most monotonous lives are commonly thought to be directed and controlled by men, a little thought will disclose the fact that the most highly controlled societies are far more to the advantage of mothers and their children.

Although they may appear to be the victims, it is older women who benefit most from societies in which little is ever allowed to change. They are capable of directing their apparent male rules from cradle to grave. They even choose and tutor their successors.

I began to realise early in teaching how very effective schools are in driving great crude nails of fear and guilt into children's hands and feet.

Forgive the harsh imagery. The pain and damage are real. The majority are crippled doubly. Fear makes them unwilling to offer kindness to others. Guilt—especially of 'not succeeding' in societies in which all are expected 'to succeed'—leaves them unable to deal calmly with the unpredictable trials of life: often involving dishonesty, injustice, unfairness.

Above all, they can no longer think for or say of themselves: *"I am who I will be!"*

Moses might well weep.

All great ideas are first ignored, then scorned, and are then described as having always been entirely obvious.

Here is an entirely obvious idea.

Only the exploitative, the legalistic, the unimaginative, and the mad want war.

Upwards of one half of the followers of the world's religions want to overcome their guilt and their fear, and do not want war. We can show them that God *cannot* inspire war.

If you are interested in helping me create a charity to promote this entirely obvious solution to the world's wars, please start thinking NOW.

To explain more advantages I shall write just three more essays: 'How to be honest'; 'How to be just'; 'How to be fair'. In them I shall try to show how every religion began as and embodies First Religion.

And then, dear friends, I will STOP!

Love to you all, Colin.

On Staying Honest

There are two reasons to stay honest. Although apparently very different from a scientific perspective, from the spiritual standpoint they are much the same.

The first reason will be the most essential to most people. Let us start, however, with the most unlikely.

The simplest organisms on our planet are single-cell amoebae. They are about the size of that last dot, and absorb nutrients from grains of sand smaller than themselves. Then they stick the grains around themselves to construct a protective shell. They make, in fact, a house.

How unlikely!

Now I am perfectly able to accept that this is due to nothing more than a chance. In the case of such very simple creatures, this might require only a relatively few instances over several billions of years. But since I am also inclined to be sceptical, I am also prepared to say: *"I don't know how it does that: but it seems to me to require rather more than chance."*

It appears to me that the simplest explanation for the amoeba and its house is that the cosmos is governed by a number of fundamental laws: which make life inevitable.

That we do not know them all is unimportant. We, and the fact that an amoeba can build its house, are the evidence that they exist. This is called the anthropic principle.

I have never wished to believe that we are as subject to selection for survival as any other organism, and that this is very likely to be as ruthless, as merciless, and above all just as hugely wasteful as any other natural process. Still being sceptical, I must also accept that what I have not wished to be true may be true.

Selection was the name of the process by which Hitler murdered seven million, Stalin killed twenty million, Mao Zedong beat, starved, and worked to death over forty million.

In these and other genocides, the anthropic principle was reversed. It was not random. The process was selective. In the end, it was no more than vicious human spite.

Can we do no better?

Suppose, for a moment, that you do have that which most atheists, including dear old Russell, derisively refer to as your soul. How might this be understood in modern terms?

We suppose that we are conscious. Specialists are unable to agree that we are. Some explain that the illusion is not more than a product of the more fundamental necessities of existence: in simple terms, of eating, shitting, fucking, and sleeping, the habits we share with other animals.

Are you shocked by shitting and fucking? Try not to be. My father, who never swore, and who never otherwise used Anglo-Saxon vulgarisms, one day described the basis of life to me in exactly these terms. I know now that he was deeply disappointed by his own life and that he no doubt believed he was explaining a deep philosophy to me; that I should therefore ignore all the high-falutin' rubbish that Richard Feynman also mockingly called 'feelosify!' and accept this fundamental truth: life has no purpose.

Some specialists believe that consciousness is functionally unnecessary. The amoeba, we may suppose, does not have it. We can live without it. And without free will.

I am prepared to agree that, for those who lack more curiosity, this is very likely true.

But I doubt that Bach would agree. Or Mozart either.

I would rather imagine that the soul is a portal into consciousness through which, ultimately, we—some of us—may be selected for survival.

And the evidence for this belief includes instinct, music, and mathematics.

Is this impossible? No. Is it repugnant? Of course it is repugnant, horribly so. It is likely to mean that this portal must be discovered and kept open until the very instant that our mind's consciousness ceases to anchor us to the presentamen of reality which we have been obliged to share with billions of others: and that, if it is not kept open, it will not connect with any possible higher level. Do you want to bet it isn't there? Wise decision: poor judgment.

But if it is true, what will be the consequence for most of the billions of others?

They will have no future at all.

The apparent cruelty of Darwin's theory led Russell to declare: *"Henceforth the soul's habitation can only be safely built on the foundation of unyielding despair."*

I think he is wrong. In at least one respect our variation is more hopeful. It is, for example, more respectful of intelligence, even at the level of amoebae.

But in another respect, it is more cruel.

For us the responsibility is personal. It means learning to use one's intelligence as honestly as possible *with the intention to survive.* It means being ready to abandon whatever is expected: especially what one has been told to expect, to do what is necessary.

Without this: no survival.

This, therefore, is the most far-fetched, selfish, and cruelest reason to learn to be honest.

It is cruelest because most people will never know what is required. Most people today are ruled by elites who, above all, do not want them to learn to use their intelligence or their honesty to their own benefit. This is how it has ever been.

'It is a great beast' is how Alexander Hamilton described America during its foundation, proposing that the rich retain control. *"It is a great beast, turbulent and changing; seldom able to judge or determine what is right."*

So much for ideals.

What now of the more mundane reason?

Here we run into other difficulties. My father was possibly much like yours. Honesty was as natural for him as breathing. This produced a problem for me, for he simply could not believe that anyone could honestly have any opinions different from his own.

That I might develop such opinions filled him with dread, and, as I grew older, with rage. His efforts wore down the affection between us—and, I regret most of all, my respect for him—so that by the time I was thirteen or so we were hardly speaking.

As soon as I could, I became independent. At the age of 17, I joined the Army.

What a relief! Within a year, although still nominally a private soldier, I was marching around acres of boot-polished tarmac with up to three thousand others, all equally speechless, all never required to express any personal opinion, and revelling in my new freedom.

Although I would not discover for several years, shooting had already lost me my high-frequency hearing. I never noticed this, but the result on the drill square, especially if the command was unexpected, was that I might be a millisecond behind the rest of my platoon.

This mattered little to me, but deeply to our drill instructors, Sergeants Hall and White, who consequently christened me Yogi. My best chum was Denison, an Academy cross-country runner, fast and fleet of foot. In the battle-dress which we wore daily, I was approximated to a cube. He was half my size. They christened him Boo-Boo.

Despite me and Boo-Boo, they caused our platoon to win the drill trophy in that first year, and as we crashed back to our billet in spine-jarring synchrony, we could have died together for the glory of it all. The purpose of military service is to prepare young men to die together: not necessarily for their commanders or for their country, but for each other.

Honesty matters more to soldiers than any other virtue. It is more important than courage, intelligence, knowledge, wisdom, or decency. Sooner or later it decides life or death. Being lied to is therefore unforgivable. A soldier would readily hang any commander who lied to him and his mates.

In most respects, the soldier's life is otherwise easy. He is dressed, housed, fed, reasonably paid, kept, at least when young, superbly fit, and allowed to make few personal decisions. It is true that there may be very few occasions or reasons for him to be dishonest.

But then, one day, some over-excited, over-testosteroned politician decides his moment has come to demonstrate his own belief in destiny, his own unflinching moral courage: and lies.

And the next month, you may be another Joe Bonham.

You don't know Joe?

Joe is lying in a hospital bed without face, mouth, eyes, arms, and legs.

Unable to communicate with anyone, he wonders:

"Did anybody ever come back from the dead, any single one of the millions who got killed, did any one of them ever come back and say, by God, I'm glad I'm dead because death is better than

dishonour? Did they say I'm glad I died to make the world safe for democracy? Did they say I like death better than losing liberty? Did any of them ever say it's good to think I got my guts blown out for the honour of my country? Did any of them ever say, here I've been rotting for two years in a foreign grave, but it's wonderful to die for your native land? Did any of them say hurray I died for womanhood and I'm happy? See how I sing even though my mouth is choked with worms?"

(Cited in his lecture 'Taking Soldiers Seriously',
by Professor Cheyney Ryan,
Oxford, 22 May 2012)

A modern writer describes more succinctly what young men and women expect for offering their lives in service to their country.

"Duty is a transaction. We owe them. They owe us a solemn promise to risk our lives and limbs if and only if there is a damn good reason. We like to feel some kind of good faith somewhere. Now it's all political vanity and electioneering. You can try, but you can't bullshit a soldier."

(From the novel, *'Nothing to Lose'*, Child, L. 2008)

It seems to me that the main obstacles to honesty are trust, loyalty, patriotism, faith, ignorance, fear, laziness—and, most of all, expecting what you have been told to expect.

Since they almost always act together, philosophers have argued for millennia how to separate them logically. I doubt that there is a way. Human nature is just too complex.

But I learnt recently two versions of a story which may help us here.

In 333 BC Alexander the Great was confronted in a little place called Gordium by a huge knot suspended from two poles. He was told that it would be undone only by the future ruler of the world.

Alexander is 23, barely five foot tall: just a boy. In one version, he draws his sword and cuts the knot in two. This must appeal to many politicians.

First, identify the enemy: then slice him up. Electioneering!

But big knots don't cut so easily.

He would have had to jab and hack and saw.

It would have been a long and tiring business, ending in a mess of severed strands.

In another version, recalled by Plutarch, Alexander took down the knot, grasped its ends, and simply pulled: until the rope lay untangled at his feet.

How could he have been so confident?

His mother had always told him he was a god.

He wanted to show that knots can be untied.

Simple honesty can undo many knots.

This is the second version.

But honesty—today—is only for stupid people.

Isn't it?

Smart people learnt to tie knots, not to undo them.

Don't they?

We learn how to make people believe that we know what we are doing.

Don't we?

'Leave it to us', we say,

'Trust us to do what is right!'

And they do!

Not understanding that we define what is right.

As whatever is good for us.

And honesty as whatever we can get away with.

Believing in 'truth' is for mugs.

And anyone who believes differently from us

Hasn't grown up.

I think it's time I showed you where all this started

Oxford, March 2010

Epilogue I: How It All Began

THE SOURCE

I wish to propose for the reader's favourable consideration a doctrine which may, I fear, appear wildly paradoxical and subversive. The doctrine in question is this: that it is undesirable to believe a proposition when there is no ground whatever for supposing it true. I must, of course, admit that if such an opinion became common it would completely transform our social life and our political system; since both are at present faultless, this must weigh against it.

Bertrand Russell, *Sceptical Essays, 1928*

What mathematicians call an existence theorem [is] *a demonstration that what is thought implausible exists.*

Carl Sagan, *Contact, 1985*

The room is small, clean, brightly lit, about ten by fifteen feet. On the left was a plain barrack-room metal frame bed. Ahead, in the right hand corner, is a washbasin on the wall; above it a mirror; above that a strip light. The main light is coming from a very bright bulb in a plastic shade hanging from the ceiling. The bed is already made up. The sheets and counterpane are drawn taut; there is a clean pillow; the inner sheet is turned down, but not folded open.

The room itself is in the corner of the building and has two windows. There are curtains, but as I enter they are not drawn. The one on the left only looks into dark trees, but the one ahead looks out over the inky waters of the Solent. I go to it and look out. There is little to be seen except the lights on the distant shore. (The Royal Victoria Hospital was built at the command of Queen Victoria to care for the wounded of the Boer War. It was then used in the First World War. During the Second World War it was occupied by the 28th US General Hospital. It was closed and mainly demolished in 1979. The grounds are now a park.)

I have already realised that this building is a wing of the much larger building. That is where they would keep any soldiers who have become psychotic. So far as I know I am the only officer here. I have certainly seen no-one but the corporal who politely served me dinner.

I undress carefully, deliberately performing ordinary actions. I have neither toothbrush nor razor. Indeed, I have nothing but my uniform. Perhaps I can borrow them from the corporal in the morning. Meanwhile the hospital has put out common pyjamas and a thin towel. I pull on the trousers; button the jacket up to the neck.

The room is warm. The building now seems completely silent. If I opened the windows, I would hear the wind in the trees, perhaps even the sea.

But I am far too preoccupied to do this. I go to the washbasin, press the switch to turn on the light above the mirror, and examine my reflection. I look calm, but serious.

I am very serious. I can think of no way out of this problem, and this is what is annoying me most. I am used to thinking my way out of difficulties. The first thing I need to know right now is not how to think, but how to act.

What behaviour is appropriate? This place appears completely open. I saw no-one on duty downstairs, and I have just walked back from the railway station through the grounds. An NAAFI shop is still open by the back gate. That was the only sign of life. There is no guardroom. I could simply walk out of here.

Where would that leave me? *On the run!* Clear proof of instability. Is it sane to wait here until the doctors have decided what to do? They have clearly not initiated this action; that much is clear from Colonel Ferguson's anger: *"I am having nothing to do with this."* He seemed honest. But, of course, he would. It could be just his professional indignation: *"I have no clinical notes for you."* Should that matter so much?

Doing nothing is rarely a good option. Soldiers who wait for the enemy to decide to attack generally end up wishing they had decided to act first.

I had seen a pay-phone by the NAAFI shop: [Navy, Army, Air Force Institute: the British equivalent of a PX.] I know no friends who could speak to the government, let alone deter it in any action already decided on. There was Bernard Levin, of course. I had sent him a copy of my paper. He would understand at once. He had made himself famous defending Soviet victims of state-directed psychiatry. Now this seems to be directed at me.

Levin has powerful friends. But it is Friday evening. Even with a phone, it will be impossible to reach him, or anyone, except via their private number. Was this planned as well, that I should be effectively incommunicado—unless I run?

Let's stick to the facts.

Here are the facts.

One: I had tried to tell this lazy, stupid government to deal with the Irish as people, not criminals as criminals. I had never really expected to be thanked for this, not even by the Irish, for I had pointed out their weaknesses, not their virtues. I had expected to be noticed, probably court-martialled. Then explaining my reasons might prevent more people being killed.

Two: I missed a simpler alternative. I have let them trap me like a bug under glass. Now they can squash me flat at their leisure, scrape me down the drain. No court-martial; no public hearing. And even whether I am sane is no longer a question for me to answer. These people will answer. And if they decide that I am not, they will then also decide what to do about it.

Three: There is no defence. This is the beauty of it—strictly, of course, from their point of view. If I had been accused of something criminal, then I could be locked up; but I would also have the right to a lawyer, someone to add his arguments to mine. Once there is a medical opinion, the only other opinions that matter are those of other doctors.

Although in these few minutes I have only vague ideas what might still happen, and although I have no wish to distract my thoughts by dwelling on this, I had no doubt that my situation was very serious. It could easily be fatal. Psychiatric medicine has moved on from pushing a spatula in over the eyeballs to scrape out the frontal lobes to 'rectify', actually destroying, the personality, but only just. Used often enough, electro-convulsive 'therapy' can be just as destructive. And then there are the drugs.

The truth is that I had not more than a vague notion of the possibilities from general reading, but all animals have an acute sense of peril. Just now I was holding down my animal sense in a corner of my mind, where it was trying to bite through its chain.

Four: This little exercise had been planned for some time. It must also have started at a very high level. To order any person to be tricked into entering a psychiatric hospital must require considerable political bounce.

This was what was worrying my saturnine Scotch colonel: as it should. He was being tested as well. This was why his anger had fired up so readily with mine. But who the hell had I annoyed so much that they would take risks like these? Many people go crazy at some time in their life; nevertheless the taint of involuntary psychiatric medicine—and I was no volunteer—can destroy a person's credibility forever. Surely I am not this important!

But, there is still five: The colour-sergeant who had punctiliously returned my salute at reception this afternoon had been expecting me—and not for 'hearing tests'. The corporal who had been sent along as my "driver's guide" had known it. The only thing that might be holding up this process was the caution of the colonel, whom I do not trust. His anger seemed genuine: but perhaps only because he had not received the nonexistent notes; which anyone with sufficient knowledge could write up without my participation. Standing in this quiet room, I challenge my own reflection. Sure, I have been arrogant. But I would stand by what I had written. The problem in North Ireland was never a military problem. It was fundamentally a social problem. To use more force to solve a problem created by a lesser force is not just stupid, it is dangerously stupid. Unless the larger force—the Army—can completely eliminate the lesser, Irish nationalism as represented by the Provisional IRA and its million-strong supporters—which, I had argued, was impossible—the social problem could only get worse.

By circulating this opinion I had clearly extremely annoyed someone very high up in the government. But whoever that was, he could only have initiated this response. Who is now controlling it? I had the nasty feeling that it may not be controlled at all; which meant that the limits to which it may go have not been fixed.

So who is in charge? Well, I am. Of course, I am. Without me, and particularly without my dangerous sense of duty, none of this would be happening. And where in fact does this sense of duty come from, I ask myself—so that, even when you think it is your own government that is wrong, you have to challenge its power and its authority?

I am still standing here looking at myself, wasting my energy trying to analyse this problem. I still need a solution. To save myself, to save my own sanity, I need to know what has been impelling me to take these risks. Suddenly, I know.

What happened next happened very fast. About three years later I wrote down the details for a small group of philosophers in Cambridge, and they published this account in their journal. A copy is in the archives of the British Museum. The original text will be found there. The following is a little longer, but is not very different.

I was still coldly furious; not at all in a panic, not afraid, still determined, somehow, to win. But then, whilst I looked at the face before me, I became suddenly aware of something I had not often, or perhaps had never, openly acknowledged: that I was impelled by something else to take the risks I had.

It was not just my new ambition to be noticed as a writer, together with the confidence that my judgment was better than that of my superiors, together with some sympathy and anger at the waste of lives, together with a hatred of all this political pretence and infantile posturing.

There was as well a kind of responsibility which drove me. I felt abruptly a shift in my own mind: a decision made and, with it, certainty. Beyond any possibility of saving itself by anything expected of it, a trapped animal may sometimes do something completely—even insanely—unexpected. What I suddenly knew I could do was not rational, yet I was perfectly certain it would work. I had only to do it. That, I was sure, was the important thing. Don't pause; don't check.

I was not at all accustomed to doing anything without first thinking out all of the consequences first. This time I did. I turned from the mirror, knelt beside the bed, clasped my hands, bent my head, and I said, actually quite angrily: *"I need some help."*

The effect was astounding. There was an immediate cessation of all the perceptions of kneeling in the room. There was a tremendous sensation of forcible displacement, of acceleration to a velocity. Before there was time to realise more, I knew that I was passing out of the region of solar space. I knew this quite distinctly. It seemed to me that I was already at a great height above the solar plane, travelling outwards at a terrific speed. The speed did not diminish. It seemed to increase so that I was passing through the galaxies which were like streamers of mist, radiating a faint heat.

And then I stopped. It was dark. I knew that behind me also there was nothing. It was as if I had reached a boundary. I had time to realise that this loneliness was perfect. I was poised in emptiness, waiting. But then I knew I was not alone. I felt an inexpressible relief at this. At first there was no consciousness of a presence. Instead there was a consciousness of having entered the dominion of a presence.

148

I began to comprehend its character.

Whereas the displacement had been swift, this appeared slow. And yet it seemed to increase, exactly matching my ability to comprehend it. The difficulty of describing it is due to the fact that simultaneously it was expanding from a centre which was discrete and distant, and yet it was also all around. It had a vastness and a centrality. I also knew two things at once. It was familiar: there was no strangeness about it. It was a person and of the same kind as I was. Perhaps it is wrong to say it was gigantic. The scale defeated comprehension. It was as if I had been brought across the whole extent of the universe, or the picture we have of the universe, and at such a speed, simply to understand that this was greater. It was greater because its scale included all that I had seen as the world includes its grains of sand.

I then received two signals: a salutation and an enquiry. The salutation was both an acknowledgement and a greeting. It contained much that will be difficult to describe. It was an acknowledgement as of kind to kind. It affirmed possession. This was as a statement, unarguable, undeniable, complete, and absolute. It was as if to say: *'You need no more protection than this.'* Yet with it came a blaze, a force of love, of pride, delight, of comradeship—with such a shock that I might have laughed aloud with the joy of it.

'You are of me,' it told me as well. This was the kind of love that, perhaps, men always dream of, and yet which is always beyond them to contain, even to express. I think that the nearest to it is that kind of love that men in battle feel for each other; and even for an enemy whose courage is a shared thing. Therefore it was no soft love. It was as hard as the blow of a fist, as strong as the grip in darkness, seizing, gripping to the bone; a grasp of comradeship; a blow of love. It was a caress, and its strength was its tenderness. What could have destroyed, smashed back into oblivion, stretched out, touched, steadied, and held. Here was a strength to do anything, perhaps which did everything. But here it was in check. Its very power was balance. It included everything— and yet it was outside everything. All the principles, all the

polarities lose their meaning. Human affairs are nothing. Good and evil are human affairs. An absolute is the absolute, which is everything.

The enquiry was then simple. I was asked what did I want. I could not have drawn three breaths. My presence was my question. I wanted to know what to do. I heard the answer: as clearly and distinctly as a strong voice speaking into my ear. It seemed to me that a voice did speak to me; as if a man stood close beside me at my shoulder, to the right. "BE HONEST."

And then I was back in the room, and opened my eyes. Nothing had changed. But I had changed. For me a world had changed. First there were other matters to decide. I said, aloud again, *"That was God"*. It sounds foolish. It was pronounced, in delight and with astonishment, but for a purpose. In these few moments ten years' of unbelief, and increasing certainty, had been swept away. I had learnt to trust my own judgment; now what was my judgment to make of this? The centuries of scepticism and rejection that I had learnt and made my own, all this had gone. I wanted to hear my own voice. There was a difference. I got into bed and lay there. The reconstruction would have to wait. I wanted to leap up and find someone to tell.

But that would have to wait. First of all I had to consider the answer I had been given.

The more I considered it the more empty it seemed. How had honesty ever helped? How would it help now?

I scrambled out of bed and knelt again. Now, consciously, I was breaking my own rules. Never ask for help. Now I expected a response. I wanted to know, what did it mean? How, be honest?

This time there was no shift. I was conscious of the presence, but only as if at a great distance. But once again the answer came from outside. It seemed to form in my mind as if I had to read the words with great difficulty. *'Be of good cheer, for no harm can come to an honest man.'* I knew without doubt that I read this correctly. Still it made no sense. Worse, it was plainly false. Honest men were harmed daily. It seemed that there was nothing which so attracted violence as honesty.

After I had lain again for some time debating this in my mind, with increasing dismay, I knelt and prayed a third time. The third time there was nothing at all. I was alone in the room and the room enclosed me in quietness. But then I did understand what it meant. It was something that I could understand by my own intelligence: and that therefore I should discover by my own intelligence.

At the same time, while I attempted to hold it back, to deal only, in these moments, with the matters of immediate concern, realization of what I had learnt, and a beginning of an appreciation of the gift that had been made to me—this pressed in and would not be ignored. I realised that only through honesty may one know God. The quality that God acknowledges is honesty. And to know God, by honesty, or even to acknowledge God unknowingly, by honesty, is to be put beyond the powers of man to harm, for nothing is as important.

That night, surprisingly, I went to sleep almost at once, and slept as soundly as a child. It was only five days later, three days after the formal tests had begun—by which time, as Ferguson told me later, he and his team were already convinced that I was perfectly sane— that I began to question my recollection of the events.

I was sitting in the officers' wing garden at the time, for on the south coast it was still warm enough in November. What I needed to know was if there was anything I could remember which could not have come from my imagination. The plain fact was that although the entire experience would have needed an extreme effort of my imagination, there was still no doubt that it might have.

I began to realise that, whilst I had distinct recollection of the initial visual impressions accompanying the displacement, there was no trace of anything I had seen, as opposed to felt, in the final encounter. This seemed very odd.

Slowly I realised that my memory did contain a definite impression. I think now it had been there continually, but it was so strange and uninformative that I had not noticed it, or I had even refused to notice it. Indeed, I could make no sense of it then as I examined it. I rejected it and sought again for something that would make sense. But all of this was to no avail. The image continued to persist clearly, without any addition to help me understand it. I can see it now if I recollect it. It makes very little sense—as it made no sense to me at the time—if I describe it as a visual image. And yet that is what it was, so I must.

What I saw was an intensely black sphere, neither radiating nor reflecting light; not completely free, but as if a third enclosed from the base in the darker background apparently of space itself. This was the source from which what I had experienced had seemed to appear.

Somewhat later I would like to discuss whether this particular insight is also important. I think possibly that it is, and also very probably that it is not as it at first appears. [I made nothing of this particular insight in that year of 1972, nor in 1975 when writing this account for the first time for the Epiphany Philosophers.]

Many years passed before I caught the end of a radio interview in which the famous American cosmologist John Archibald Wheeler declared, with some asperity, for this was his field: *"Of course, everyone calls them black holes, but they're not holes at all. They're spheres!"* Some years later I learnt that Stephen Hawking believed that they may also radiate a faint light, only be visible against the darkest background. As J.B.S. Haldane once remarked: *'My own suspicion is that the universe is not only queerer than we suppose, but queerer than we **can** suppose.'* Alternatively one might accept that we cannot see what is, but only what our minds allow us to see.

Experiences like mine may be far more common than we may suppose. Alternatively, they may be just as rare as history seems to suggest—or, perhaps, although it amounts to much the same thing, as rare as authorities may wish us to believe.

What matters ultimately, it appears to me, is not what the experience says in itself, but what effect it has on one's life. If it changes one's life at all, then, clearly, it is important to the degree that it does this—but whether it changes it for good or ill is actually not something that the individual can decide entirely alone. Ultimately it can be determined by its fit with history and the present.

13th July 2012

Epilogue II

Dear Friends,

And to those of you who have just joined our class: welcome. I no longer know how many of you there are now, or from where you have come, but you are very welcome at a time, but especially now, when I believe I have made the most important discovery of my life: and, quite possibly, of yours.

An unknown-unknown is now known. Being known, it cannot necessarily be manoeuvred into a corner and knocked on the head, but it can be handled more intelligently.

My original intention had been to write three final essays in the past month, summarizing our progress in securing our children's sense of their own worth, simply by encouraging them to be honest, fair, and just.

I worked hard on the first essay, but I could not like it. I could not throw off the feeling that something was missing. Despite this worry, half a dozen drafts winged across the Atlantic to my saintly editor: who corrected my spelling, questioned my logic, found my typos; and sent them back again.

We were ready to publish, when I realised that it was just not good enough. Pretending to be a giant-killer, I was armed with the equivalent of a wet paper bag.

I have realised for many years that I have—we have—an exceedingly powerful enemy. No: I have not become paranoid; quite the opposite, as you will see.

But possibly I *was* paranoid with good reason.

I had thought my first idea was wonderful. It was simple, elegant, easy: to show my pupils how to learn mathematics as it was first supposed to be learnt: through debate, then argument, leading to general—but not always total—agreement.

This simple change does far more than allow the whole class to engage in understanding mathematics. It restored honesty and

153

fairness and, yes, justice to our classroom. It would do this in any classroom from which an increasingly muddled education has leached away the qualities essential to responsible citizens, and instead rewards dishonesty, selfishness, avarice, fostering indifference in those who have and anger in those who have not. *Circumspice!* (Look around!)

I believed this discovery, so simple and so obvious, to be capable of changing education everywhere for the better. I still think so. But then I made another: this was precisely how democracy was established in Greece two millennia ago.

An Athenian who could not argue reasonably was made to feel that he had failed in his duties as a democratic citizen: as he had. Athenian democracy lasted for nine hundred years. How long will ours? Political divisions in all our supposedly securely democratic societies are becoming increasingly hostile to debate; increasingly extreme in their slander; increasingly sure that the other is a more threatening enemy than any from outside.

There was some interest shown by educationalists in France; more in Germany; still more in Hungary, where it is taught at university; more still in the US, there too; a little in Qatar and Jordan.

With the encouragement and financial support of the Qatar Foundation, which sent a delegation of its own teachers, I organized a conference in Windsor Castle. I was supported by six international professors of education. At the last moment, however, a British professor of mathematics education asked to be invited.

Although I knew that she disagreed with me, I assented cheerfully: why not?

I was, of course, naïve.

Deploying all her confidence and authority, she objected repeatedly throughout our presentation, then attached herself unfailingly to the elbow of the most senior member of the Qatari delegation, in order to continue *sotto voce* at every further opportunity.

We never discovered what it was that she told the senior member *sotto voce*. But when frequently interrupting our presentation of the

Socratic Methodology she informed the Qatari delegation that our approach, of teaching children to learn mathematics through arguing with each other was nothing new. Every British mathematics teacher already used it: occasionally. It could never be an improvement, however, on the tradition of mathematics being taught, as always had been and should be, via the instruction of a confident, fully-qualified, inventive and energetic mathematics graduate standing in front of the class.

She brought along one of her own protégées to give an impromptu demonstration. I wince now, remembering how we were trumped so blithely. I allowed her to do this.

It was a miserable experience: akin to quaffing cyanide.

For this is precisely what the delegates wanted to hear. Education through instruction has always been the tradition in Muslim schools.

Their relief was palpable. No need to change! Just buy more computers!

I never heard from the Foundation again. It withdrew its support without a single further word. Perhaps it felt that I had tried to fool it. Perhaps its thanks went elsewhere.

This was the end for me of four years of hard work. It was over. I got up. I brushed myself down, thanked my good friends, and shed my tears alone.

But the loss to the world is incalculable.

With this one single malignant, short-sighted, and self-serving stroke, Britain, Europe, and the United States lost the opportunity to provide the hundreds of millions of the Arab Spring with the educational basis their children desperately need for a stable democratic future.

Meanwhile neither Britain, Europe, or the mighty United States of America can lure enough fully qualified inventive and energetic mathematics graduates to teach in its schools in the way that it has always been taught: which fails.

Because of this, Western science is failing. So are our democracies.

There have always been enemies of new ideas. This is a given. But, as years passed without any further success, I began to realise that I had been far too modest in trying only to restore honesty and fairness and justice to education.

The problem is far bigger. The Beast is a danger to mankind.

I knew all of this when I sat down to write a month ago. I also knew that, in all the years I have been pursuing it, I did not know how it did so much damage. I did not know why. I only knew how to recognise it from the harm it does.

I told my editor that I was stuck. I needed to think again. But I had tried that for decades. It was time for a little humility. I needed help.

"Ask, and it shall be given unto you; seek, and ye shall find."

It took the whole of the month for some of the best minds of the past two millennia to pull me up short; to tell me to look around; to look at them, at their history, at the present now: to understand how people are so easily made to believe that they already know all that God, or providence, or their university, expects them to know. But this is just the twinkle in the eye of the Beast, just a lick of his tongue. He can do far more. He has been able to convince people throughout history that they are pre-ordained to invade and conquer or exterminate other people, replacing their way of life with their own.

How is this done? By what dark powers is this achieved? I still did not know.

But lurking in the shadows of my thinking was always that terrifying poem by the Irish poet, William Butler Yeats. He clearly had a notion similar to mine. Do you know this?

The darkness drops again: but now I know / That twenty centuries of stony sleep / Were vexed to nightmare by a rocking cradle, / And what rough beast, its hour come round at last, / Slouches towards Bethlehem to be born?

(A hint: all the stress is on 'vexed': this is when the Beast wakes up.)

You are all, of course, my helpers, but in the past month the following have been of special importance (alphabetically): Flavius Valerius Aurelius Constantinus Augustus; J. M. Allegro; Albert Camus; Felipe Fernandez-Armesto; Sigmund Freud; Robert Graves; Frank Harris; Thomas Hobbes; Soren Kierkegaard; A. A. Milne; Henry David Thoreau; Friedrich Nietzsche; Thomas Paine; Plato (for Socrates); Bertrand Russell; William Shakespeare; St Augustine; Shlomo Sands; Roger Scruton; C. P. Snow; Baruch de Spinoza (actual and other); Jonathan Swift; Sun-Tzu; Voltaire; W. B. Yeats.

Be assured that 99.8% of the writing is mine: but without the pointers, the nudges, and an occasional hard shove, from one or more of the above, I would have given up in despair.

I am asking you to read a great deal. I will split the whole into Facebook essays. This won't make it shorter; but unless you read them all, you will not be able to share my astonishment as my errors have shown to me, one after the other. I will try to make clear how my thinking was changed, by whom, or by what; but what I was able finally to understand was not seen by any of the above.

Only four of the above lived in our nuclear age. None of the others could imagine the dangers we have created for ourselves. They are aptly summarized in the last sentence of Felipe Fernandez-Armesto's magisterial history of the conflicts between every country in the world in the past thousand years: *'No earlier age had access to awareness of such a comprehensive menace, or of such an awesome chance.'*

None of them will show you that the path to Armageddon was opened by whoever first made a besom of twigs and began to *scritch-scritch-scritch.*

This is what woke the Beast, with all its powers.

Stay with me.

Colin

Next: The True Nature of the Beast.

THE TRUE NATURE OF THE BEAST I: THE CHASE

Dear Class,

I am no longer the man that I was. My conceit has been diminished; my hubris has been punctured. I have been humbled.

The proof that I survived is here. And the consequence, I am happy to report, is glorious.

My intention had been to use a summer month to write three final essays [Ed. Hah!] to summarize our progress with teaching children that they have a natural and incorruptible right to be honest, just, and fair.

Although I worked hard on the first of the essays, and in spite of a number of drafts sent to my editor, nothing seemed right. Then, rather than publishing, as I had hoped to do, I was submerged in an avalanche.

My friends came together to show me that I had been pursuing the wrong beast.

I should have realised what was wrong. I should, for example, have remembered the importance of this story from the biography of one of the most profound English philosophers, one with whom, incidentally, I identify most readily—Winnie-the-Pooh, the Bear of Little Brain.

One day, Pooh was following some strange tracks in the snow around a spinney (that's a small wood of young trees, grown too closely together to see through) when he was joined by his small friend Piglet.

"Now look here," said Pooh. He pointed in front of him. *"What do you see here?"*

"Tracks," said Piglet. *"Paw-marks."* He gave a little squeak of excitement. *"Oh, Pooh! Do you think it's a-a-a Woozle?"*

"It may be," said Pooh. *"You can never tell with paw-marks."*

Clearly their possible Woozle must be now on the other side of the spinney.

They set out to confront it.

A deep tragedy is about to unfold. It is an extremely instructive tragedy, similar to Hamlet, or Macbeth, for it reveals the most important truth about the quest for truth.

Namely, don't decide what you are going to find before you start.

For this, basically, is what I have been getting wrong. I have been chasing a beast that I created, and ignoring multiple warning signs all the while.

Fortunately, although I am separated from my editor by thousands of miles of ocean and the entire Appalachian Trail, I have other helpers: as you have seen.

On trial for his life, Socrates, a stone-cutter by profession, teases his accusers by reminding them that he did not always make up his mind for himself. He had the benefit of his *daemon,* who always tried to prevent him from making mistakes. And besides his wife, Xanthippe, who bore his three sons and made sure he was decently clothed, he had also a spiritual mistress, Diotima, who had first claim to his heart, and who instructed him in philosophy.

Some classical historians think that Diotima was Aspasia, the beautiful and intelligent mistress of Pericles, patrician leader of Athenian democracy, who all the other high-born Athenian ladies whispered was a whore.

I can hardly call Pooh my daemon, and he is certainly no Diotima. I think of him as more like Baruch de Spinoza, the Amsterdam Jew whom Russell called 'the noblest and most lovable of the great philosophers'. He was excommunicated by his synagogue (Whoops! He is here already! I read the reason two minutes ago in my biographical dictionary.) because: *'he identified God with the ultimate substance of the world—infinite, logically necessary and absolute—which has mind and matter as two of his attributes'* (Chambers Biographical Dictionary, 1990). The saints are always with us.

In the margin of Russell's text there is also a scribbled note of mine of many years ago, possibly in 1977. It reads: 'Well, well— difficult to know if I ever read that before and assimilated it. I think not.' The reference is to Spinoza's own words: *"The mind's highest good is the knowledge of God and the mind's highest virtue is to know God."*

Bertrand Russell goes on to comment: *"Intellectually, some others have surpassed him, but ethically he is supreme. As a natural consequence, he was considered in his lifetime and for a century after his death, as a man of appalling wickedness."*

So, you see, we are all either whores or corrupters of youth. Spinoza died aged 43.

But let us go back and look for a few more warning signs.

In 1959 an unusually thoughtful man called Charles Percy Snow published a famous book entitled: '*Two Cultures and the Scientific Revolution'*. In it he described the lack of communication between scientists and nonscientists, together with his fear for the future.

We are in his future now, and the problem has got worse. I described in *'Oxford High Jinks'* the attempts of a high priest of science, Dr Richard Dawkins, and a high priest of faith, Dr Rowan Williams, the Archbishop of Canterbury, to agree with each other on even the most basic notion of how they might agree. And they could not.

My sympathies were about equally shared. I never imagined that the theologian would defeat the scientist; but I thought that Dr Williams might better explain his faith, as I thought I could.

On the other hand, Dr Dawkins is hardly less dogmatic. He had recently introduced the baleful notion that religions act like a virus on human minds, taking possession of their intelligence, turning them into thoughtless zombies.

I could see his point. But I also thought that, as a highly respected biologist, he should never have proposed the existence of a virus which could not possibly be physical.

Let me now attempt, in outline, and with respect, to offer alternative lines to both.

As the Archbishop of Canterbury, I would have observed, mildly: *"I hope we can agree together that all societies need a common morality. To be most effective, this should be learnt by all; approved by all; tested by all; sustained by all; learnt as children by all. Without this common moral accord, the unity of any society can be shattered by a first determined blow and fall apart.*

"The history of all religions shows that the great majority of people benefit emotionally from their religious beliefs. Some still find them intellectually challenging. It has recently been proven, scientifically, that many live longer, happier, more peaceful lives. Over the centuries their gratitude has built great cathedrals and humble chapels. There is not a village without its church.

"The Church of England was established by King Henry VIII, rejecting the authority of the Catholic Pope, to provide the British people with just this support.

"I am ready to concede (remember that I am doing my best to speak as a high theologian) that some of its principles might now need re-examination, even reformulation.

"It is certainly unfortunate, for example, that Jesus is most commonly remembered today for suggesting that it is glorious to be poor, whilst to be rich is unfortunate.

"But we must remember that in Jesus' time the elite identified entirely with Rome. The middle class, a few thousand merchants, a few dozen itinerant rabbis like Jesus himself, were insignificant.

"All the common people were poor. Of course he had to comfort them: to tell them that they should be grateful for being poor, that this almost guaranteed a smooth trip to heaven. This is what they needed to hear: and it is just as true now as then."

He might also concede—well, I doubt an archbishop would do this; so I will—that this very fundamental message of the Christian church has also had an unintended consequence.

This is found in Britain too, but is most obvious in the United States, where it is clearly held as an obvious truth by many who are so unfortunately rich: doomed to a very rocky ride, followed by a long wait in a vast, cold, gloomy hall, echoing with the anxious moans of billionaires and the squeaks of their lawyers preparing their plea, but still defiantly declaring: they'll be *'damned twice to hell, and back again, if Jesus H. Christ, Our Lord and Our Redeemer, is going to be made out to be a goddamn Socialist.'*

No, that wasn't the archbishop. That was just me going off the rails.

"Anyway!" I might say, scrambling back to the somewhat higher moral ground. *"Anyway, that is what religions can do, and that is the mission of the Anglican Church, and this is what it does; and, were it not for the unfortunate incursion of so many other religions into our sceptered island, this precious stone, set in a silver sea (ahem! Shakespeare), of so many religions which do not agree with us at all, I for one would have no fears for the future."*

Now here I am as Dr Dawkins.

He is, by the way—as I have said before, though some would disagree—a remarkably polite, elegant, and nice man, so that it is very hard to make him appear otherwise.

"My dear Archbishop, thank you. So you are not ready to admit that all religions, not least your own, ruthlessly exploit people's credulity and fears, just as much as any tenement landlord cramming yet another penniless immigrant into yet another fetid room; that your beliefs depend on evidence that would only convince a five-year-old; that you are fundamentally a business, even more like a Las Vegas casino that promises to make everyone rich, in the end, whilst skimming off its profits; that only guilt and fear keeps the money coming in.

"As for more peaceful! You have challenged me by suggesting that irreligious governments, especially in the past century, have murdered more people than ever religions have. This, of course, is true. But I will remind you that in every case the actions of these governments were justified scientifically. Now we see that errors were made. But it is the very great virtue of science that it can admit to its mistakes and then moves on. Can you do that?"

The Archbishop, being required to reply: *"No."*

Dr Dawkins: *"I thought not."*

The Beast cannot be a part of this kind of raree-show. I did not intend to make this trivial. But it is trivial.

We are looking for something like the monstrous devourer of nations in Goya's paintings of the Spanish civil war.

To find it, we must look further from the present into the past.

A Letter from Greece 20th July, 2012

Dear Friends,

Here is the second part of The Beast. It comes to you from the blessed island of Naxos, sacred to the memory of Ariadne, who, you will remember, saved Theseus from the Minotaur, her monstrous half-brother, in his labyrinth, but was then abandoned by him there. Gerald Durrell thinks that the experience may have unhinged him, where she was more happily found by Dionysius, who fell in love and married her.

Amongst his most recent meticulous corrections (it was *Henry IV*, Act 3, Scene 1, and not 2) I received a mild check of my own from my editor over in Georgia: that I should not claim to be the *only* person alive to have my experience.

In the first place, as I try to say later: there is good reason to suppose that all individual experiences are precisely that, and that, inevitably I suppose, we try to make sense of them by matching them with a more general, even universal, corpus.

But you should also know how often, and how fervently, in all the years that I hesitated, and even before I began teaching, I wished, oh, how I wished—I may even have prayed—that someone, anyone, more than one, and braver—might take the responsibility from me. It never happened. Why? Then one may justly answer, with resignation: 'God knows.'

Colin.

27th July 2012

THE TRUE NATURE OF THE BEAST II: FIRST CHECK

I was not trained as a scientist to a very high degree. The reverse can be said to be true. After I achieved my engineering degree, the army began at the beginning, starting with orange-white hot iron pulled straight out of the roaring coals of a blacksmith's furnace.

This is absolutely the best training for an engineer. Give me good steel, and I could still make you a horseshoe, or well-tempered sword. Chains are rather harder: all those links.

But, despite my humble background, I like to think of myself, in spirit, as a scientist.

Which was, of course, the heart of my dilemma on possibly being the only person alive able to confirm the truth of Jesus' assurance in reporting his relation with his God, the reality of Muhammad's experience, or the reports of other witnesses from world history.

This responsibility did not so much frighten me. I simply felt myself to be totally inadequate. What help is it to know how to hammer hot iron into a sword?

And the list is shortening. Abraham is now considered a myth. So, possibly, is Moses. Other milestones are toppling. Even Israeli historians now accept that the Exodus, on which the moral right of Israel to exist is supposed to depend, never could have happened; therefore there is no longer any need to continue thanking God for killing all the Egyptian firstborn. The crossing of the Red Sea was not necessary. Moses did not need to carve the Law on tablets of rock on Mount Sinai. The walls of Jericho never fell down. The Jewish nation has experienced many transformations. In the face of endless hardship, it has had continually to reinvent itself around the matrix of myth and culture.

Many Christian theologians now question the historical reality of Jesus. Others shrug away the Resurrection. His miracles no longer impress as they once did.

But, and as is indeed true in my case, what most suppose is 'reality' is far less important than demonstration.

Here is a demonstration that convinces me: When they challenged him: *'He bent over and wrote on the ground with his finger, then straightened and said to them, "Let whoever has not sinned throw first."'*

No-one who is not at once in that room with the frightened girl, the excited men, the sweat, the dust, her fear: with him—whoever does not at once know that this is real, will not be very good, I suggest, at distinguishing reality from twaddle.

Only Muhammad is now wholly human. Human with all his simplicity as a spokesman of God; human as a warrior, offering friendship to enemies; most human of all, in forbidding his followers ever to think of him other than as a man.

He could only be appalled by the idolatry attached to his name today.

Most convincing of all, however, is the captivating account of the response of his wife's blind uncle, Waraqa bin Naufal bin Asad bin 'Abdul' Uzza bin Qusai, to his nephew's story. It is essentially the moment when Muhammad first understands the difficulties before him.

After he had heard, Waraqa sighed, and said: *"I wish I were young and could live up to the time when your people would turn you out."*

Once again, I can feel that I am with that anxious young man.

He looks younger than forty. His wife, Khadija, has already pulled a rug over him. His head is in her lap, one hand is in hers. There is wind; a flickering lamp; wild shadows; then this exchange in whispers: *"Will they turn me out?*

The old man shakes his head, reaches out to touch him: *"Never did a man come with something similar to what you have brought but was treated with hostility."*

A little less than fourteen hundred years later, aged twenty-nine, I became a member of this dangerous club. You know now the circumstances. If I had been anywhere else, I suppose, it might have been worse. I was well supported. It could not have been better arranged. Even I was left convinced that I was not mad: not before; not then; not later.

But we may all report delusions. And we all may be privately mad, with no obvious signs at all. These are trivial questions, really. But there is another: a very deep question. It is whether we are identifying our own intense, enduring, entirely individual and purely metaphysical experience with the same source. Could we be mistaken?

There is great potential for harm in persuading others that their reality is exactly the same as that of others. More than anything else, this is how modern science resembles mediaeval hokum.

To avoid this danger, we look for demonstration. And we are not alone in insisting: *'There is a history in all men's lives, figuring the nature of the times deceas'd; the which observ'd, a man may prophesy, with a near aim, of the main chance of things as yet not come to life, which in their seeds and weak beginnings lie intreasured.'* (*King Henry IV*, Part 2, Act 3, Scene 1, Shakespeare, W.)

Compared with the multiple madness of humankind today, all fixed around some totem of reality, some blood-soaked altar, some patch of land, some notion of liberation and freedom, our simplicity is surely to be treasured. So also, possibly, courage.

But science rightly demands more than courage. It insists that no experience can be accepted as the basis of general knowledge unless it is repeatable, on demand: not only by the first witness, and the next, and the next, and the next; until it can be experienced by everyone.

And there's the rub.

We cannot order up the experience which: *'seem[s] to give an insight deeper than the piecemeal knowledge of our daily life. A life dominated by this insight, we feel, would be a life free from struggle, a life in harmony with the whole, outside the prison walls built by the instinctive desires of the finite self.'* (*'The Essence of Religion' in* 'Basic Writings', Russell, B.)

There has always been a different reason for my continuing to try to communicate what my own insight meant and still means to me.

It is, to put it simply, that I am haunted by the spirit of Baruch De Spinoza.

I try to read widely. I usually think that I know what I need to know.

Spinoza may not agree.

'Yes, yes, that's all very well,' he mutters testily. *'NOW LOOK AT THIS!'*

Under my nose, almost always, he presents a book: usually open at the page; sometimes as if a finger is pointing out the line. He always knows that I will understand. This is so irritating. It provides him with some amusement. He sucks his teeth. He misses his synagogue.

These events are common. Occasionally they are shocking; that's when then you might hear me mutter, angrily: *"Just what THE HELL is going on?"*

They have never been delivered with such urgency.

It seems now that this was necessary to head me off from attempting to nail the wrong beast: the beast the world is trained to fear, the beast which grows stronger every time it is defeated.

A few weeks before, I had read a long article on Islam in a scholarly Jewish journal by a respected British philosopher, Professor Scruton, of Oxford and Harvard.

He begins with a blood-chilling line: *'The West today is involved in a protracted and violent struggle with the forces of radical Islam'.* (Azure Magazine, No. 35, 2009)

The violence he sees as unavoidable. The reason is that: *'Traditional Islamic society sees law as a system of commands and recommendations laid down by God. These edicts cannot be amended. Law, as Islam understands it, is a demand for our obedience, and its author is God. This is the opposite of the concept of law that we in the West have inherited. Law, for us, is a guarantee of our freedom. It is not made by God, but by man, following the instinct for justice that is inherent in the human condition.'*

The 'instinct for justice' sounds promising. It accords with our views. But I think he is wrong. He believes in the reality that is described by texts: as fanatics do. He should look for demonstrations. They say that liberal Islam, personally mediated Islam, is the world's fastest growing religion. And that radical Islam is dying.

A week ago there was a long discussion on Islam's future between a German Salafist and a young Muslim woman. This was reported in *Die Zeit.*

The Salafist declared that his possession of an encyclopaedia of Islamic laws and proscriptions, covering every aspect of life, meant that he enjoyed the supreme privilege given by God of never needing to think. His authority was given to him by God.

His young opponent was unimpressed. Imagine a hundred million young Muslim women being similarly unimpressed. They do not have *Die Zeit*. They have their IPads.

At the end of my street lives a young woman, who appears most mornings wearing long black robes with a letter-box slit for her eyes.

She looks extraordinarily elegant. Doubtless she enjoys her little daily triumph.

It is the wrong demonstration.

I trust that someone will tell her that dressing modestly means not attracting attention in any way; perhaps also that she should never be outdoors at all without her father, uncle, or her little brother.

Of course this is also trivial. But it is important. Multiply again by several hundred million, and this is the future.

A young man had resigned from a Salafist group. Later he tells his fiancée why he still believes in its ideals. She listens, and tells him: *"I may not be able to argue with you, but I know what you are saying is simply bulls***. And you know what? So do you."*

I have argued in previous essays that the apparent subjection of Muslim women by Muslim men has always been required by the women. It provides them with the security to bring up their children safely.

Al-Qaeda cannot see it, but outside its training camps, radical Islam is dying. First: because Muslim women are realising that they no longer need or want to spend their lives indoors. Second: because young Muslims, young Jews, and young Christians, even possibly even Mormons and Scientologists, are no longer trusting texts.

They look for demonstrations.

There is just one more clue from the past.

I never noticed it before. I nearly missed it here.

Jesus knew the Evil One, who showed him all the lands of the world, and promised him dominion over them. Not minds. Jesus refused.

Is that a clue? Is this our Beast?

Perhaps he looks now different.

Perhaps he offers different powers.

Colin

THE TRUE NATURE OF THE BEAST III: TRYING SOULS

So our Beast is not religious, nor is it atheist.

I look at its tracks again: still maddeningly real; maddeningly unclear.

Then I was struck by another dangerous thought.

What divided religion and atheism?

Russell once declared: *'All Western philosophy is essentially a footnote to Plato'*, a remark also made by his previous teacher, then his colleague, Alfred North Whitehead.

And how did Plato triumph: not forgetting his teacher, Socrates?

They raised logic above mysticism, logic above emotion, and, yet more precariously, logic above intuition and imagination.

Which led us, as Bertrand tells us, to find that *'mathematics— rightly viewed—possesses not only truth, but supreme beauty—a beauty cold and austere.'*

But there is another, very different, kind of beauty.

"I am the stag," sang a British poet in about Plato's time.

Sing this, softly:

I am the stag: of seven tines / I am a flood: *across a plain /* I am a wind: *on deep lake /* I am a tear: *the Sun lets fall /* I am a hawk: *above the cliff /* I am a thorn: */ beneath the nail /* I am a wonder: *among flower /* I am a wizard: *who but I / Sets the cool head aflame with smoke?*

Take a breath here. Now shout:

I am a spear: *that roars for blood* **/ I am a salmon:** *in a pool* **/ I am a lure:** *from paradise* **/ I am a hill:** *where poets walk* **/ I am a boar:** *ruthless and red* **/ I am a breaker:** *threatening doom* **/ I am a tide:** *that drags to death* **/ I am an infant: /** *who but I / Peeps from the unhewn dolmen arch?*

Another breath. Now whisper:

I am the womb: */ of every holt /* **I am the blaze:** *on every hill* **/ I am the queen:** *of every hive* **/ I am the shield:** *for every head /* **I am the tomb:** */ of every hope.*

This is who we are. Creatures of emotion. Our blood is hot. We need intuition, imagination. We cannot trust logic to find the truth. There are perilous gaps in logic.

In 1901, Russell wrote to a famous mathematician, Gottlob Frege, to ask him an odd question. Bertie was 29. Frege was 63. It had taken Frege twenty years to write his first acclaimed volume on mathematical logic. His second volume was ready to be published.

Russell's question was certainly odd, but not mischievous. He asked if Frege would deal in his second volume with 'sets of sets that are not members of themselves'.

Frege was appalled. They were certainly not in his second volume.

They were logically toxic. They could not exist.

Actually they had been around for a long time. Bertie only gave them a family name.

How can any statement be a member of a set that is not a member of itself?

'This sentence is false'.

You can write it. It appears to make sense. But if it is true, it must be false. If it is false, as it says it is, it is also true! This is how logical statements are written. It presents itself to be a member of the set of true statements. But then it states that it is not. Oh! So, actually it says it is a member of the set of false statements. But it cannot be false if it is true.

Poor Frege! His second volume was published, but he never wrote again.

My own lessons began the day I took down Russell's *'Basic Writings'*, published in 1961. I bought it in Bristol in 1968. I wish I might have met him. He lived in a remote part of Wales, where he died two years later aged 98. I doubt very much that he would have been interested to meet me.

Now I was looking for his help.

It is a big fat book. Some scribbled notes I must have written in Ireland. Several of his 'technical' essays are still very hard; but I wanted his views about education. I hoped we might agree.

'No man can be a good teacher unless he has feelings of warm affection towards his pupils and a genuine desire to impart to them what he himself believes to be of value.

'The thing above all that a teacher should endeavour to produce in his pupils if democracy is to survive is the kind tolerance that springs from an endeavour to understand those who differ from ourselves.'

This was all good stuff. Then, leafing back a few pages, I was struck dumb.

Russell wrote this in an essay of 1926:

'One generation of fearless women could transform the world, by bringing into it a generation of fearless children, not contorted into unnatural shapes, but straight and candid, generous, affectionate, and free. Their ardour would sweep away the cruelty and pain we endure because we are lazy, hard-hearted and stupid.'

I must have read that forty years ago. But what an impossibly quixotic, romantic, hopelessly impractical notion that would have seemed forty years ago!

Until six months ago, when I wrote in my Christmas letter to you that the world needs: *'Mothers to begin to tell their children always to know that they have a right to be honest; and always to know that they have the right to ask questions. This would soon produce a generation of young messiahs.'*

That was a shock. In ninety years the absurd has become the obvious!

More amusing was a newspaper cutting I had used as a bookmark. It told another interesting story:

ARMY PATIENT IN SEA CHASE

Three soldiers had to be rescued from Southampton Water last night after they got into difficulty chasing a patient from the Royal Victoria Hospital . . . who swam into the busy sea lanes. The patient swam strongly through the heavy swell. He was overpowered one and a half miles out to sea and taken back to hospital.

One must admire 'overpowered one and a half miles out to sea'. I doubt that I would have been able to swim that far. I might, however, have been more inventive.

But this was still a distraction.

Suddenly I muttered: "Paine!"

An old copy of Thomas Paine's *'Rights of Man'* was once my father's. His proudest boast, which I heard often as a boy, was: *'An Englishman can think what he likes; and say what he thinks; and write what he likes; and fear no-one!'*

That was true eighty years ago. It is still true in America: largely due to Thomas Paine.

Tom Paine was a Quaker, born in Norfolk about 1740. He had been a corset-maker. His writing inspired two democratic revolutions; got him into endless trouble; made possible by my father's pride.

His words also helped an English gentleman called George Washington to stiffen his soldiers' rebellion against their German-speaking king and his craven English parliament. *"These are the times that try men's souls: the summer soldier and the sunshine patriot will, in this crisis, shrink from the service of his country; but he that stands by it now, deserves the love and thanks of man and woman."*

But what could possibly be the same now as in Paine's lifetime?

'That there are men in all countries who get their living by war, and by keeping the quarrels of nations, is as shocking as it is true; but when those who are concerned in the government of a country to make it their study to sow discord and cultivate prejudice between nations, it becomes the more unpardonable.

'When I contemplate the natural dignity of man, when I feel for the honour and happiness of his character, I become irritated at the attempt to govern mankind by force or fraud, as if they were all knaves and fools, and can scarcely avoid disgust at those who are thus imposed upon.'

These sentences fly off the pages.

What *has* changed? What is *unchanged?*

Is the Beast only greed?

A very different book was returned to me, unprompted, a week before.

It was my 1964 Christmas present to myself.

It was described by US Supreme Court Mr Justice Levy in 1925 as *'unquestionably obscene, lewd, lascivious and indecent, and filthy, and disgusting, and utterly revolting.'*

Clearly this is why I bought it.

Clearly Mr Justice Levy read the same parts.

'My Life and Loves' is the biography of a very curious individual called Frank Harris.

I realise now that I might have had a happier life if I had applied his instructions of how to give, eventually, females of any age, colour, and experience the most complete passionate, sexual pleasure that they are capable of.

Frank Harris was born in Yorkshire in 1856. In New York in his teens, he found work as a bootblack and bellhop in the caissons of the Brooklyn Bridge. After a year or so later, he *'bought a shotgun and a Winchester rifle and a revolver'* and *'two days* [later] *we set out, ten men strong and two wagons, to cover the twelve hundred miles to New Mexico, to buy six thousand head of cattle at a dollar a head and drive them back to Kansas City.'* He had yet to become an aide to the Russian General Skobelev in the Russian-Turkish war.

All of this made him a very confident young man. G.B. Shaw wrote of him: *'a man of splendid visions, unreasonable expectations, fierce appetites . . . savagely contemptuous of people who wanted nothing splendid done.'*

In England he was soon the editor of a highly influential journal.

Everyone wanted to know him. Many feared him.

But who else, when the British Empire was increasing faster than maps could be drawn, could have written: *'I loathe wars and the combative aggressive spirit of the great conquering race, the Anglo-Saxons with their insane, selfish greeds* (sic.) *of power and riches.'*

And by 1904: *'the worship of wealth in England reaches a point beyond anything seen before . . . . The people of England have come to look on starvation and suffering as part of the social order.'*

It appears that our Beast only ever grows stronger.

'After World War II we chose to militarize in order to jump-start a lagging post-war economy, sucking our taxes into obscene military budgets, with rampant corporate profiteering from "endless war". The US is hooked on war. Its so-called "economy" is so tied into the vicious cycle of ravaging the world for oil, feeding the war machine with our taxes, then going out to ravage for oil again. A small group fills its pockets while the vast majority are vulnerable to their desires.'

We are at last beginning to understand that the Beast is a part of the social order, everywhere.

But who controls it?

29ᵗʰ **July, 2012**

Breaking News:

Dear Class,

In the past few months I have felt like Alice falling down her rabbit-hole.

The aim has been to understand what drives people to kill not a few people, but millions of people: eagerly, as if it is obviously necessary, inventing new reasons and new ways to kill more.

This impulse has never been defeated. It is active now. It appears only ever to grow stronger. This is the impulse, in us all, that I have called The Beast.

None of the usual suspects is old enough, simple enough, or sufficiently greedy. The last characteristic is most specific. Once it has persuaded people to start killing, they will continue killing until there is no-one left to kill. Then they may begin to kill one another.

In the end I am pretty sure that you will find The Beast so familiar, and so terrifying, that you will be ashamed. I think that everyone will be ashamed. In future, when anyone declares: "This is a reason for war!" others will be ashamed and will say why.

Then they may take his dummy away.

I have just posted Part III of the story. I want you to share my puzzlement, disappointments, surprises, but, finally, the horror of recognising that hundreds of millions have died for the most common and ordinary reason of all.

Meanwhile, there is something important that you can do for me!

Earlier this year I talked briefly in Oxford with a Vice-President of the European Commission, Mr Maros Sefcovic. He has many responsibilities as Vice-President, but is particularly interested in the future of the European Schools and of democracy in Europe.

I reminded him that the European Schools are supposed to *'foster tolerance, co-operation, communication, and concern for others throughout the school community and beyond'.*

In other words, the European Schools are supposed to foster democracy. But, I explained, this is hard to achieve when education primarily through instruction soon divides young people into the few who understand, the many who pretend to understand, and the rest who understand nothing at all.

And this, I also pointed out, is fair explanation why confidence in Europe has collapsed. European societies are divided into just these three groups. Greed and dishonesty are rife. No-one trusts anyone else. This is catastrophic for democracy. How can trust be recovered? Only through education.

I told him of our work at Culham; where you learnt mathematics with me by reading explanations directly from the text-book, discussing these together, deciding together on a satisfactory understanding, then choosing problems yourself to see if you had: thus learning *tolerance, co-operation, communication, and concern for others.*

Mr Maros Sefcovic asked for more information. I sent it to him; then forgot about it (being busy with The Beast). I returned from a five-day holiday in Greece last week, to find a letter from Mr Sefcovic telling me that he has asked the Secretary-General of the European Schools to examine the information that I sent him *'so that it can be discussed during the next Joint Teaching Committee meetings in mid-October'.* He continues: *"I am sure the Secretary-General and the Joint Teaching Committee will pay your reflections all the attention they deserve."*

This is a hugely important opportunity. I hope they may at least direct one of the larger European Schools to try our approach with their young mathematics classes for just one period a month for a term to judge for themselves and their teachers whether it is worthwhile. Nothing ventured: nothing gained!

Love to all, Colin.

[I never did hear from the Secretary-General, or the Joint Teaching Committee.]

The Next Day:

At the rate I am progressing, some of you will be grandparents before we reach the right true end. I am also getting close to my sell-by date. I have therefore followed Part III immediately with Part IV. In this I describe the most poisonously divisive statement in history: until Marx's manifesto, which aimed to negate it. The tracks are unmistakable. Produced by a military genius, his followers organized ruthlessly to transform the desperation of millions into power for themselves. Another two thousand years of wars followed: because of one man's power; his parasites' greed; and the fact that now hundreds of millions can be frightened into believing that nonsense has meaning. Marx called religion an opiate. It is more of a placebo. Part V follows shortly.

PS Marx didn't get it right either. He forgot avarice. Avarice is important. I remember, possibly badly, a comment by the Russian nuclear scientist then political dissident Andrei Sakharov: *"The snow drifts everywhere, but the wind in Russia always blows one way."* The young people of Russia, of all the previous USSR, deserve to see this change.

THE TRUE NATURE OF THE BEAST IV: SCAM

Dear Friends,

I think we are now ready to look again at the torpedo that caused poor Professor Frege to sink into oblivion; but this time (get ready for a pun!) at greater depth.

From this will appear an explanation of everything described so far.

Although now named after him, it was unfair of Russell to claim that he had discovered 'his paradox'. It had been described in 1869 in its most basic form in a volume on deductive logic by another mathematician, Thomas Fowler, of Corpus Christi College in Oxford. There it appears as a classical epigram: *'Epimenides, the Cretan, says "All Cretans are liars"'*.

Epimenides lived around 600 BC. He is said to have helped Solon revise Athens' laws and to have kick-started its democracy. We need such people now.

Another curious form of the same paradox is the Moebius loop. One side of a flat tape is given half a turn and is then joined to its underside. It is still a surface: which—'as any fule know'—must have two sides. But now outer and inner surfaces have become one.

This delighted me as a child. Sadly, no-one explained its deeper significance.

Actually I don't know that anyone has noticed this before.

The secret of these, usually quite simple, statements is that our natural expectation to understand them is defeated when they contain a denial of their own existence or truth.

Imagine, for example, asking for a brick wall to be built without bricks.

You should expect your builder's immediate response.

Simpler still is: *'This sentence is false.'*

Simplest of all: *'Wrong.'*

These apparently straightforward statements defeat our understanding because they are actually all nonsense. Although this would help the rest of us, mathematicians and philosophers have too much pride actually to call them nonsense.

Instead they call them 'inconsistent'; or, possibly, 'non-demonstrable inferences'.

Russell, Frege, Wittgenstein and others were surprised to find more of these sterile little maggots wriggling and squirming on the great pale bosom of formal logic.

We shall discover, however, that their variety far exceeds those found in formal logic, and that the creative force behind them deserves our respect. Some of them are just silly. Some are only intended to confuse. Some may cause nations to collapse.

The Federal Reserve, for example, although composed of banks, is not a member of the set of banks. Dollar bills are called money. Money should have intrinsic value. Dollars have only the value they are recognised to have: otherwise they have none. Dollars are members of the set of money, but dollar bills are bills.

Once one has struggled (as I have) to understand where the literal or logical half-turn has been made, one starts to see more of this nonsense, more inconsistency, more nondemonstrable inferences, everywhere. Another interesting oddity is zero. Is it a number, or not?

Few of these statements are as elegant, however, as that which caused Pooh to become suddenly so hot and anxious. Let us return to high drama.

He had understood the tracks in the snow to be a clear and simple statement. They had been made a short time before by two Woozles, who must therefore be just ahead.

But now, as he cooled his nose, this has become abruptly inconsistent. *Qua* Woozle—statements, one might say—or, more precisely, *qua* statements about two Woozles—this once clear and simple statement is no longer a member of itself.

"*FEETH!*" Pooh exploded, stamping his foot, causing Piglet to jump once again, raising a cloud of powdered snow which, falling down and clinging to his fur, transformed him from a cuddly old bear into a kind of ursine Ezekiel.

"*Feeth!*" he repeated, and sneezed: and with even more alarm Piglet heard the accents of Pooh's ancient clan in his next to sepulchral whisper: "*A thurrd craitur has jined th'ither twa!*"

"*Oh, Pooh!*" cried Piglet, hoping that it could still be consistent. "*Another Woozle?*"

"*Naw,*" said Pooh, "*it maks differen' merks. Eether we hae twa Woozles an yin, a' micht be Wizzle, ur Twa, as i' micht be, Wizzles and yin, if sae tis, Woozle. Le' us geh on t' follae 'em.*" Most will know the rest of the story. Let us leave our two friends wondering how to deal with three Woozles, or two Woozles and a Wizzle, or two Wizzles and a Woozle.

The point of our model is that any statement shown to be inconsistent can be believed only by faith.

No test can prove any inconsistent statement true. This is, however, a test of faith.

A modern example is the conclusion of the Nicene Council of 300 bishops called together by the Emperor Constantine in 325, and required by him to decide the true, final, absolute statement of Christian faith: the most important event in the history of what is now called Christianity.

Flavius Valerius Aurelius Constantinus Augustus was the most successful fighting general in Rome's history. He had crushed the Franks, Alemanni, and Visigoths and won two civil wars.

He now aimed to end the religious confusion in his Empire now increasing between its pagans, the Jews, and these new Christians the Jews had spawned.

Far more important was to ensure the loyalty of his soldiers.

They knew him as a fearless leader. Many had died protecting him.

Now he would make his own blood theirs.

He would become the Messiah promised to the world by both Jews and Christians.

His Empire would be their Kingdom of God.

The bishops of his Council were bitterly divided.

But they also knew what he expected.

Constantine wanted results.

Two years later he would order his wife to be boiled to death for disloyalty.

Then he killed their son.

He had ordered that one day of every week was to be dedicated to the sun.

This pleased the pagans.

He wanted much more for his armies, and for himself.

Wherever his legions made camp, they dug a ditch around it. Given time, they built a wall above the ditch. Given more time, they planted sharp stakes in the ditch, a crown of fearsome thorns to draw any attackers' first blood.

The plan was as familiar as his hand. He wanted a ditch, wall, thorns.

First he would steal the Jews' old god. It had certainly given them courage once, but then let them be defeated. Their rabbis' new main industry was now inventing ever more prescriptive laws aimed at preventing other disasters. According to the old intelligence reports which Constantine now read, they had wanted Christ killed because he told people that they were not to be trusted: *"You hypocrites!"* Jesus told these 'teachers of law': "You *clean the outside of your cup and plate, while the inside is full of what you have got by violence and selfishness! You strain a fly out of your drink, but you swallow a camel."* (Matt. 23.25)

Constantine must have realized that it was mainly their anxiety that their nation might be destroyed even more that kept the Jews together. Sometimes he thought that if they lost all their reasons to be anxious, they would only create another reason. They needed to be afraid.

I can imagine him thinking like this:

'They still believe their god especially favours them.
Even a small child can see this makes no sense.
Well, let them drown in their ink-pots.
Or disappear somewhere else.
Meanwhile everyone knows that their god
Separated the light from dark,
The sea from land,
Created everything that grows, swims, crawls, flies, or runs.
Such an immensely powerful god
Must belong to the entire world.
To everyone in the entire world
By trying to keep Him for themselves.
The Jews simply did not honour Him enough.
Now I, Constantine Augustus, will honour Him
As He deserves
By making Him known as the only God
Of all the people in the world.
My new bishops will awe them by the powers
I shall give them.
They will smother any questions,
Smooth over all dissent.

And any really awkward bastards I will crucify.
Their wall will be the resurrected Jesus.
His cross was good for me in battle.
My soldiers liked it too.
Now it will hang on walls everywhere.
A wall defining my Empire.
And, finally, this Jesus, now in heaven,
Must stay there.
He cannot return.
I'll make him the son of my new God.
Later still: also equal to God.
Hah! Let the logic-choppers break their teeth on that!
Later still one God: eternal, indivisible, invisible; never human again.
And they should even share some holy blood.
Without light there is no life: the light of life; that will do.'

There is actually no report that Constantine actually told his bishops what he wanted. I doubt that he needed to: *'He just sits in that great purple cloak, just waiting . . . .'*

Once they understood the power he would be giving them over the millions in his Empire, they required only two further councils to affirm that the old god of the Jews was the father of their resurrected Jesus; that Jesus has also become a god; that the light of their faith would sustain their everlasting life. All this, provided all tax was paid.

They thus produced the formula by which Christians to this day identify themselves.

Their God is Father, Son, and Holy Spirit, one, eternal, indivisible.

Fifty years later, Saint Augustine, a man of high intelligence, wrote dolefully: ". . . *Dictum est tres personae, non ut aliquid dicretur, sed ne taceretur*": *'When asked what are the three, human language is found inadequate, and there are no terms to express them: yet it is said that there are three persons, not in order to say something, but because we must speak and not remain silent.'*

Perhaps he thought it might avoid schism.

Sixteen hundred years later, after sixteen centuries of schism, torture, massacres, and burning, the English philosopher Thomas Hobbes wrote, very carefully: *'Which Insignificancy of language, though I cannot note it for false Philosophy; yet it hath a quality, not only to hide the Truth, but also to make men think they have it, and to desist from further search.'*

No doubt Constantine meant well.

Hitler had a similar idea.

Both created a religion for their armies centred on themselves.

Both believed they were divinely inspired. There are, however, two deeper questions: What idea did they share?

Why does such nonsense succeed so well?

7ᵗʰ August 2012

Announcement of Part V

Dear Friends,

One of the rarely mentioned pleasures of teaching is not the satisfaction of knowing that your pupils have actually learnt something, for this may happen only rarely: but that **you,** the teacher, have!

In this case, I admit that the lesson has been somewhat over-long, seven months. I apologise most sincerely for this. I never thought it would take so long.

I should have realised that it might. The problem has defeated many before me. I set out to discover the true name and nature of The Beast: by which I mean the habit of war, rape, and rapine that has plagued humanity for so long that makes that very claim of 'humanity' questionable.

In Part V of my treatise, which I have just posted, I think, finally, I have done this.

When I was a young cadet many years ago at The Royal Military Academy Sandhurst, the British equivalent of the United

States' West Point and France's St Cyr, I was taught the orthodox explanation of Karl Marie von Clausewitz, writing in 1833, that 'war is an extension of foreign policy'. This was adequate in the 19th century. It still explains, to a degree, the two world wars. It is probably still being taught to young soldiers today. But what it fails utterly to explain is war on a truly massive scale within a country by its government on its own people.

There have been ten genocides in the past century. *The Economist* of December 2011 provides a useful list. The illustrious first, second, and third, are, of course, Mao Ze-Dong, with a handsome score, as Stephen Fry might chortle, of at least 50 million; followed by the man of steel, Stalin, with 20 million; then our own Adolf, although with around 12 million; and, coming in at a weak fourth, a *very* dark horse indeed, King Leopold II of Belgium, whose plantations in the Congo took the lives of 8 million whilst making Belgium rich; and finally, Hideki Tojo, military dictator of Japan, who is credited with 5 million, although some may have been vaporized by courtesy of Los Alamos and the USAF.

You think my humour is in bad taste? Not at all! This is the first part of this lesson.

I do not claim to have found a perfect explanation. But, if you will look at my possibly less-than-perfect explanation, I hope it may persuade you that the cause of the next genocide—and, you may be sure, there *will* be more—will not be the remarkable moral courage and historic foresight of a uniquely gifted leader—which is what all of these charlatans would want you to believe—but is rather due to a very ordinary, usually unimportant kind of mental twitch, which those named above were able at the time to communicate to many others, usually able to manage, for example, the railways, just as they felt the same kind of twitch.

People began to die, shortly after this, like insects. The simile, by the way, is apt. It is extremely common for the organisers to refer to their victims' death in terms appropriate to a short-tempered housewife trying to clean her kitchen on a bad-hair day.

And is this now disgracefully dismissive of the deaths of over a hundred million innocent people? Not at all! My aim in Part V is to persuade you that when the next damn fool declares that he has got a plan to rid his golf club, his church, his mosque, synagogue, town, nation, his nation's neighbour, the world, solar system, galaxy, and universe, with, of course, your help, of another million or so undesirables, you will know what his real problem is.

Just give him a pat on the head and a toilet brush. This is the work he needs.

THE TRUE NATURE OF THE BEAST V: MOMMA'S BOYS

It was getting darker, and colder: and Piglet realised that they were about to circle the spinney for the fifth time.

"I say, Pooh" he began, but only a squeak emerged. He tried again. "I say, Pooh. Could there be more Woozles in these woods?"

"Hunnerts," replied Pooh tersely. "Mebbe mahr."

"Well," Piglet suggested, "if there are so many, and if so many others are looking for them, why don't we just wait for others to tell us what theirs looks like?"

Pooh snorted. "Humph! Dinna fash yersel!" he replied. "They all want keek. But they hasna! Hev feeth!" He pointed at the icy rut they were now following. "This yin is oors!"

*

There are 19 major religious groups in the world. Each has many subdivisions, often hundreds. There are at least 30,000 independent Christian churches.

One consequence of this great diversity is that what anyone believes to be true depends, generally speaking, on where they are born.

Young people are beginning to notice this.

We must all suppose that all these groups hold that their understanding of God, if not perfect, is not as imperfect as that of the others.

Everyone is therefore saying that it is not a member of the set of numbers in which it is included by the others: or vice-versa, that it *is* a member of the set of numbers in which the others refuse to include it.

Ardent pessimists take this as evidence that human minds are so defective that we may not be able to stop destroying ourselves.

An alternative view—one which I will consider later, in *'Mr Darwin's Nightmare'*—is that there is a deeply buried impulse in the human psyche to ensure that we *will* destroy ourselves.

However, before we get to this possibility, we have first to deal with the present, in which two nations, both deeply proud of their ancient culture, both certain that they embody God's intentions, both ready to rectify what they regard as God's unfortunate mistakes, are ready to erase the other's existence: at whatever cost to the rest of the world.

This is the real situation, children. We will be part of that cost.

My own first mistake was to suppose that national wars were always caused by these inconsistencies. But these have generally been old-fashioned wars, fought by the armies of relatively well-defined enemies. The last two world wars were of this kind.

We need now to look for something far more modern: at the complicity in the murder of millions of ordinary people by ordinary people, usually for no other reason than a kind of erotic excitement: the thrill of virtually guiltless murder, rather like Erica Jong's 'zipless fornication'.

In 1704, in his funny and profound *'Tale of a Tub'*, Jonathan Swift suggested that the cause of this wilder kind of violence may be infectious vapours *'ascending from the lower faculties to overshadow the brain, there distilling into conceptions for which the narrowness of our mother-tongue has not yet assigned any other name but madness and phrensy.'*

In the early 1920s Freud: *'reached the conclusion that . . . besides Eros* [his name for the drive to survive], *there was a death drive, and the interaction and counteraction of the two could explain the phenomenon of life.'*

To this he added later: *'The libido has the task of making the destroying instinct innocuous, and it fulfils the task by diverting that instinct to a great extent outwards . . . . The instinct is then called the destructive instinct, the instinct for mastery, or the will to power, a perhaps much more recognizable set of manifestations.'*

An ex-soldier may think in terms of conflict. But is this so natural for the mild-mannered discoverer of the unconsciousness?

Is it necessary for there to be two Woozles striving to defeat the other?

These questions make me pause. Is it possible that there is a real Satan: a destructive instinct, a will to power, an instinct for mastery, capable of encouraging whole stupidity, cruelty, evil, destruction everywhere? Could it also have a physical presence? Could it be worshipped? How would such idolatry appear? How would this be enforced?

Absolute certainty is actually quite rare. Here is some:

'The Jews are the scourge of humanity. If any nation, for any reason whatsoever, tolerates one single Jewish family remaining amongst them, it represents a core of infection that would bring about renewed decay.'

Or this: *'We are a master race which must remember that the lowest German worker is racially and biologically a thousand times more valuable than the population here.'*

Or this: *'I did not think I was justified in exterminating— that is to kill, or to order to have killed—the men, whilst leaving their children to grow up to take revenge on our sons and grandchildren.'* The children must be killed too.

And then: *'Killing children is also permissible if they stand in the way. There is justification in harming infants if it is clear that they will grow up to harm us. Under such circumstances the blow can be directed at them, and not only by targeting adults.'*

Statements like these, by Rudolf Höss, Commandant of Auschwitz, are buried in my mind like frozen twigs under the snow, crackling under my feet, too muffled to be heard.

Some kinds of madness we can try to understand. But we are obliged to accept that a psychopath in our culture may be a respectable moral authority in another. All this is part of the rich tapestry of life.

Within which, the mystery remains: by what magic can a majority rapidly be made to believe that a minority no longer has the right to life: that they must now be treated as a horrible disease; for millions to be scrubbed, scalded, scoured out of existence, leaving so little trace that later it may be denied that they ever existed?

I spent a quiet evening reading of the happiness of Henry David Thoreau in the little hut he built himself by Walden Pond: *'tight-shingled and plastered, ten feet wide and fifteen long'*, sharing his pleasure that his new home, with its new-sawn logs, was just as clean within as without.

Then Baruch followed with a collection of Friedrich Nietzsche's essays.

There could be no greater contrast of vision and style. Or so I thought.

I began, obediently, to read once again the raving of the man who, with terrible consequence, urged: *'all creators to be hard. It must seem bliss to you to press your hand upon millennia as upon wax.'*

Some years ago I sat on the balcony of his house in Naumberg, a beautiful mediaeval town. He must have sat in the same place, perhaps in the same chair, when already paralysed and already insane. One day, he promised, his name would be *'associated with something frightful, a crisis like no other before on earth'*.

I only felt a great sadness. His boasts were perfect Nazi fodder.

The truth is that Nietzsche scoffed at German nationalism; loathed anti-Semitism; deplored 'Darwinism'; jeered that Germans would never become a master-race; and called Christianity *'a hangman's metaphysics'*.

What he really wanted was to sweep away all the mawkish sentimentality and moral pretensions of his contemporaries. He believed his writing would inspire new generations to reject formal religions—hence his cry "God is dead!"—in order to learn to think honestly.

This is what he believed would create *'a crisis like no other on earth'*.

Despite his dislike of all things German: *"I am,"* he insisted, *'a pure-blooded Polish nobleman, in whom there is not a drop of bad blood, least of all German.'"*—he naturally spoke German. He wrote in German, especially when reporting that his mother and sister's treatment of him: *'fills me with inexpressible horror: an absolutely hellish machine at work here, operating with infallible certainty when I am most vulnerable'.*

Every man can imagine this hellish machine: his mother and sister's endless cleaning, dusting, and scrubbing around him; the unspoken accusation that he should have made more of himself; that he had become a disappointment, and is now a burden.

In Germany, this kind of behaviour is called *Putzfimmel.* It describes the behaviour of people driven by a horror that *nothing* is as clean and ordered as it should be: who will not rest until all is as clean and ordered as *they* require.

Nietzsche called his sister, Elizabeth, an anti-Semitic goose. Her revenge—or perhaps from frustrated pride—was to edit his writing into the Nazi's bible.

He admired Buddhism for its 'hygienic thinking'. He was sure that teaching children to think hygienically would soon rid humanity of its ancient plagues of exclusive religions and their divisions. It seems never to have occurred to him that the quickest way to stop a plague is simply to kill everyone infected by it.

But none of this occurred to me in reading. As I have said, I was only saddened.

But the next morning I woke with a start: *knowing* that I knew!

That the Beast is just Nietzsche's hellish machine writ larger: familiar, ordinary, merciless. Children! Write down this word. It spells genocide:

D-O-M-E-S-T-I-C-I-T-Y

The drive to achieve perfect domestic order is found in men as in women. Sufficiently obsessed in the home, such persons are called *Putzteufeln*—literally "cleaning devils" (what we might refer to as "obsessive-compulsive cleanliness freaks"). They are likely to have loved a mother who kept her house and home in order against all odds.

Could Hitler and Stalin both have had mothers like this?

Given enough power, such men will attempt to order the lives of millions, and millions will be eager to obey them. Orwell first noticed how their actions are soon also domesticated:

"People are imprisoned for years without trial, shot in the back of the neck, sent to die in camps; this is called 'the elimination of unreliable elements'."

The true name and nature of the Beast is pathological domesticity.

The will to mastery and power first appeared when someone made a broom.

On the smallest scale, it means getting everything 'just so'.

On the larger scale, it means killing millions.

And Momma's boys will *always* know how to do this best—with love.

PART VI: MR DARWIN'S NIGHTMARE

Dear Friends,

I fear I have bored many of you to silence. I'm sorry. Let me offer you a little nightmare.

Some weeks ago I opened Felipe Fernando-Armesto's history again and found two lines of a poem which I had not noticed before: *'There may always be another reality / To make fiction of the truth we think we've arrived at.'* (in *'Millenium'*, Fernandez-Armesto, F., 1995.)

Every page of history is an illustration of this. Some certainty dies every moment. The wise man always accepts the simplest explanation of the evidence; then searches for new knowledge in the most obvious direction. The wiser man also keeps the crazier alternatives in mind and knows that new knowledge often comes from the least obvious direction.

Here is the nightmare.

*

"Wake up, Winnie! Wake up, Winnie! They're here!"

My initial irritation at the use of my old school nickname was soothed by the realisation that my good friend Huxley was bending over me and pointing—with, I noticed, a slightly shaking hand—at an enormous *object* on the lawn at the rear of the house.

From my earliest years of observing beetles mating in the Cambridgeshire fens (or of watching, far more recently, the great Galapagos tortoises attempting their own nuptials in a way that, on the one hand, is strikingly similar, but, on the other, is spectacularly different: not least because of the huffing and puffing of the labouring male in his efforts to climb onto his chosen mate, while their massive carapaces clunk and clash and screech together, while the object of his passion, far from yielding gratefully to his need for urgent consummation, stretches her outraged neck far beyond the usual limit, bawling like a branded heifer, wagging her pointed purple tongue), I have cultivated the habit, essential to science, of objective observation.

I saw at once that the object on my lawn was altogether different from mating beetles or copulating *Testudinidae* (that is, from tortoises). More imagination might be needed.

My first surmise was that Huxley had arrived in some kind of balloon. Yet it seemed altogether too *solid,* and he was already hurrying towards it, muttering: *"They promised to wait until you arrived."*

Who were they?

Then we were *inside*: inside a brightly lit room with curved walls. As we entered, my eyes were drawn at once to the two curved windows at opposite ends of the room.

They could not *be* windows. On the right was a remarkably vivid portrayal of deep space: of total blackness and a scatter of wonderfully bright stars, unaffected by atmosphere.

On the left, no doubt by the same artist, was an image of what could only be the Earth itself: a ball of exquisite blue and white against the same panorama of black space. This, in actuality, could be visible at a distance of many thousands of miles. What genius of imagination!

"Mr Darwin!" I was being welcomed in the more usual manner as Thomas gently urged me further into the room.

We had obviously arrived during some kind of committee meeting.

Six figures were seated at the long table. Another was standing. All wore cowled gowns. It only seemed a little odd that they *all* looked rather like Thomas. This hardly disturbed me as I realised, with some distaste, that the figure welcoming me far more closely resembled my most fervent critic, His Grace Bishop of Oxford, the Very Reverend Samuel Wilberforce, also known, because of his invariably unctuous manners, as Soapy Sam.

What is he doing here?

"Mr Darwin," he repeated, in a markedly friendly tone, "how *very* kind of you to take notice of our little experiment. Since we are not likely to return until," he made a curiously deprecating gesture with his right sleeve: it seemed rather empty of hand, "it is all over, it seemed to us only correct, if I may so express the sentiment, to share results, expected and unexpected, ah, *collegially.*"

As if now prompted by a sharp kick beneath the table, another figure rose beside him, whilst the real Thomas, the balloon Thomas, the Huxley Thomas, always the contrarian, whispered to me urgently: *"Winnie, old chap, it might just be better, to hear this, if you was sitting down."*

I found that I was at once sitting in a fine leather library chair, very comfortable.

"Erm," the new Thomas began. "Mr Darwin, you will have realised from, erm, your own work that nothing really evolves *entirely* by chance. Our main interest is in extremely primitive social development. A short time ago,"—Huxley whispered, *"three million years ago"*—"we modified one of your planet's relatively intelligent mammals so that they could learn faster, remember more, and would therefore be able to share more complex ideas."

"And that," His Grace interrupted, "was *all* that we intended. But an *unauthorized* change was made by our young colleague here which is very likely to spoil both our empirical experiment and your own prediction that, absent sufficient predators to force it to evolve in an entirely new direction, the human race—and you will understand that we do not use 'human' pejoratively—is not equipped to survive."

"But, erm!" his young colleague seemed to have recovered his nerve, "usually we accelerate this process by preserving one of the original traits of the, erm, apes,"—Huxley whispered: *'of your apes, Winnie'*—of violently disliking any of their related sub-species who are not exactly like themselves, in shape, smell, sound, or behaviour, in fact in any way at all."

I found myself now able to respond. "You cause them to make war!"

This young alien—this was bare-faced cheek: treating people like rats!—was perfectly unabashed. "Then we can sooner study how long it takes them to multiply, increasing their numbers for war, to begin fighting over resources and develop more powerful weapons, until, by accident or design, they exterminate themselves."

"Always happens," another offered. "Bigger brains makes all species more aggressive. They never learn."

"Indeed," said another. "But there should be room for the *un*expected. The unexpected," he elaborated, "is the unexpected."

"Yes!" young Frankenstein responded eagerly. "That's what I decided to change."

"Do, please," this was Soapy at his most unctuous, "tell us, again, precisely: what you changed. I am sure Mr Darwin would like to know how you are going to destroy his life's work," he paused with evident satisfaction, "and his hard-won reputation."

"Ah, well, you see, I left the very great majority alone. But I took just a few of the young females, and I did a little more."

I was now accustomed to their telepathy. At this point the entire committee took a deep breath telepathically. One tutted, also telepathically.

"What exactly?" asked Soapy coldly.

"Ah, well! The core population will still enjoy violence as usual: with no self-control beyond immediate appetitive gratification. I simply inserted a different form of our species-transforming virus into the females' mitochondria."

"But," another interrupted crossly, "it's all supposed to be over by Friday."

Huxley whispered a second translation: *"He means soon"*.

"Well, of course. But although the great majority will certainly go on breeding heedlessly, enslaving and exploiting the weak, indifferent to inequalities, even praising the value of inequalities; in general behaving like Englishmen"—I hoped Huxley would object at this flagrant slur on our national character, but perhaps he agreed—"in these few females I inserted a segment of DNA which causes violence to be thought of as equivalent to infantile incontinence. This segment will be passed on through generations of women: unpredictably, because of so many rapes, think only of the Sabines . . . ."

"Yes, yes," Soapy interrupted again, "I wrote that report! But now," his next question was asked with an openly triumphant glance at me, "what exactly do you expect to achieve?"

"Ah, well: that's the point. From time to time these women's uniquely different offspring will pop up in all parts of the world, more or less at random, and will attempt to persuade the others *not* to multiply regardless, *not* to hate each other, *not* to make war— and thus, possibly, *not* to destroy themselves. This will be their new survival strategy."

"Hm!" The response was not encouraging.

"Huh!" came from another. "I'll tell you, and this is from my experience, that wherever one of your young lads or young lassies appears, our standard models will happily beat them to death. If they attack anyone who speaks, looks, even *smells* different, it is just too horrible to imagine what they will do to anyone who deliberately *disagrees* with them."

"Yes, well," the young bio-geneticist conceded. "That will certainly happen. We have seen it happen already. Anyone not sufficiently well protected soon gets scragged. Only one has not."

I noticed Soapy wince. But young Frankenstein was hurrying to reveal how he had reduced the likelihood of our species committing suicide, which is indeed the logical outcome of my theory. "But every time this happens, every stoning, hanging, burning, every time one of their children is cut in pieces, the

194

women get more annoyed; and women, as we know, always talk together to share each other's secrets."

"And to compare men," a voice chuckled, "always unfavorably."

"So?" Soapy was now intrigued: as I was. "What will this change?"

"In talking together, the females will get angry at being used to produce half-wits who only want to kill, and will protect their children instead."

"Oh, obviously!" wailed Soapy. "Oh, obviously! Men have been slaughtering each other for countless generations. Now they can destroy their entire planet; and you think women can stop them! We will have to come back to bury the remains!"

Young Frankenstein had no time to answer.

"Charles! Charles!! You've been asleep in the garden again. Do come in! Dinner's ready."

I found I was still holding my tray of earthworms. I had been measuring how quickly their casts could raise earth levels. A simpler problem.

I met Huxley again a few days later. I did not discuss my dream with him.

But it left me with a question: Have women *ever* been able to change men's lives?

I must write my next book about this!

PART VII: TO KILL THE BEAST: SOULS

After months of effort, it is an enormous relief to see The Beast is finally unmasked.

And what a surprise! Not religion, not greed, industry, science, ideology: stupidity, of course, as always. But we have realised that to start any properly organized genocide it is only necessary to remind the majority of people of the form of instruction they obeyed as children: *"Time to stop playing, children: to throw out the rubbish: to make everywhere clean and tidy!"*

The imperative is subliminal; the excitement contagious; the guilt shared.

But how shameful not to have seen that Hitler's determination to make his Reich *Judenrein,* for example: cleansed of every trace of Jewish blood, is mirrored by the determination of ultra-nationalistic Jews to ensure that their new Israel contains only Jews.

All cultures which believe in inheritable identity can become ambitious to become genetically pure. This is clearly no more than our own genetic programme: like breeds with like.

We now know why people take an active or neutral part in genocide.

We have realised that their impulse is natural.

The obvious question is: can so natural an impulse have a natural antagonist?

Let us look at this question now.

I cannot pretend to have had a very exciting life; but it has persuaded me that life has purpose, and that the universe, rightly understood, to imitate old Russell, can either be a total hindrance or an active partner in achieving that purpose.

This last will already mark me out as unscientific. The most confident spokesmen of modern science never tire of telling us that life has no value, no purpose, and that the universe has not the slightest interest in the existence of any life anywhere.

The first of my contrary insights, now of forty years ago, gave me to understand that I had a duty—this, of course, is outrageous, but it is also true—to save mankind from this depressive madness: for depression seems endemic to the entire human race.

Such insights are, unfortunately, also so rare historically; or are so rarely reported as to have a nearly mythical quality. About 280 AD, for example, a pupil of Plotinus, a philosopher subsequently influential in Christian and Muslim theology, wrote that his master had achieved it *'three times with great effort and relentless discipline.'*

I am personally doubtful of the value of all that effort and discipline. I rather favour the lack of effort of William Blake, who claimed: '*I am in God's presence night & day / And he never turns his face away*'.

Apart, however, from such instances, safely remote in time, such events are far too commonly claimed by frauds, the honestly deluded and the obviously mad, so that it is intellectually suicidal to make such a claim today. What is necessary is to find solutions to our problems. Loving one's neighbour as oneself is not such a generous ideal amongst the psychopathically inclined.

I am no longer sure that humankind can be rescued, but on my study wall is an image of Winston Churchill who orders me in his inimitable growl: *"Nevah, nevah, evah give up!"*

You have been experiencing the second insight throughout this long odyssey.

I will come to the third presently. It is without doubt the most astonishing and the most universally transformative. It also tells us how The Beast can be killed.

But first: *'Farewell to Reason'* is the title of a book by a delightfully provocative thinker, Paul Feyerabend, another philosopher I wish I might have met. I thought I had left his book behind in France, and was therefore delighted to find it again shortly after I had identified The Beast.

I felt sure that Feyerabend would have something interesting to say, opened his book at random—let me repeat: *at random*—read at once, at the top of page 11: *'The assumption that there exist universally valid and binding standards of knowledge and action is a special case of a belief whose influence extends far beyond the domain of intellectual debate. This belief may be formulated by saying that there exists a right way of living and the world must be made to accept it. The belief propelled the Muslim conquests; it accompanied the Crusaders in their bloody battles."*

Hell's Teeth! He wrote this twenty-five years ago!

Typically, he then buried it under such an avalanche of wordy abuse that its importance could not have been noticed. He failed to explain this 'belief' as we have: a universally subliminal imperative that in modern terms can lead to hacking people to pieces with machetes, fitting suicide vests on candidates for paradise, or ticking the next list of drone targets.

But he had the gist of it, right there.

I was still frowning over this loss of priority, but also pleased to find his support, when my eye was caught by another name at the bottom of the page.

'Enlightenment', wrote Kant, 'is man's release from his self-incurred immaturity. Immaturity is man's inability to make use of his understanding without directions from another. Self-incurred is this immaturity when its cause lies not in lack of reason but lack of resolution.'

Two inputs of genius on one page!

Should this be regarded as another deeply curious form of enlightenment; or should it be supposed that this is another kind of madness? It is time to decide which.

The fact is that these events are utterly absurd. I have invented Spinoza to disguise them with drollery. But they should not happen. Since they do happen, repeatedly, urgently, intelligently, as if provided by an entirely separate intelligence, they deserve far more serious consideration, even if their cause may appear as impossible for our minds to understand.

For years I have been accustomed to this 'trick', as I have called it myself; of being able to pick up almost any book, opening it at random and finding, sometimes at once, usually within a few pages, some connection with my own thinking, sometimes a flat contradiction.

It is always uncanny.

My friends call this having 'a prepared mind'.

Undoubtedly this is sufficient, up to a point. But in the past few months I have had the sensation of having information forced on me continuously: of such quality, relevance, continuity, at such a rate, that it becomes entirely inadequate.

Experimenting with mescaline in the 1950s, Aldous Huxley reported that it opened 'the doors of perception', through which limitless knowledge seemed accessible. Unfortunately, such knowledge seems not to connect too well with what the rest of us think of as reality.

My experience has been far more ridiculous than he ever experienced: as if another, far higher intelligence has been desperate that I should '*nevah, nevah, evah give up*'.

It actually feels—hold tight!—as if I have a cosmic partner who knows virtually every facet of human knowledge; and, even more preposterously, tells me where to lay my hand on it.

Is this farewell to free will? No. I am still in charge. I can always stop!

I have great respect for that careful man Darwin. I had already sketched my story of his nightmare, wanting to point out how dangerous it is for man for only the fittest to survive: and finding, incidentally, that footnote from Nature by accident.

Then I learnt that Feyerabend recognised our Beast.

Then I read Kant's fierce rebuke: precisely equivalent to the inner *jihad* that Muhammad requires of us all.

Then I knew that I must explain how this can be achieved.

And, as before, I had no idea how to begin.

Both Darwin and Nietzsche have been accused of destroying faith in God.

Both may be fairly said to have damaged faith in religions.

But Darwin wrote privately: *"Another source of conviction in the existence of God connected with reason and not with feelings impresses me as having much more weight. This follows from the extreme difficulty or rather impossibility of conceiving this vast and wonderful universe, including man with his capacity of looking far backwards and far into futurity, as the result of blind chance or necessity. When thus reflecting I feel compelled to look at a First Cause having an intelligent mind in some degree analogous to that of man: and deserve to be called a Theist."*

His theory of evolution by incremental changes supported the belief that if all natural processes could be studied on a sufficiently small scale, they would all become explicable as due to incremental changes within cells. Once their genome was known, all would be known.

This confidence recently took a knock-out blow.

The human genome was expected to have a uniquely complicated structure: a structure well able to explain why human beings are so very different, say, from sea urchins. Unfortunately it does nothing of the kind. It is instead very difficult to explain why we are all not sea urchins.

The difference between our DNA and that of the sea urchins is far too small.

There has to be another way for information to tell the cells what to do. Often the most devastating question is simple. I noticed an eminent geneticist asking recently: *"The genes must explain development, but how can they, since every cell of a multi-cellular body contains the same genes?"*

The story is often told of a distinguished mathematician who was about to board an omnibus when he realised that one abstruse branch of mathematics was connected with another. In that moment, he later reported, and although it took him much trouble later to prove it, he was absolutely certain that it was true.

Later that evening I was driving up the Woodstock Road, when the same certainty came to me, and I heard myself say aloud: "THE SOUL!"

An absurdity to science, an empty vessel in theology: here is the next step in understanding your world, and yourself.

The Soul receives; the Mind connects.

The Soul supplies prepared minds with intelligence in the form that they will recognise: as art, music, mathematics, text.

The Soul is the organizer of our cells.

The Soul is the natural enemy of The Beast.

31ˢᵗ August 2012

To: Jamie MacFarlane

Dear Jamie,

Thank you for joining our Facebook group. You are most welcome! Of course I remember you. I hope your memories are as pleasant as mine.

Although all of that last is true, what I always yearned to do as a teacher, as I am sure many teachers must, was to tell my classes: *"You know, and I know, and I know that you know, that I am supposed to teach you all this rubbish"*—and one brave girl once told me that is exactly what I should do: but this was integration. *"What I really want is to persuade you to disbelieve everything that you will ever be told is true until you have tested and proved it for yourself. And this includes anything I tell you!"*

Gautama Buddha taught this subversive doctrine 2500 years ago. Rene Descartes tried once again—in historic terms—more recently; and I have just finished another of my essays for 'Children for an Honest, Just, and Fair World' in which I try to give another reason.

Even more recently a number of distinguished Western philosophers have written solemn treatises insisting that a war with Islam is inevitable: even necessary.

They seem not to have noticed that in this they are being no more imaginative than the late Mr Osama Bin Laden. They only differ on which outcome is inevitable.

Curiously, whilst both agree that their fundamental difference is religious—ignoring the differences of hundreds of forms of Christianity; dozens of Islam: and now there are the Mormons!—they all agree that every human being possesses something of absolute importance called a soul.

But then they only explain *why* the soul is so important in the vaguest possible terms. Don't you find this seriously odd?

Here they are straining to go to war, are even already at war, and they cannot explain the function of the most important element of faith: in which they all believe!

This should be a bit of a worry to the moderate followers of religion (of all types). It must be a source of real anguish to the more extreme. I do know that many young people tell me that they are so disillusioned that they have turned away from religion (of all types) in despair, sometimes in disgust.

In my latest essay, APOCALYPSE, I try to show why everyone does in fact have a soul, should know they have a soul, why they must also learn to use it consciously: not only because it provides us with mental and emotional depth and strength, but because the fundamental purpose of the soul is to prevent us from becoming slaves (of all types) and going to war at the behest of stupid people (of all types) for silly reasons.

Let me know, if you have time, what you think. Colin.

4ᵗʰ September 2012

Dear Friends,

I wish there might be a way to discover how many of you are now reading these essays of mine. I would be content with only one, for in finding things out there are two levels of pleasure: first, the pleasure of the discovery; second, the pleasure of sharing it with others (or the other). But 'Apocalypse', the essay I have just posted, is very different. It contains a discovery, which I found at first delightful, but which soon filled me with horror. I need also to warn my one—or possibly more—readers that it may also be very dangerous.

It is a remarkable coincidence that on leaving the Army, I went to work for a man, a retired doctor living alone on a remote Scottish island, who, I subsequently learnt, was a great-grandson of Charles Darwin. He needed an engineer. I was good at mending fairly simple machines. I am proud of the fact that we became friends; even more grateful for what I learnt from him. He seemed to have the same qualities as his great-grandfather: modesty, caution, wide knowledge, high intelligence, and a shrewd sense of necessity.

Of 'Apocalypse' I believe he would say, as did Darwin of his theory of evolution, that an explanation may not necessarily be complete, but it is at least sufficient when it explains all the currently known facts. He would also maintain, more fiercely: "If it isn't provisional, it isn't science!" I offer you now a provisional theory to explain why our world is divided, both internationally and nationally, into implacably hostile groups, only able to treat others as permanent enemies.

My explanation is simple, but deeply disturbing. It is that these unhappy people have lost contact with their souls: for, as I further theorise, it is the function of the soul, ignored by science, neglected—very understandably—by all the religions, to supply the conscious mind with insights, inspiration, and above all, modesty, caution, and doubt.

Now, dear reader(s), if you are brave enough, read on!

PART VIII: APOCALYPSE: A SCIENCE FOR SOULS

Dear Friends,

'Apocalypse' (from the ancient Greek, 'uncovering') means a discovery which transforms understanding: in modern terms, a paradigm shift.

Religiously, it has been described as 'a revelation of knowledge previously hidden from mankind by falsehood and misconception.'

This will disappoint many who expect an apocalypse to destroy the world. This will not happen. We will only destroy some misconceptions of religions and science. The rest of the world will remain intact.

Let me offer a *'mise en scene'*, a suitable scenario.

After they had battled terrible storms to enter the Pacific, the early explorers felt that they had found a limitless world. We now know that oceans cover half the Earth, and we can guess how much they affect our lives.

Its storms may be likened to the consternation of physicists almost a century ago on realising that the universe is not ordered in accordance with either their intuition or logic. *"I have no doubt,"* the British scientist J.B.S. Haldane wrote in 1927, *"that the universe is not only queerer than we suppose, but is queerer than we **can** suppose."*

It has got queerer since, and its queerness affects more than anyone has ever imagined.

My latest discovery is apocalyptic in revealing a new world of connections between ourselves; in telling us how our thinking has evolved in the past; in showing us how we continue to draw from a great ocean of inspiration in the future.

It changes who we are.

Virtually all we have discovered until now has required little more than an exercise of the mind in connecting known facts. Winnie and Piglet would have found their Woozle eventually: just as we did in recognising that genocide and other aggressive wars require only a majority of people conditioned to obey mother's orders, some eager momma's boy to become a surrogate mother, and a few million other people to be selected to be turned into smoke.

Many other mysteries can be resolved in much the same way.

Simplify; clarify; connect.

Why, for instance, is it impossible for the leaders of the world's religions to agree on a common cause?

The answer requires little effort. It is because they are old men.

Is this too simple? Reflect for a moment. They *are* all old men.

What is it they want?

Respect; deference; obedience: that no-one challenge their authority.

How do they achieve this? Through oppression, fear, guilt, imprisonment, torture, execution. They are without respect for reason. They also insist that the synchronised grovelling before them is demanded by God.

So far, so good. Our discovery has no respect for mentally fragile old men. If there are any old men robust and honest enough to want to help, it will find them out.

It is like finding another Pacific.

If it can be supported by evidence, it will change everyone's future.

If it is an evolutionary change, many young people will feel it already.

But how hard is it to demonstrate that the soul is the source of inspiration?

Not hard at all. You are likely to use your own soul every day. But there are some serious misconceptions, if not misdirections, in the way of recognising that you have.

Turn to our most authoritative dictionaries, and you may be puzzled to find that they define your soul as: *'the essence of identity, the spiritual or immaterial part of a human being or animal, regarded as immortal.'* (Oxford) Or: *'the immaterial essence, animating principle, or actuating cause of an individual life.'* (Webster)

Your soul is immaterial, immortal, animating, actuating.

Just what is this supposed to mean? How immaterial? Why immortal? When does it animate? What does it actuate? What, above all, does it do: by itself?

The answers to these questions should divide religions and science. Curiously, both are mute. Science finds no use for the soul. Religions insist on its existence, but allow it no purpose. We need to know why.

All philosophies divide. Some philosophies can be expressed as shibboleths: freely pronounced by some, a stone in the mouth to others. Most memorable is the first. After the Gileadites under Jephthah defeated an army of Ephraimites, and its defeated fugitives asked to cross over the Jordan, Jephthah's men said, 'Say "Shibboleth".' But they could only say "Sibboleth". Forty-two thousand never crossed to the other side. Such simplicity!

Let us now attend to the shibboleths of science and the religions.

That of science was first pronounced by a mathematician, philosopher, writer, and occasional soldier, Rene Descartes, often called the Father of Modern Philosophy.

His first intention, sustained throughout a long life, was to demonstrate that everyone has the capacity to doubt anything, except that they can doubt.

From this Descartes derived his own shibboleth, "I think, therefore I am".

This establishes the existence of the thinking mind, therefore the existence of the thinker, both being possibly independent of God.

Despite this close approach to heresy, Descartes fought for Catholic supremacy in Europe over the rebellious Protestants. And the year before he died, he also wrote a long tract to the Princess

Elizabeth of Bohemia, whom he admired, entitled 'Les passions de l'ame'.

A kybosh, from the Hindoo, is a metal plate used to extinguish embers.

Descartes' 'Les passions' was the kybosh of the scientific soul.

It is clear from his text and his philosophy that Descartes meant by soul what we would now call consciousness, and that he meant by 'passions' what we now call emotions. In addition, he insisted that emotions are passive—hence 'passions'—being the product solely of 'animal spirits' and therefore far below any intellect.

Paradoxically, he appears to have made no effort to understand how his mind—how any mind—can think thoughts which no other mind has entertained before. He also appears to have been content, as many Christians are content, to entrust the care of his soul to his priests. I wonder if he ever asked our questions.

I want now to suggest that the corresponding shibboleth of religions, although much older, may be expressed in an equally simple Cartesian form: "I feel, therefore I exist."

The difference, you may imagine, will be crucial.

I further suggest, if you have imagined, that you have just drawn this insight from your soul.

The obvious difference is that 'I am' is a statement of instantaneous being, and the image of reality developed by science after Descartes was primarily concerned to establish universal laws true in every instant of time.

But in Descartes' frugal dictum is, also crucially, an element of moral instantaneity. It commands those who accept it to doubt the motives of anyone who tries, on any authority, to tell them how to behave.

Ecrase l'infame! "Crush the villainy!" the French revolutionaries shouted: against priests and aristocracy equally. But the reason they wanted was soon guillotined too. The majority of Europe's millions would still rather be impassioned—in precisely Descartes' sense—by guilt and fear than try to rule themselves.

Admittedly, there is no harder rule. For societies still bemired in history, with very little sense of Kant's resolution, of Descartes' moral instantaneity, or of Darwin's capacity '*of looking far backwards and far into futurity*', it becomes unimaginable. Only in America were these initial conditions fulfilled.

Most contemptible was—and is—the refusal of Europe's established religions to encourage people to look into themselves, to find the source of inspiration from which their faith was born, to discover their own apocalypse.

Only the prophet of Islam sufficiently trusted his followers' intelligence to tell them that their first responsibility is to connect the mind with the soul.

Irresistibly tempting to far less confident priests is to condition their people to experience irruptions of atavistic fear that anyone in their church, mosque, or synagogue may notice their lapse in obeying an otherwise meaningless regulation that they or their predecessors have invented precisely to keep them fearful.

Does this appear sufficient to keep billions of people in thrall? The old men know their industry. It is sufficient. They have had ample practice.

Making his own attempt to reveal their mischief, Sigmund Freud called his own analysis 'archaeological', supposing that he could dig down through millennia of spurious inventions to reach solid reality.

"*STOP!*" he has an invented opponent shout. "*Our culture is based on religion . . . . If people are taught that there is no all-powerful, all-righteous God, no divine world order, and no life after death . . . everyone will follow his anti-social, egotistical drives without fear or inhibition . . . [and] chaos will return!*"

Freud responds: "[Although] *the human intellect is powerless in comparison with human drives . . . yet it does not cease until it has gained a hearing. [Its]* primacy *undoubtedly lies in the far, far distant but probably not infinitely distant future.*"

He is even more relaxed concerning religious tantrums: "*Once such remarks were certain to earn one a curtailment of one's earthly existence and a greatly accelerated opportunity of gaining experience of the afterlife. Writing today entails no danger.*"

This will surely amuse some of you. Freud died in 1939.

But we still wait for the guardians of Christian souls to tell their faithful that they are more than empty markers.

"STOP!" bawled His Holiness, and the red hats below him rippled like nervous poppies.

"How many of you imbeciles support this idiot notion: to expect me to announce that the souls—pah!—that the soul of any honest mind can open to God's inspiration? We have spent a thousand years replacing That Man by the only proper symbol of our Holy Church, by the babe in his Holy Mother's arms! Have we not burnt every heretic who ever claimed the same? Our only defence is faith!"

Contrite, the poppies hung their heads.

Whenever the "I think" of the mind connects with the "I feel" of the soul, intuition becomes an insight. This proves Descartes' other insight. It prevents us from being slaves.

PART IX: HATRED

Dear Friends,

You will notice that occasionally I now write 'we' instead of 'I'.

This is not because I have developed delusions of royalty.

I started after one of you wrote to me recently to express your appreciation. I replied with my own thanks, then added: *"But you are also part of the programme!"*

Since then I have recognised a deeper reason.

I have been helped in writing these essays by a process which might be acceptable in a religious seminary through the careful reading of its holy books.

Beyond the realm of saintly revelation, this process has to transgress most of the laws of physics: at least as these laws are presently known.

I confess that I do not understand how this works. I only know that it does.

However, when I rescue smaller forms of life, this is called compassion.

It may be that compassion motivates this programme. Perhaps we are being helped by some higher consciousness out of compassion for its smaller forms of life.

And perhaps I should begin to call it 'The Programme'.

Although we had to leave Winnie and Piglet still searching for their Woozle, we now understand that aggressive wars, and genocide, commonly depend on a mixture of mental laziness, childish obedience, and reckless ambition.

The basic requirements are a society anxious to regain its sense of order; a ruthlessly ambitious leader telling them they can restore order by obeying the equivalent of their childhood instruction to 'clear up this mess'; and a weaker nation or vulnerable minority, to be 'cleared up'. It may appear deeply heartless to explain the deaths of millions in terms that might describe a pantomime: an audience; a hero, the kind I have called a Momma's Boy; a surrogate mother; and a wicked witch.

Unfortunately this is how people do behave.

But why are they so eager to accept such nonsense?

Why can't this supposed 'higher intelligence' keep them sane?

Or, as Freud might have asked: What happened to your *Life*?

At this point, I was distracted. I had begun looking for a better definition of a word common to all cultures, especially important to religions, but only vaguely defined.

The word is 'soul'.

What exactly is 'a soul'?

As mentioned above, the Oxford Dictionary defines it as: *'the essence of identity, the spiritual or immaterial part of a human being or animal, regarded as immortal'.*

Webster says it is: *'the immaterial essence, the animating principle, or actuating cause of an individual life'.*

I was puzzling over this when it occurred to me, an authentic insight in itself, that the soul can be understood as the faculty of intelligence which has evolved to supply the conscious mind with insights and inspiration, to encourage modesty and caution, and—above all—to invite doubt of whatever is certain.

This was a first glimmer of sense, for this definition contradicts none of the above. It does explain, however—and more completely, I think—what they all seem to want to mean.

The usual explanation of religions is that God places a soul in a body as its life is created, and takes it back when its life ends.

Surprisingly, they are then far less informative about what the soul *does* in the lifetime of a body. Apparently it just hangs around.

Any parent would tell it to find something useful to do.

The basis of our theory—our provisional theory—is that the soul has evolved to 'actuate' and 'animate' every new insight, inspiration, discovery, and invention. It is responsible for every advance of human knowledge.

This is how it makes itself useful.

It may then also be perfectly understood as: *'the essence of identity, the animating principle or actuating cause of an individual life.'*

But we can now press our understanding further.

It must now be clear that a mind without free access to its soul can do only what is has been shown, can believe only what it has been taught.

It will become stuck in an eternal present.

This is our Old Testament default position: the origin of Leviticus.

It also explains why so much modern education fails: in most cases badly.

When a child is learning from another child, you will hear one say to the other: *"Just show me what to do or what to say. This is all I need."*

If teachers do no more than this, they fail their pupils. Children can develop as individuals only if they are encouraged to maintain free access to their soul. To keep this channel open they must be allowed and encouraged to argue, to doubt, to invent, to disagree. They must know, as I often told my pupils: *"Some of you, right now, are certainly cleverer than I am. Find out how you can prove it."*

Unfortunately even the most benign governments would prefer a majority of their people to think only as they are taught, to believe only what they are shown, to pay without protest for wars which ruin them.

Or, more crudely: '*If you want a vision of the future, imagine a boot stamping on a human face—forever.*'

This was George Orwell in 1948. He also remarked, as famously: '*In a time of universal deceit, telling the truth becomes a revolutionary act.*'

So: our question has now become: how can people created by God in his own image—and yes, I do believe this—be persuaded to stamp on their own faces?

And our answer is: by being separated from their souls.

Evolution is haphazard. It is unlikely that everyone should possess this faculty to the same degree, or be able to use it freely. The majority of people want an eternal present. They hate having their reality disturbed. They will eagerly stamp on new ideas, and on their proposers. Perhaps we need more help.

Let us start with the fact that children are always asking questions.

This means they have active souls.

We know how they behave.

Young people are more likely than their parents to retain active souls.

We know how they behave.

But they question too.

And the web now allows them to share their ideas.

Even so, it still takes courage to begin to think for oneself. Very often we must first rebel against those who have loved us the most, and whom we have loved the most: our parents; our teachers, our guides. This is too hard for many.

In a recent book on the 'wars' in Iraq and Afghanistan, both of which conflicts having been invented by our very own 'Momma's Boys' a young army volunteer imagines the relief of '*never needing to make a decision again*'.

I used to know this feeling. I was rescued from it by the mad hospital. Not everyone is so lucky. I am frequently amused to read of deeply serious intellectual debate over what consciousness consists of. Is it necessary to be actually conscious of being conscious?

In his now famous book *'The Origin of Consciousness in the Breakdown of the Bilateral Mind',* published in 1976, and at first much derided, the Princeton University psychologist Julian Jaynes suggested that before about 1700 BC humans were not conscious of being conscious at all. They simply did whatever was necessary as occasions required, without being actively conscious. This is rather like driving a car on a well-known route—or even occasionally, and even more alarmingly, on an entirely new route!—without consciously noticing what we are doing.

Human consciousness, in other words, was to Jaynes a product of human evolution.

But what is it as a mental activity? The answer seems obvious to me. We are actively conscious when we are being obliged to think deliberatively about anything: but we are only fully conscious when we are actively challenging, and replacing, previous habits of thought.

From this definition of mine—but I don't suppose I can be the first to propose it—it follows that many people today are still essentially unconscious. They have not yet been touched by evolution; or they are so frightened by its demands on them to *think*, that they would rather retreat into whatever cultural bunker allows them to feel secure until the spasm has passed.

The truth is that we think or we die.
Cultures in which history
Only justifies the present
Separate mind from soul,
Which is the seat of compassion.
The people of these cultures
Are caused to believe they are
Superior to the rest of mankind.
The rest, by their definition,
Are sub-human.
Treated with derision,

Contempt, even with horror,
They can be brushed aside,
Without further care.
Believing that all others are enemies,
They love themselves extravagantly.
They will never make peace.
Whatever the cost,
Their faith will prove them right.

Such ideas are typical of millenarian philosophies. They motivated the wars and genocides of the past century. They survived the death camps. They are typical of the religions run as industries, needing income, never new ideas. It fits extreme forms of all religions. It fits all dictators, tyrannies, ideologies, failing democracies. In a particularly apposite passage in his philosophical essay on Western philosophies, Russell suggests that *'The Jewish pattern of history is such as to make a powerful appeal to the oppressed and unfortunate at all times. St Augustine adapted [it] to Christianity, Marx to Socialism. To understand Marx psychologically, one should use the following dictionary:*

Yahweh = Dialectical Materialism
The Messiah = Marx
The Elect = The Proletariat
The Church = The Party
The Second Coming = The Revolution
Hell = Punishment of Capitalists
The Millennium = The Communist Commonwealth'

And adds, somewhat more cryptically: *'A similar dictionary could be made for the Nazis, but their conceptions are more purely Old Testament and less Christian than those of Marx.'* I must have read this in 1968, and forgotten it. It appears later in these essays.

In the voodoo religion of Haiti, those unfortunates whose souls have been taken from them are called zombies.

Welcome to Zombie World!

According to this crude analysis—crude, but, I think, effective—many people, everywhere, have badly damaged souls. They cannot doubt. They love and hate extravagantly. They are easily persuaded that anyone challenging their ideas must be destroyed. They cannot see their own servitude, their loss of dignity.

Tom Paine would despair.

I realised that this is why our world is divided into so many hostile camps.

I realised that this multiplicity of hatreds is virtually ineradicable. So many have tried to explain its dangers. So many have failed, and, having failed, have been destroyed.

Suddenly I was horrified.

I was not really concerned that I would make billions of enemies. I was more concerned that billions would be hurt. People do need hope, and belief in a faith, almost any faith, however high the price, is a source of hope.

I was also tired. I made a cursory search for a name which had intrigued me: Rumi. I knew little about him. I had the notion that he had been a Sufi poet, perhaps another Omar Khayyam. I decided to look again in the morning.

Once again I slept uneasily, dreaming of Dan Brown's albino assassins, of *fatwas* like autumn leaves, of being poisoned by polonium.

Next morning, The Programme was waiting.

Sharon Bussell had sent me an article by Tarek Heggy, a famous Egyptian analyst of Arab affairs.

Its title is: *'Political Islam versus Modernity'*. It is doleful reading.

'Just as Marxism presented a nemesis for pluralism . . . political Islam can do nought else . . . . The Islamist is dominated by the thought that he is 100 percent right . . . . How can this not be the case given that God himself enters with him in[to] *all epistemological, cultural, economic, political, legal, and constitutional arenas?'*

Unhappy to be so accurately confirmed, I now looked for friend Rumi, and found: *'The inner world is invisible to the senses, and*

yet is real and eternal. Once your heart becomes pure and clear,
it will become a mirror on which pictures will appear from beyond
this earthly realm . . . . Knowledge about religion is like borrowed
money. It does not belong to the one who possesses it. Ignore
danger and walk freely through places that others avoid.'

I had been horrified, and frightened.

Horrified, because it seemed I could unite so many angry tribes
only by offering them a new target for their hatred.

Frightened, because this new target could be none other than
myself.

Reading Rumi helped me to realise that there is a better way.

Instead of inviting hatred, I can offer hope.

God is indeed all-merciful.

It is always possible to retrieve lost souls.

I believe I know how to do this.

*

Dear Friends,

I have usually been able to post a new essay every month. The
latest is extremely late. I begin therefore with an apology.

There are three reasons for the delay. The first, that I have been
quite seriously ill. Then I was asked to write a chapter for a new
textbook for mathematics teachers to be published early next year.

And this resulted in the most exciting discovery of my life.

Once you know it, you will be able to explain, as examples:
why Jews, on average, are more clever than the rest of us; why,
on average, the rest of us are even more stuck in the past than they
are; and, best of all, why religions are more like the product of
cooking recipes than the product of divine inspiration. If they *were*
the product of divine inspiration, they would be all the same.

In my previous essay, I borrowed some lines from a famous
Sufi poet of the twelfth century, Jalal Rumi, who wrote: *'The*
inner world is invisible to the senses, and yet is real and eternal.
Once your heart becomes pure and clear, it will become a mirror

on which pictures will appear from beyond this earthly realm . . . .
Knowledge about religion is like borrowed money. It does not
belong to the one who possesses it. Ignore danger and walk freely
through places that others avoid. '

The heart, as he would certainly know, keeps us alive. We should
expect some ability of our mind to make any inner world visible.

In 'Hatred' I identified this ability as our soul, and suggested
that there is so much violence in the world because, to one degree
or other, nearly everyone's soul is damaged.

But what exactly is this soul? Is it physical, or metaphysical?
Is it really no more than a songwriter's cliché: *'You gotta have*
so-o-o-u-ul!'? Or could it be like the dark energy currently
puzzling scientists? Could it even be a connection between the
intelligence of the universe and our minds, which have not yet
evolved enough to recognise?

I confess that I ended 'Hatred' with no clear idea. It was, if you
like, another Woozle. But I have written before of feeling that there
are other authors working through me: showing me facts I need to
know, pushing me onwards, occasionally showing me that I am
wrong.

Although, half in jest, I have called this The Programme, its
support has been so reliable that I was sure this last essay would be
written: that all would be clear in the end.

After twenty failed attempts, I was no longer sure. The
Programme kept pushing me back to recall when, thirty years
ago, I first began to explain to some of you that the brain has two
nearly independent minds. Our right brain remembers patterns or
routines. This is really all it does. It will remember bad routines
just as happily as good ones. Only our left brain can ask questions
and correct mistakes.

But its stubbornness was infuriating. I needed something new,
not lessons from the past!

Almost exactly forty years ago I had a nearly identical
experience as that of the Prophet Muhammad. He had to survive
many dangers to create Islam. He was a superb left-brain thinker.
He saw that his greatest obstacle to creating unity amongst the

Arabs was that the different tribes worshipped different idols and lived by different routines. This was why they could not unite.

As soon as he was able, he smashed their idols; then he gave them new instructions to prevent them dividing again; and Islam was born.

Imagine a grand piano falling onto a cobbled street. *Crash! Bang! Thud! Tinkle-tinkle!* This is approximately the sensation of realising that his solution is still valid today.

This is what The Programme wanted me to see! We are still worshipping different idols. The cause is elementary. For hundreds of thousands of years our ancestors survived by learning routines. We are addicted to routines. Our idols are routines. We worship especially those which allow us to believe that we are exclusively favoured by God, are especially important to history, to the future, to 'progress', or are in any other way different from the rest of humanity.

Unless we learn to use our left brains more wisely, we will continue to be enslaved, as most of us are now: by the need of our right brain to continue imperfect, divisive routines.

Colin

1st November 2012

THE SOCRATIC METHODOLOGY, MATHEMATICS, AND THE SPIRITUAL REVIVAL OF HUMANITY

Part One: Where to Start

It was only after he discovered that his parents' murder was the result of the wholesale corruption and criminality of Gotham City that mild-mannered reclusive billionaire Bruce Wayne decided to make it his duty to cleanse Gotham of its criminals and fraudsters, and of all the political chicanery and injustice that kept them free.

Today it is hard to imagine any ordinary person unaffected by the collapse of common spiritual values and common morality that Western societies have recently experienced.

This is no longer the stuff of comic-book heroes. It is here and now.

The moral values which once everyone accepted as natural, the values which made our countries prosperous and safe, the moral values which encouraged young people to believe in their society, and in their ability to succeed through honesty and hard work, these moral values are now scorned by the new mega-rich as strictly for the ninety-nine percent: not for them.

It is also hard to imagine a more unlikely saviour of these values, of honesty, humility, resourcefulness, and self-reliance, than the average mild-mannered mathematics teacher.

I am sure most of you are seen in this way by your colleagues and your pupils, even by yourselves. Waiting within you, however, is a hero or heroine, fully equal to Bruce Wayne and Barbara Gordon (even as played by Ms Michelle Pfeifer in black latex).

Let me explain what makes mathematics teachers uniquely able to save their pupils from losing confidence in these simple values and sliding down the slippery slope into self-disgust and moral degradation.

The first reason that makes this possible is that mathematics is culturally neutral. Every major civilisation throughout history has played some part in its development; so that every modern nation feels proud of sharing in its present development.

The second is that mathematics is the only truly universal subject. It is taught in all countries, in all schools, in all languages, with the same practical intention of enabling proficient students to continue to work with others anywhere.

The third is that mathematics is itself essentially a language of argument. It should never be taught to youngsters as a plethora of mysterious rules to be applied without question and without understanding, but to encourage them to develop their skills in critical, informed, and receptive argument. This is essential in understanding mathematics properly. It will prepare them for study in all other sciences. The same skills are vital for democracy's health and success.

The fourth reason is that the teaching of mathematics has never imagined having any moral consequence. As a science, of course, mathematics has none. But, as we shall see, its teaching can have very great and inescapable moral consequences. The choice is only whether it will be bad or good. My purpose in this chapter is to argue that teaching mathematics as if it has no moral, social, or ethical consequences has been indispensable in wrecking our democracy, in giving power to the fraction of our societies interested only in increasing their own privileges and wealth, and in making a cheap joke of the notion of government 'of, by, and for the people'.

The fifth reason is that mathematics lessons have never before been used deliberately in this way. It is, in a most important sense, invisible. It is the equivalent of Batman's cloak.

Given all these positive conditions, it will be obvious that mathematics teachers, knowing at firsthand the moral and ethical demands their training made on them, and wrapped, at least for the first few critical years, in their cloak of invisibility, are most able to restore the spiritual and democratic values of any country. And if the people of any nation under God want this to happen, they must surely arrange for its mathematics teachers to be instructed in the best way to succeed!

The first step is to become acquainted with the Socratic Methodology which I developed whilst a Head of Mathematics in the British European School, UK, together with Dr Hartmut Koehler, Director of Studies, Stuttgart LEU, Germany, with support from Professor Eva Vasarhelyi, Director of the Department of Mathematical Didactics, Eotvos Lorand University, Hungary, and Professor Dr Hani Khoury, Chair of Mathematics, College of Continuing and Professional Studies, Mercer University, Georgia, USA.

It is strange now to remember when I first became dissatisfied with the way I was teaching mathematics.

This was over thirty years ago. I had been appointed a head of mathematics of the British European School outside Oxford, one of twelve international schools created by the European Union and teaching multi-national, multi-lingual, mixed-ability pupils for the European Baccalaureate, preparing them for university entry anywhere in Europe and the US.

This was not only a highly prestigious position; it also provided me with almost complete pedagogical freedom and official encouragement to find a way to teach mathematics better.

It soon became apparent to me that I was held to be a highly successful teacher—hence my appointment, aged 36—because I was actually so highly successful in teaching the majority of my pupils to be obedient: whether or not they understood what they were doing. The more obvious this became, the more disgusted I was with myself. Surely I should achieve more than this!

Still more serious was my increasing realisation that I was also responsible for my pupils' moral degradation. They had all come to me as eager young innocents: incapable of meanness, incapable of sustained deception. Within a few years, this would change: permanently, disastrously.

Given the freedom I enjoyed, I was able to stand back and reflect on the results of my teaching. I had been trained to teach at the School of Education of Cambridge University, one of the most highly-regarded in the world.

How could there be anything wrong with the methods it had taught me to use? My pupils did well in their exams. This must surely mean that they understood what they were doing!

The hardest obstacle to my own understanding was to accept that it was I who was failing. I was finally obliged to face the truth.

The truth was that only a very few actually did understand.

The even nastier truth was that I was obliging the majority of my pupils to learn to conceal that they did not understand. I was forcing them to be systematically dishonest. Most were just copying, more or less accurately, my instruction. Copying, for them, was 'understanding'.

A much smaller fraction always could understand my instruction as I intended. They were being obliged to believe that the others were stupid or lazy. As a result of this they were not only learning to be contemptuous of anyone less able than themselves, but also to be selfishly unwilling to share their achievements.

And finally—as even I had to admit—there was always a bewildered remainder being simply left behind. Because of the relentless pressure, which all teachers will know, to 'finish the syllabus', once they fell too far behind I had no time to help them. At first only confused and disappointed, they would become increasingly angry with me and contemptuous of the system.

It became irresistibly, and painfully, obvious that in my classroom I was creating exactly the same three mutually distrustful, mutually contemptuous divisions visible in the breakdown of civil responsibility and individual moral confidence in our societies.

These divisions have been created in children before they even leave school. They enter societies already divided by previous generations. How easy then for unscrupulous politicians to tell them, as they have repeatedly told their parents, that all the faults of their society, all the obstacles they faced in their individual lives, are caused by the dereliction or delinquency of one or other of the other divisions, or both. Societies become ever more polarised as political rhetoric becomes ever more poisonous. Decent debate becomes impossible: becomes, in fact, unwanted. Democracy dies.

I decided either to quit a job that I had begun to detest: or learn to do it better.

This turned out to be spectacularly easy and astonishingly enjoyable, both for me and my classes at all ages from 11 to 18. My senior pupils had always passed their exams. Although none had chosen to be math specialists, for the next fifteen years they continued to achieve amongst the highest average Baccalaureate grades of all thirteen European schools.

More to the point, when they left my final class they knew how to continue to study and learn unsupported.

Unsurprisingly, my more orthodox European colleagues were horrified by my temerity: even more by my success. Their noses were being kept firmly pressed to the grindstone by their individual national inspectors and were obliged to continue teaching just as they had at home.

In contrast, my British inspectors were usually either historians or geographers. Either they did not realize that what I was doing was heretical, of, if they did realize this, were not anxious to get into a fight.

In consequence, I was left alone.

3ʳᵈ November 2012

Dear Friends,

I have now posted the first part of my text-book article. The rest will follow at easily digested intervals.

Meanwhile my email system has buckled under the weight of so many best wishes for my recovery and offers to help. Thank you all; and I may follow up some of those offers to help: Thank you especially, Lucy! I am also delighted that you all appear to appreciate our latest discovery: thank you especially, Tine.

Powerful ideas are always very simple. Usually they come as a shock because they have not been noticed before. Make no mistake. Ours is a world-changing idea! I will try here to reduce it as much as possible so that you can play the part of peace-maker. This is always guaranteed to upset the most people!

Here is the back-of-a-matchbox version.

Our ancestors' need for routines in order to survive has left us all with an addiction to routines. They are learnt and stored in our right brains. Many routines remain essential for everyday life. But our right brains would like everything to be routine: with no need to think, question, change. This is how our ancestors lived for hundreds of thousands of years.

Much has changed. Our groups are much larger. In order for us to feel secure within a group; to feel that our group's identity is secure; and that our group is more important than others, our right brains have developed very specific routines to serve these needs.

These group routines are the cause of much cultural, religious, and political conflict. This is no accident! Their purpose is to ensure that other groups are irritated, provoked, and angered. Such responses then reinforce the group's belief that its identity must be asserted ever more vigorously: even to the point of being ready to kill anyone who refuses to acknowledge its importance.

Such extreme reactions mean that a group's identifying routines can best be questioned from within: by young people who have learnt to enjoy the ability of their left brain to question, criticise, judge, and correct.

Only they can see that the identifying routines, or rituals, serve no other purpose except to divide, exclude, irritate, and to provoke: even to make war unavoidable. To free their minds of the right brain's control, they must learn to use their teeth, the names of which are: Who? Where? Which? How? Why? Why not? What if? Whose?

And, sharpest of all: *Cui bono*? (Who benefits?)

Colin

6ᵗʰ November 2012

THE SOCRATIC METHODOLOGY, MATHEMATICS, AND THE SPIRITUAL REVIVAL OF HUMANITY

Part Two: Saving Democracy

Every year I would begin by explaining to my youngest pupils how best to help their brain to learn intelligently and critically. This would be their first lesson—of less than an hour.

Within another month they would be proving its truth for themselves:

"I want you all to hold out your two fists, pressed together in front of you. This is almost exactly the size and shape of

your brain. You see that it's divided into two almost equal halves. Almost equal in size: but with very different powers. Approximately—remember that I say 'approximately'—the right brain learns by remembering what it has seen or felt as patterns, of what it has done as routines; meanwhile the left side knows how to hear, how to speak, and how to ask questions. We may say that the right side remembers what has happened; the left side is capable of understanding why it happens. Most of the time the right side's memory is very accurate: this is how you learn to ride your bike: but, if you make a mistake, it will remember this mistake very accurately too, as part of a routine. How many of you have found, if you have once spelled a word wrongly, you seem to spell it wrongly again, and again? This is when we say a routine has become, what?—thank you!—that it has become 'corrupted'. We can get it 'uncorrupted' only by asking the left side to find the mistake. The right side cannot do this!"

This explanation was readily understood by even the youngest children because it corresponded completely with their own past experience. I then went on to explain what would happen in their near future.

"Until now," I would continue, *"you have learnt almost all your arithmetic and reading and writing and spelling as routines. Many of you could go on learning mathematics with me like this. You might all be entirely successful—for another two or three years—and then, and I absolutely guarantee this, most of you will start to fail. Why do you think this would happen? Thank you, again! Because you would have been using less than half your intelligence; trying to pack everything you need to remember into your right brain as routines, without any understanding of why they work; and when, eventually, they begin to fail, as they will, you will have not the least idea of why they fail, or how to make them work. You will find that many grown-ups remember this. You may hear them say: 'Oh, I was never any good at mathematics at school. I soon found it was too difficult for me!' What do you imagine happened to them? Let's suppose that every one of you has an IQ of 110. What is one half of 110? Thank you: 55. Do you*

know what people with an IQ of 55 can do for themselves? Not a lot! Thank you. Even with the best training, someone with an IQ of 55 will remain permanently aged about 8. Do you remember what you could do aged 8? This is what will happen to many of you if you don't start to learn that mathematics is not just a lot of patterns, a lot of rules, a lot of boring routines. It is a great adventure, very nearly the greatest adventure that human minds have ever begun; and to take part in this adventure you must learn to use all your mind: which means you must learn to question, to argue, to criticise, to love to be criticised—for this is learning too—above all to doubt that anything is true until, as if you are pinned on an ice-face with nothing but a hand-spike to save you, you must put your faith in it in order to move at all. This is the adventure of mathematics. In order to learn mathematics properly, you must learn to use the left side of your brain: this side. This is where your brain keeps its ability to listen, to talk, to discuss, to argue, to disagree, and to think seriously about disagreement, because sometimes the other will see what you do not see. Then you need to be honest enough to be thankful for being told you are wrong."

"Sometimes," the White Queen famously told Alice in Wonderland: *"I think of six impossible things before breakfast!"*

When I first announced that I planned to teach my pupils to learn mathematics by arguing its explanations and statements within each class, my own British colleagues were immediately, and loftily, dismissive. *"How can they possibly learn anything by arguing about mathematics? They don't know any mathematics. They will just end up fighting."*

But what seemed impossible to them turned out to be easiest of all!

I turned for help to the National Literacy Trust in London, which provided me with the following statistics. They represent the approximate ability of the average child to retain knowledge after different kinds of class activity:

1. **Listening 5%**
2. **Reading 10%**

3. **Audio-visual 20%**
4. **Demonstrations 30%**
5. **Discussion 50%**
6. **Practice by doing 75%**
7. **Explaining to others 90%**

Many people—above all, many parents—continue to insist that 'proper' teaching must emphasise mainly the first three activities. Whole classes, of any size, should learn by listening or reading (silently), or by watching their teacher writing or drawing diagrams on a board and (also silently) copying this down. The teacher is totally in control. The class is totally occupied. There is no fooling about. There is no talking. Everyone seems to be busy.

Of course such lessons always appear impressive. But how many are learning anything? The hard fact is that the first three activities can be twenty times less effective than the last three.

Their exclusive use by any teacher will spell only disaster for children.

Modern classes of youngsters will always contain a few who find it difficult to understand the meaning of even a single sentence. Most, of course, can read, silently or aloud. They recognise the words. They can also pronounce them. The crucial fact is, however, that many just *do not comprehend what the words actually mean.* By the end of a paragraph they may be completely lost.

We blame such children for being inattentive, for being bored, disruptive, and even destructive. And they often are. Do you remember how often you were bored?

In truth, their situation is really terrifying. They sit through lesson after lesson in a daze. They may act as if they understand. They may have learnt to do what is praised, very often without the slightest idea of why it is praised. They have come into school with almost no experience of reasonable conversation, of the use of language to communicate, of the need for tolerance of mistakes, for patience in constructing comprehension and achieving agreement.

This is not their fault. Almost certainly they did not choose to be like this. Nor do they want to fail. But unless they are taught to understand, they *will* fail. It is inevitable and terrible to watch. It is also entirely possible to prevent it from happening.

The most effective lessons will be those in which you ask selected children to read a text aloud, to show their comprehension by explaining in their own words what it means, to demonstrate their understanding by discussing their ideas with others, and then by using those ideas.

The reason for this is not difficult to understand. Knowledge is created through associations. The brain best remembers whatever has caused it to combine the most functions, whatever has caused it to notice or create those associations.

Sitting silently whilst listening and watching a teacher— however talented the teacher—does not do this. Reading and listening, reading aloud, discussing the meaning, searching for a better explanation, giving examples, explaining to others: these use far more energy; they involve many more functions of the brain, create many more associations. How many more? We can give a rough approximation. Up to twenty times more energy, functions, and associations: which is why reading aloud (and then explaining) makes it far more certain that your pupils will learn!

Whatever their age, they should also hear much of the explanation you have just read. If it has convinced you, you should be able to convince them. Incidentally, the first time I dared to begin reading aloud with a senior class, I did not do this. Within minutes, there was an explosion of rage. One girl slammed down her book. *"We're not supposed to be able to read this rubbish, and understand it,"* she shouted angrily. *"It's your job to teach it to us!"*

"Listen," I replied, as calmly as I could manage. It was obvious that the rest of the class agreed with her. *"Within a year you will be sitting alone in a study bedroom in some university, and in the room with you will be a pile of books."*

I paused whilst the rest of the class contemplated this possibility, real for them all.

"There will be no-one else in the room. Unless by then you can open books and read them, with understanding, you might as well be dead. Now, pick up the book—and read."

The lesson continued successfully. But I should have tried to explain this first.

This I now recommend!

*

Next: Zombie Land.

Possibly the 8th November 2012.

Dear Friends,

I have just posted on Facebook the second part of this long final essay. I hope that some of you may find it useful.

Its aim is to teach your own children how to release the power of their left brain to question, to criticise, to present alternatives to orthodox and failing routines.

Most civil societies, even more naturally, all military organisations, would prefer to teach right brains to imitate and obey routines without question.

In societies strongly fixated on even more traditional routines, it is likely to be far more dangerous to teach many children to think for themselves.

Nevertheless, I assure you, one day they will thank you for it: if you, and they, survive. I wish the last were only light-hearted, but this danger now affects us all.

Yesterday evening I sat in St Peter's College in Oxford to listen to the previous Director-General of the BBC, now Chief Executive of the New York Times, Mr Mark Thompson. I was seated, incidentally, in the front row and beside Sir Roger Bannister, the man who ran the first 4-minute mile and is now an eminent medical man.

Mr Thompson spoke for an hour with force, knowledge, wit, and clarity; and whilst he was speaking, Moira, Lady Bannister, drew an exquisite portrait of him in red biro in her notebook. (You didn't need to know that. I thought I might impress you.)

His speech was entitled *'The Cloud of Unknowing'*.

You may know that this is the title of a famous work of Christian mysticism written anonymously in the latter half of the 14th century. Its underlying message is that *'the only way to truly "know" God is to abandon all preconceived notions and beliefs or "knowledge" about God and be courageous enough to surrender your mind and ego to the realm of "unknowingness," at which point, you begin to glimpse the true nature of God.'*

This is a fair description of what happened to me: almost exactly forty years ago to the day. I may refer to it again in the final signing-off. It would be a pity not to use it.

Meanwhile, of course, you didn't need to know that either. Sir Roger told me that cutting down on the steroids that I am being obliged to take: *'may give you strange ideas'*.

Strange ideas, I assured him, I do not need.

We have to deal instead with a reality so strange that a generation ago it would have been unimaginable. When a nation as heroically powerful, as powerfully idealistic, and as globally important as the United States of America is divided into two almost exactly equal, wildly vehement, fiercely inimical halves over such a momentous decision as to how it shall be governed, I think it sensible to recognise that it has got itself into a virtual civil war.

Thompson's explanation is that it has become so polarised because the majority of its people neither want nor will allow others to engage in civil and critical discourse. They resort to routine stereotypes, childish insults, labyrinthine conspiracies, appeals to greed and fears. He said the same of Britain, incidentally; and much the same of other countries: but nowhere else is it so disastrous.

Welcome, I wrote some months ago, to Zombie World. Here is Zombie Land.

After his speech I spoke briefly with Mr Thompson. I told him that these mutually suspicious divisions are created in schools, most of all by mathematics lessons: the selfish and uninterested; the greedy and dishonest; the angry and bereft.

A true intellectual is always able to listen. I wonder if he heard me.

Love to you all, Colin.

*

24ᵗʰ December 2012

TO WISH YOU ALL
A MERRY CHRISTMAS
AND A HAPPY NEW YEAR

Here is a Postscript to my 2012 collection of essays for the Facebook group 'Children for an Honest, Just, and Fair World' entitled 'Educating Messiahs'

"Metaphysics, or the attempt to conceive the world as a whole by means of thought, has been developed, from the first, by the union and conflict of two very different human impulses, the one urging men towards mysticism, the other urging them towards science. Some men have achieved greatness through one of these impulses alone, others through the other alone. But the greatest men who have been philosophers have felt the need both of science and of mysticism: the attempt to harmonise the two was what made their life, and what always must, for all its uncertainty, make philosophy, to some minds, a greater thing than either science or religion."

From *Mysticism and Logic*, Bertrand Russell

Over three billion people today follow various forms of Judaism, Christianity, and Islam.

The foundational reports of these religions of a universal intelligence as a personal guide are now many centuries old. The rarity of further reports has always made it hard for young people to sustain their mental and spiritual balance. A modern report, persuasively substantiated and unbiased towards any tradition, would do much to help them do so.

Such is the aim of this report.

It once seemed that nonverbal behaviour is mainly mediated by the right hemisphere of the human brain, whilst the left hemisphere is usually responsible for language.

A more modest suggestion is of two structures, characterised in much the same way, but without being physically fixed; which will also explain the plasticity of damaged brains.

Following this suggestion, the structure which insists on conformity and stasis in all social behaviour may be called the Colonial Mind; whilst the structure with the courage to attempt to escape from it by inventing and practising new behaviour may be called the Adventurous Mind.

As in the case of the colonial powers, the Colonial Mind will be expected to place high value on previously successful patterns of behaviour. These will range from personal habits to public rituals, to automatic applications as varied as military drills and car driving, to near subliminal logic, as in mathematics and other sciences.

Since understanding, formulating, and expressing language requires invention, both logic and illogic, criticism, and other forms of mental risk, the Adventurous Mind is prepared to do more than attempt to break free of its colonial servitude. Being capable of envisaging imaginary realities, it may even attempt to exceed human perception entirely.

In doing so it may be thought to emulate the behaviour of that other faculty of mind, in earlier time called the soul, supposed to be capable of the direct apprehension of the universal intelligence on which the above religions are based; possibly including those even more ancient traditions in which this intelligence is the entire cosmos; possibly including the random probabilities supposed to direct evolution.

Forty years ago an interesting experience of high imagination was reported by a patient in a military psychiatric hospital. He was a young officer in his late twenties who had threatened severely to embarrass the government. The government ignored its legal prerogatives and had him tricked into entering on pretext. Once there, he found himself a patient, without any freedom whatever.

After some weeks of tests and observation, the hospital staff found him perfectly sane. The government was obliged to accept their report, so that he left the hospital unharmed.

No apology was offered. Soldiers do not sue.

But the account of his experience on the first evening of his detention was later accepted as truthful by a group of eminent University of Cambridge philosophers. They advised him that his report would only antagonise other philosophers, would especially terrify other theologians, and they advised him to remain silent. They insisted only that his account be preserved in the British Library.

He accepted the good sense of their advice: but only because he knew he had nothing useful to say. It is no longer enough to claim to have climbed a ladder to heaven. There must be more.

Forty years later he can now explain why modern education is failing disastrously to develop and harmonise the two metaphysical impulses described by Bertrand Russell as together a greater thing than either science or religion; how, as a consequence, Colonial Minds are made the most savage oppressors of dissent and reckless agitators of war; and how best to encourage and support billions of Adventurous Minds to join with others to make peace.

It is technically possible now to create a full-spectrum electronic simulation of his experience, producing a vivid approximation of his experience with light, sound, and movement.

Published globally, this simulation would help revive the expectations of Adventurous Minds everywhere whilst confirming the truth of the reports of ancient Adventurous Minds. It would save them from being led into useless conflict with each other by

Colonial—or Unconscious—Minds, and show them that life has indeed a purpose.

Many of you will have read this account already. If so, you may wish to skip my seminar.

The first rehearsal took place on 6th December 2012 in my usual classroom in the Esporta Gymnasium in North Oxford. After I invited anyone not wishing to participate to leave (but none did so), those present were: G., female, 40, Buddhist-Christian; H., male, 40, Muslim; Y., female, 30, Muslim; S., male, 70, Sikh; D., 30, Agnostic; M., 40, Atheist; A., female, Christian, 50.

I began by pointing out how odd it is that whilst all religions affirm the existence, intelligence, nature, purpose, and, above all, the power of God, few—among them the prophets Isaiah and Ezekiel—in all the thousands of years of recorded history, have ventured to describe a personal meeting with God. I proposed to describe such a meeting.

"For this," I explained, *"and for reasons that will soon be obvious to you all, in a moment I will need Isaiah* [as I called him] *to stand against the door facing me."*

Since Isaiah is both very large and very dark, he would block almost all the external light. Since I had previously given him a copy of my report, in 'Source', he would also know what to expect.

S. was already shaking his head: *"We do not need any evidence for the existence of God. God is invisible but everywhere. We only need to clear our minds and he will recharge us with goodness."*

M. growled: *"I don't believe in any God. Religions just exploit people for greed and power."*

It was very hot in our small room. It is, after all, simply a sauna, about ten feet square. I had recruited everyone now present for a seminar. Now Isaiah was waiting to play his part.

First I explained how I had accused the then British government of sacrificing people's lives from political cowardice; how I learnt later that one of the journalists to whom I had sent my paper took it to one of the government's senior officials and told him: *"This is one of yours. You'd better fix him."* This was probably what made the whole absurd affair possible. Each was trying to impress the other. They were the tigers. I was supposed to be the goat they tied to a tree. Imagine being that goat.

At the end of three weeks—of being found perfectly sane—I was told later by the hospital's military director, Colonel Ferguson, that he had been instructed to begin treating me as soon as I arrived for schizophrenia.

Schizophrenia is a deeply frightening, totally disabling, permanent mental illness.

The most frequent treatment was to pass high-voltage electric shocks through the patient's frontal lobes. Alternatively, a surgeon might push a thin instrument rather like a screwdriver through the thin casing of the upper eye-sockets into the frontal lobes and oscillate it violently. I would have been reduced to a drooling wreck.

Fortunately, Ferguson had too much integrity: and smelt a political rat. *"I tell you what, Hannaford,"* he told me in our first interview: *"I'm having nothing to do with this. Do all that I tell you, and I will get you out of here untreated and unharmed."*

In our final interview he said: *"As soon as I met you I could see that some bloody fool had made a bad mistake."* It was then that he told me also that I had been betrayed by the very man I had most respected and trusted. I wrote to him some years later to ask if this was true. He replied that it was: *"but it doesn't seem to have done you much harm".*

I had been allocated a small bedroom. Through its windows I could see the lights of ships at sea. They might now be on another planet. I crossed to the mirror over the sink and examined my reflection.

I looked surprisingly calm. Actually I was very angry. I had been stupid and badly fooled.

I was now stripped of all social identity. I had been a senior captain. I was used to being treated with respect. I was supremely fit and confident, physically very strong, mentally alert, trained to deal calmly with stressful situations.

Now I was just a psychiatric hospital patient: no longer a person, just a thing.

This is a very frightening transformation.

Even more frightening to know that it may be made permanent.

And suddenly I knew that this was intended.

Now I continued my narrative:

"Without a moment to reflect, I dropped to my knees, put my hands together as in prayer, and said, angrily, *'I need some help.'*

"The effect of this demand was utterly astonishing.

"I was immediately above the solar plane, travelling outwards through skeins of galaxies like distant mists until, abruptly, I arrived at the edge of the universe. This took no more than five seconds.

"There was nothing in front of me now but total blackness. I had just time to wonder what I was doing here when I realised that an enormous presence was emerging out of the black space in front of me and was rushing towards me, growing ever larger, until—with a physical blow—"

At this moment, on cue, Isaiah fell solidly against me, his broad muscular chest hitting mine, his strong arms embracing me, his dark head beside mine.

As best I could, I continued: "I was embraced by this enormously powerful being. He let me know in the first place that he was hugely delighted by my confidence; then spoke directly into my mind" (and not, as William Blake would say, organically): **'How can you be afraid? You are OF ME!'**

"Then he asked me what I wanted. I told him: to know what to do.

"And this time I heard distinctly two words, here by my left ear, urgently again but as if amused: **'Be honest!'**"

On this second cue Isaiah released me, and I sat down, with a bump, on the bench behind me. Around me the others were watching with various degrees of surprise. *"You see,"* I told S., *"at first I thought this was just intended for me; and indeed it did help me persuade the hospital staff that I was sane; but later I realised that it is meant for everyone; that honesty is the nature of the goodness with which God can charge our minds."*

Then, mainly to M, I observed: *"And this is also why you are right not to believe to be true what you do not know to be true. Only accept to be true what you have experienced."*

There was little more to be told. I thanked Isaiah for his help, and I also explained how I had tried twice more that evening to understand how *'being honest'* can actually protect anyone from harm, since honest people are being beaten, tortured, imprisoned, killed every day.

There were no further flights across the cosmos. The answer, I realised, was what must have given many immensely brave men and women the courage to accept hideous torture before their deaths. They believed that no ultimate harm can be caused to the soul: as we might now say, the Adventurous Mind, and that this embrace by what may also be imagined as a physical manifestation of that supreme intelligence is the supreme reward.

"But finally," I reminded my small and very hot audience, *"it must be understood that none of this could actually have happened. An actual demonstration would require control of physical laws which we know, or which we believe that we know, are utterly incorrigible. It would have to extend beyond the boundaries of Newtonian—and Einstein's—reality altogether and access non-ordinary dimensions of existence."*

We know that this is factually impossible: therefore it did not happen factually, it was an entirely imaginary journey to meet an entirely imaginary being.

There is, however, one tiny problem with this strictly sensible assessment. When Bertrand Russell was once asked what might possibly induce him to believe in the reality claimed by religions, he replied, in effect, that he would demand to perceive the physical truth of an established mathematical theory for which such perception is accepted as being physically impossible.

This might be imagined to have been the case, for example, of the Higgs boson, which was eventually 'perceived' due to the efforts of a major scientific collaboration costing many billions.

I continued with my explanation: "When, three days after the events just described, I had a short time alone, I was puzzled to realise that whilst I had these indelible physical and audible memories of my meeting and being embraced by this being, whom I certainly identified as the god of the Jews, Christians, Muslims, and others, I could not recall seeing anything in the blackness of space before its presence began to unfold before me.

"Then I realised that I had in fact a perfectly clear visual memory. The difficulty of accepting it was simply that it made absolutely no sense. It was of a perfectly black sphere glimmering exquisitely faintly against the background of perfectly black space.

"It was not so much that I could see so much light, as to know that it was there. It also seemed to me that this was where God had come from, possibly to where he returned."

This remained a puzzle, but unimportant, for at least another twenty years. In all this time I was too busy learning how to teach mathematics at the British European School as Russell would have approved: *"One of the chief ends served by mathematics, when rightly taught, is to awaken the learner's belief in reason, his confidence in the truth of what has been demonstrated, and in the value of demonstration."* (*Mysticism and Logic,* Russell, B., p. 63)

Then I was listening one day to a BBC interview of Professor John Archibald Wheeler, the American physicist and cosmologist who had established the mathematical existence of something called black holes. This may have been in 1990, after the publication of his book, which I soon bought: *'A Journey into Gravity and Spacetime'.*

Suddenly I heard this gravelly American voice declare, with distinct asperity: "Anyway, they aren't black holes, they're black *spheres!"*

Of course they are. Massive stars which have exhausted all their fuel must collapse under gravity until all their mass shrinks to a dimensionless point, creating a gravitational sink from which not even light can escape. Some cosmologists now surmise that there are very many of these throughout our universe, and that each may connect ours with another universe: rather as if God has indeed many mansions!

But this did not solve my problem, now of rather greater importance.

In my imagination, I seemed to have 'seen' a black hole.

How enticing this is: not only to travel absurdly impossible distances in absurdly little time to be embraced by a god rejected by science who appears to know science better; but also to see one of the rarest of all the theoretical beasts in its native habitat in deep space, a space it has sucked clean of every particle of energy and matter!

But however it might be 'imagined', it is, for this very reason, actually impossible to see a black hole: it cannot emit any light.

I could not therefore possibly have seen whatever I imagined seeing in 1972.

Black holes, or spheres, are not visible: not even imaginary ones.

It was about two years later that a distinguished British cosmologist, Stephen Hawking, first explained that this is not necessarily true: that pairs of spontaneously created photons in space around a black sphere might propagate in such a way that one might be swallowed up and the other escape

In this case, if only anyone *could* overcome all the absolute physical impossibilities of doing so, it would be possible to actually see a perfectly black sphere 'glimmering exquisitely faintly against the background of perfectly black space'.

Just as I had imagined: impossibly.

Which, I suppose, is not only evidence of the powers of imagination, both mystical and scientific, but, if he had imagined it, it might also have been sufficient to persuade Lord Russell that there is more to heaven and earth that science has yet to understand.

My hope is that this may help many of my young friends to try to do so. I do not believe that there is any greater or finer or more rewarding purpose of a life.

Never, ever, give up!

Colin

PS Here below are the hints that The Programme kept throwing at me.

If we never write anything save what is already understood, the field of understanding will never be extended.

Ezra Pound, in the Pisan Canto XCVI
Cited by Zissimos Lorenzatos, in *The Drama of Quality*, 2000

The Prophets Isaiah and Ezekiel dined with me, and I asked them how they dared so roundly to assert that God spoke to them; and whether they did not think at the time that they would be misunderstood & so be the cause of some imposition. Isaiah answer'd: 'I saw no God, nor heard any, in a finite organical perception; but my senses discover'd the infinite in everything, and as I was then persuaded & remain confirmed that the voice of honest indignation is the voice of God, I cared not for the consequences, but wrote.'

If the doors of perception were cleansed, every thing would appear to man as it is, infinite. For man has closed himself up, till he sees all things thro' narrow chinks of his cavern.

William Blake, in *The Marriage of Heaven and Hell*, 1790

We have certain preconceived notions about location in space which have come down to us from ape-like ancestors.

Sir Arthur Eddington, in *Space, Time, and Gravitation*, 1920.

When one wakes from sleep, snuff water three times. For indeed, Shaytan spends the night in the upper part of the nose.

From *The Muslim Book of Purification*, Hadeeth 245

Three results [may be affirmed] *concerning the "quantum connection": 1. It is unattenuated: in contrast to classical (instantaneous) action, the quantum connection is unaffected by distance. 2. It is discriminating: while gravitational forces affect similarly situated objects in the same way, the quantum connection is a private arrangement between entangled particles. 3. It is instantaneous: while Newton's theory of gravity has gravity propagate instantaneously, it need not do so, and GR* [Einstein's Theory of General Relativity] *certainly involves no instantaneous gravitational action; but the quantum connection appears to act essentially instantaneously.*

Professor Tim Maudlin, Harvard U.,
Quantum Non-Locality and Relativity, 2011

The problems of the modern world arise from the fact that the realities [formulated by different cultures] *are no longer isolated from each other. Throughout most of human history a man or a woman could lead an entire life snugly within the cocoon of the local reality. Today, we constantly collide with persons living in wildly different realities. This creates a situation known as our "crisis of values".*

Robert Anton Wilson, in *Promethus Rising,* 2005

In view of these facts, the increase in interests in spirituality and inner quest is certainly one of the few hopeful developments in our troubled world. If this trend continues, inner transformation of humanity could be a major force in averting the present suicidal trend and the global catastrophe towards which the world seems to be moving at a frightful pace . . . . The spirituality that emerges . . . should not be confused with the mainstream religions, their beliefs, doctrines, dogmas, and rituals. Many of them lost entirely the connection with the original source, which is a direct visionary experience of transpersonal realities. They are mainly concerned with such issues as power, money, hierarchies, and ethical, political, and social control . . . . Carl Gustav Jung expressed a similar opinion (1985); according to him, the main function of formalized religion is to protect people against the direct experience of God.

Stanislav Grof, *The Adventure of Self-Discovery,* 1988

He [Alexander Papaderos,] *was not the light or the source of light himself, but light there is in the form of truth and understanding and knowledge—and, we might add, hope and justice and compassion—and that light will shine in dark places only if those who have it—those who know it—reflect it. That, Papaderos said, was what he was about. That was what gave meaning to his life.*

Duane E. Davis, *Light in Dark Places,* 2011

I had motives for not wanting the world to have a meaning; consequently I assumed it had none, and was able without difficulty to find satisfactory reasons for this assumption . . . . [For me] *the philosophy of meaninglessness was essentially an instrument of liberation, sexual and political.*

Aldous Huxley, *Ends and Means,* 1937

Christmas Day, 2012

Dear Friends,

When some of you asked me to start a Facebook group 'to teach everyone what you taught us in your classroom' I had a very modest aim.

It was only to explain why, as parents, you should help your children retain their innocence, meaning that they should always know that they have the right to ask questions, and the right to be honest.

This, fundamentally, was all that I tried to teach. A major reason for writing a Postscript to my essays of the past year is that I never really explained why I think this is so important. Now I have.

But in the beginning, with the inexorability of Alice falling down the rabbit-hole, the questions had to be answered.

Why is it so very difficult for people to keep their innocence; or, conversely, why is it so very easy to persuade people that they have no right to ask questions and that being honest means repeating what they are told?

This set me off, at first quasi-comically with Winnie-the-Pooh and Piglet in the Hunt for the Woozle. But then, as it became clear that this could never have a happy ending, it became an inquiry into the nature of The Beast.

By now I realised that I was really looking to find what it is that throughout human history has caused some people to believe that they are so superior to others that they can subject others to degradation, cruelty, and, ultimately, death.

To find this, of course, was also the ambition of Jesus, the hoped-for Christ, whose birthday we will be celebrating today. He wanted to find a way to bring the Kingdom of God, peace, to the whole of the Earth, and is remembered most of all for being punished by the cruelest of deaths.

It has taken me the whole of the past year to find a very wonderful answer to this question. It is wonderful because it is not strange: we have discovered it before.

Those of you whom I began to teach as eleven-year-olds will remember how I used to tell you: "Put your fists together: that is the size and shape of your brain. On the right is that half of your brain which remembers patterns" (now add: 'or whatever you are told or you come to believe is true'), "and on the left is your help in asking questions" (now add: 'and in disbelieving or revising what you realise is wrong, or that it is not necessary to believe is true').

Without your encouragement, I would never have come to realise that this also explains why some people believe they are so superior to others, and why they can then treat the others with contempt. There are only punishers and victims. Sometimes the roles are reversed.

The entrance to 'the Kingdom of God within you' is likely to be found through the faculty of mind which I have called the Adventurous Mind. It is this which will naturally make peace.

The reason that there is so much hurt and violence in our world is that the faculty I have called the Colonial Mind is generally far stronger: and it is this which will naturally make war.

Being so sure that only its pattern of reality must be respected, it is capable not only of destroying an entire country: in its furious rejection of questions, it can destroy our entire world. It was this kind of conflict between the Colonial Minds controlling the US and Soviet nuclear weapons that produced the obscene strategy of MAD: Mutually Assured Destruction.

Whilst that danger has still not receded entirely, there are now several other conflicts to be aware of between other Colonial Minds capable of destroying much of the world.

I believe we can reduce all these dangers by being able to explain them in much the same simple terms as we discovered in our mathematics lessons. On the right are stored our fixed ideas; on the left is the power to change them.

Perhaps it is not so far-fetched after all to translate this into the more colourful descriptions: on the left is the Kingdom of God and peace; on the right, the Kingdom of Satan and war.

Let us use this very simple but very powerful understanding to help create a more peaceful New Year.

With thanks and blessings to you all,

Love, Colin.

Odellia Jean Channing writes:

"Why suggest that any parts of our brains are 'fixed'? There are of course parts of the brain that are primitive and have remained unchanged for thousands of years, like the hypothalamus. But a high proportion of our brains are created by rehearsed patterns and the firing of neurotransmitters. People often try to attribute their rigidity of mind to something 'hardwired' in their brains, but really it's just more comfortable to stream than challenge the status quo. Changing people's perceptions is difficult not because they aren't able to rationalize, but because they don't want to."

Dear Ms Channing,

I am most grateful for your interest. Thank you. Before I began to write, I asked the advice of an eminent British professor of physiology. He assured me that virtually any statement about the human brain is conjectural and that, although there is still some sense in the left- and right-brain distinction made popular some decades ago, it would be better to suppose that certain distinctive functions of mind are supported by distinctive neurological structures within the brain, and that these structures may indeed be confined to one hemisphere, but may also extend into both.

As an indication of the uncertainty surrounding all these questions, his most frequent response to my questions was either: "We just don't know," or, alternatively, "I don't think it safe to say X or Y."

In this way he made me appreciate that the extent to which such supposedly distinctive functions can also be supposed to be entirely independent of other supposedly distinct functions, and the extent to which any of the structures supposed to support them are stable over any length of time must also be highly conjectural. As I think you suggest, they may be made in an instant, then dissolve.

And that the majority in any society will always prefer to accept the status quo is exactly my point. The Colonial Mind—but perhaps you would be happier if I were to write: 'The Colonial *Habit* of Mind'—can always be persuaded, or will always be able to persuade itself, and will certainly always want to believe that: 'everything is as it must be'; or 'is as it should be'; or, possibly in less happy circumstances, 'we have done nothing wrong: the natives have brought this on themselves!'

As you will know, there is some fairly good empirical evidence of the number who can be expected to exercise their Adventurous

Mind. It is about one in twenty. They may not be successful. They may be misguided. At least they may try.

I think as well, incidentally, that this has also a further spiritual consequence: 'for many are called, but few are chosen.' The real necessity is to know that you are neither the Colonial Mind nor the Adventurous Mind. You are their observer. And the moment you realise this, I believe you may feel something very remarkable happen.

With thanks and best wishes, Colin.

*

28th December 2012

Dear Friends,

I want now to introduce you to an older friend of mine, older in years and experience.

Cecil Harmsworth King always saw himself as a newspaperman. At the time that I met him he had created the largest news publishing corporation in the world. He had also published something in a book which I borrowed and which made me look to him for advice.

Cecil—Mister King, I would have called him when we talked—lived in a wonderful house on the banks of the Thames by Hampton Court Palace. I managed to get a message to him by way of his wife, and was invited to talk with him there. Later he was to give me a signed copy of the same book. I have it beside me now.

"A few centuries ago," he told me on our first meeting, *"you would have been regarded as a saint, and religious orders would have been created around you. Today you are more likely to be mocked and reviled".*

Although he was soon to offer to place all his resources at my disposal, I refused. I did not want his material help. And although we disagreed about what I should do, I had a real affection for him, and he continued to write to me regularly for several years always urging me to seek more instructions from God. I still have a box of his letters.

I liked Cecil King immensely, and I am very glad that I met him. Although he was used to considerable power and influence, he was a thoroughly good man. But he was now also an old man. He wanted to be remembered as someone who had changed the world and I could be his protégé. I could shock the world into some kind of new moral order by blazing across the sky like some heavenly portent declaring: "Be sure that God exists: I am the proof!"

This seemed to me of no value at all. I was not worried about being mocked and reviled. But there were quite a few other heavenly portents whizzing about just then. Most of them made a point of declaring that money was the root of all evil whilst collecting as much of it as they could. I also met the young Arianna Stasinopoulos at about this time, believing that this clearly highly intelligent young woman would have better ideas, but found that she also seemed to believe in the power of personal charisma

I did not. Personal charisma is what TV evangelists depend on. I wanted ideas.

That I might have become rich by playing the guru would have been a shameful dereliction of duty.

King knew this too. I have just taken his book down from the shelf and opened it for the first time in at least twenty years and found this at once concerning the most respected evangelist of that time: *'No great success, let us admit it, is secured by Billy Graham. Here is a nice man, a sincere man, trying to convince people of the truth and desperate relevance of fundamentalist Christianity . . . . It would be true to say that Mr Graham has got nowhere. This seems to me not an argument that, as some would maintain, religion has had its day, but rather that the truths of religion to carry conviction today must be proclaimed in a form intelligible to the dwellers in vast industrial cities . . . . No longer do we see shepherds watching their flocks by night. '*

Here he is in the front room of his house, sitting exactly as I remember him when talking with me. He had the habit of stroking the wing of his armchair as he does here, so that the velvet was worn away, especially on his right side.

It is a splendid book, with much to argue about, but I must get on. I learnt from him just one hugely important belief, to which, as you can now see, I have been faithful. *"I have been successful in my business,"* he told me, *"because I always tried to treat my people fairly, and I have always believed that I always have time."*

He emphasised that last point several times, and it made a deep impression on me. There is really nothing like believing that you have time. I am reminded now of Richard Feynman's similar judgment: *'In order to do good physics, you need lots of time."*

But the task of finding a new way to explain the truths of religions—and, by the way, that *is* religions plural—is much harder than he ever realised. A newspaperman would naturally always think in terms of the banner headline: and King's main British paper was The Mirror. This was part of his business too. But headlines last only a day. They very rarely change history.

Successful generals never pitch men into battle like throwing chaff into fire, and one of the most successful generals of all went further, writing in his treatise on war: *"The supreme excellence is not to win a hundred victories in a hundred battles. It is to subdue the armies of your enemies without even having to fight them."*

Who, we must first ask, are our enemies? We are. We are destroying our beautiful magical world, squandering our inheritance, destroying our children's future.

We are our own enemies. And what are our armies?

Words. Words, words, words, words! Billions and billions of words: wave after wave of words, angry, spiteful, despairing; endlessly assaulting others' ideas, and even others' right to have ideas; exulting over minor victories now and then, here and there; all noise and fury actually achieving nothing, everyone being convinced that only their ideas are correct.

How would Sun-Tzu subdue all these enemies?

This might even have seemed hopeless to him.

What is required must be obvious to everyone, fair to everyone.

What is required is to change people's understanding of themselves so that winning these endless arguments becomes not just far less important, but is recognised as a permanent obstacle to their own private mental, emotional, and spiritual health.

And we now know why this is.

We have discovered that every mind can understand itself in terms of two simple concepts: the Colonial Mind and the Adventurous Mind.

Arguments serving the interests of the Colonial Mind will always reflect its assumption that the reality that it imagines is uniquely true, and that this imagined reality must therefore be defended at any cost.

Its actions will correspond to this concept. In whatever form they take, aggressive or defensive, no possible virtue will be allowed of any other imagined reality.

The language may be different, the words different, the declared intention different, but every argument produced by the Colonial Mind will have one purpose: to discourage further thought.

You can get a real sense of this in the United States just now in the current head-butting contest between Democrats and Republicans.

This is just one of countless other head-butting contests historic and current.

Start noticing them now. They are quite literally costing the earth.

We would not survive long without Colonial Minds. They are necessary to give substance and stability to societies and must be valued and supported for this essential reason.

It is largely the purpose of the Adventurous Mind to encourage further thought.

This is why it so often leads its too adventurous owner to the cross or to the stake.

But it is also the Adventurous Mind that will develop and perfect new ideas in every field of human endeavour: in science; business; national politics; international affairs.

Only Adventurous Minds can save humankind from itself.

Meanwhile, if you want your children to have a successful, mentally, emotionally, and spiritually well-balanced, happy life, start explaining the world in these terms now.

Love to all, Colin.

*

To: The Revd Canon Dr Sarah Coakley
Norris-Hulse Professor of Divinity
Cambridge University,
Church of England

Dear Professor Coakley,

Forty years ago I was greatly helped by Professor Donald MacKinnon, and by Dean of Chapel of Trinity College, Dr John Robinson. Having read some part of your ministry, and having admired the courage you have shown in it, I hope I may now receive a similarly kind reception from you.

As you will know, both men declared that a more honest confession by priests about what they know personally, although this might not be very impressive, would serve as a great encouragement to any laity lapsed in faith to return to the church.

I had been accepted by Trinity in 1975 as a mature student, after leaving the Army and coming to Cambridge to qualify as a teacher. Subsequently I have taught mathematics for over twenty years, first in Magdalene College School of Oxford, then as a head of mathematics at the official British European School outside Oxford.

It is now possible for me to realise that I may have arrived to ask for their advice at a very bad time: for I needed help with a curious experience I had had a few years before.

It may have been the last thing they expected, but they and their friends took my report to be authentic. After I left the Army I found work on Mull, and had previously met Professor MacKinnon in Oban. In Cambridge he often invited me to take tea in your School, when he would always urge me to 'eat up all these biscuits'; and when he once took me to his college he insisted I eat both his and my portions of strawberries and cream! On a different occasion, hc pointed out a young John Sentamu to me, but no opportunity arose to speak with him.

Both he and Dr Robinson were particularly anxious to keep me from meeting any other Cambridge philosophers or theologians, Professor MacKinnon telling me with the most furious emphasis: *"There are **killers** in this University"*.

I met John twice privately, and was honoured to be invited to dinner in his rooms behind the Chapel, where he told me that my experience was 'entirely in the Christian tradition'.

But clearly—or, as eventually became clear—neither of these good men could decide what to do with me, except to advise me that it would be far too dangerous for me ever to talk openly to anyone else in future about my experience.

Instead, John advised: *'You should attempt to incorporate it in your teaching.'*

Given my choice of subject, at the time this seemed wildly impractical. Mathematics is not a very obvious partner of theology. Subsequently, however, I found it appropriate!

I retired some years ago, but when some of my ex-pupils implored me to return to our old school for a last reunion, they then demanded that I begin a Facebook group 'to tell the rest of the world what you taught us in your classroom.'

This attachment is the last of a series of essays I have written for them in the past year, in which I have attempted to explain precisely why I taught them as I did: with the emphasis, as I am sure Donald and John would have wished of me, on the intellectual, moral, social, and of course spiritual importance of being honest.

You have achieved much in succeeding them. I feel now that I am no longer in danger!

I shall be most happy if you now find my report helpful. I hope to publish it soon.

Best wishes, Colin Hannaford.

[Editorial note: Professsor Coakley did not reply.]

*

5ᵗʰ January 2013

Dear Friends,

Early one morning in late summer of 1971 I was on duty in the main Operations Room of HQ Northern Ireland. I had already spent many hours at the duty officer's desk. Partly in order to stay awake, I had spent the latest nights and early mornings writing a play.

It was essentially a long conversation between the Roman Pilate and the Jew Jesus.

All the other gospels are nearly identical, but in John's we read that when Pilate demanded to know whether Jesus believed himself a king, Jesus answered: *"I was born into the world to speak about the truth. Whoever belongs to the truth listens to me."*

"What is truth?" Pilate is supposed to have asked. John tells us no more.

I wanted to explore how they might have continued. I gave to Pontius Pilate the persona of a Greek-educated Roman bureaucrat, insisting that truths, as with Rome's laws, must be perfectly well-defined, universal, and fixed. Either this Jewish rabble-rouser was pretending to be a king: it was whispered that he was a descendant of the famous David, or he was just another clever-talking Jewish fraud. They all wanted to be the Messiah. He would soon find out.

I gave a more difficult task to Jesus. And now, in this moment: right now, with a faint prickling of the nape, I realise that this may have been the first time that the concept I have been writing about was seeded into my mind.

I asked my Jesus to try to explain to my Pilate, a rigid intellectual, but a fair man, that in his understanding, truth, as knowledge, had limits or boundaries, no laws obedient to man, that it might be infinite in extension. All that is required is a mind capable and brave enough to explore it. I wanted him to persuade Pilate that his mission was to persuade the Jews to stop believing that only they were important. Their faith might bring peace to the world: even peace with Rome.

I called my play *'Game'*. Earlier that year I had given it to a group of amateur players in Belfast. With the blithe composure of true thespians in what was declared a war zone, they had given a public reading of it which had won a favourable review in a Belfast paper.

This particular morning my play writing career was on hold. General Farrar-Hockley, famously courageous as a young soldier, had not yet arrived to be briefed by me, when a call came through from the police: *"There's a funny lookin' parcel outside the Orangemen's Hall at Castlerobin. Can you send someone up to look at it?"* This small Protestant chapel was no more than five miles away: as provocatively close as possible.

I looked up to meet a cheerful grin from the young EOD (Explosive Ordnance Disposal) officer, walking into the Operations Room. He had been on call all night and was about to go off duty.

"I heard that," he told me. *"I'll take it. Don't bother anyone else."* An hour later there was another call from the police. *"We're goin' to need some help over here,"* a sombre voice told me. *"Your young chap's bin blown t'bits."*

He was Captain David Stewardson. Aged 29, he was my senior by one year. He was not the first British soldier to die in Northern Ireland, whilst at first only trying to stop the Irish Catholics and Protestants from killing each other; but the IRA was getting annoyed that their bombs were being so successfully defused by brave young chaps like David Stewardson that they raised the stakes. They started building  booby-trapped bombs designed to kill EODs. He was their first success. They also made me feel, wrongly, but deeply, responsible.

I had been a soldier since I was 17. For the first time I felt some responsibility for another soldier's death. Of course neither of us could have known that he would die alone, crouched over a brown paper parcel at the doors of a Christian chapel.

The expectation of all soldiers is that other nations' soldiers will do their best to kill them.

But killing as a purely political symbol; and killing more or less at random, for David's deadly parcel might have been left in a shop, a pub, a cinema: this was new. This caused me to wonder what could persuade people to kill at random to advance a cause.

I had one clue. Earlier that year I had taken a call from a young man telling me he was Martin McGuinness.

At that time it would have been exceedingly foolish for anyone to pretend to be Martin McGuinness. Although still in his early twenties, he was believed to be a senior IRA commander.

He wanted, he said, to talk with a young English officer. *"You're talking to one,"* I replied. *"I just' wanna tell yer,"* his accent was strong, *"You English: you're jus' in the way. We've nuthin against you. We jus' want the Prods to go home!"*

Just for a moment I was stupidly obtuse. *"And where would that be, Mister McGuinness?"*

The answer roared in my ear. *"Back to Scotland, of course: where they came from!"*

Whoever he was, that was all he really had to say, and I can honour him for having the guts, even the candour, to attempt to explain what he and his Catholic friends wanted to achieve.

It was his earnestness and Stewardson's death which caused me next year to write my ill-fated letter to politicians and journalists telling them that soldiers could not do their work for them: that this was an increasingly bloody conflict between the representatives of two supposedly Christian religions. The world should understand that there was precious little nobility in it.

I sent my letters after the tragedy of Bloody Sunday early in the next year. This unnerved the British government even more, and it was its nervousness, together with my surprising betrayal by a famous journalist whom I admired, who recommended to a senior government member in his London club that I should be 'fixed', which caused me to be tricked into entering an army psychiatric hospital, triggering the most important experience of my life: and, eventually, these immensely laborious essays.

The Beast in the heads of young Martin McGuinness and his Irish Republican Army volunteers, and of the equally bloody-minded Ulster Defence Force soon murdering Catholics, is in all our heads.

Here is the magically simple explanation of all religious and ideological conflicts.

Catholics, Protestants, Jews, Muslims, Hindus, Baha'is, Communists, anti-Communists: all the unhappy people in the world caught up in conflict over faith, of dogma and doctrine, historically and today, are victims of the Colonial Mind.

Although I didn't name it like this, I began to explain its fundamental characteristic to some of you in my mathematics classroom over twenty years ago. Whether it inhabits only the right hemisphere of your brain or parts of both is no longer important. What is not disputable is that all minds develop a neurological structure which is extremely good at remembering whatever it is taught: but which does not know how to question or to criticize. It can only repeat, tirelessly, whatever it remembers, including any mistakes.

No doubt this structure began to build in your mother's womb. It is soon indispensable to survival. It can later become extremely dangerous to others, being likely to insist: "Everything I do, you must do too; everything I believe, you must believe; everything I say, you must say."

The playground bully starts with this premise. So do all later bullies, including parents. Freedom is an offence to their power. They will not hesitate to kill, even their own children.

This is often government policy. In Broad Street in Oxford, not far from where I am writing this, there is a crude cross of cobble-stones in the road. It marks the place where five centuries ago two Protestant bishops were burnt to death for defying a Catholic queen. As the fires were being lit, one called to the other: *"Be of good cheer, for we shall this day light a candle in England as I trust by God's grace shall never be put out."*

Even if world extinction is threatened, sufficiently obdurate Colonial Minds cannot admit they may be wrong. They may have developed a glimmer of sense that they are wrong, and may then decide that this is just another test of their courage. This is what happened in the Zionist mind, the fundamentalist Muslim mind, and the Revelation-obsessed Christian mind.

Their obsessions are like tumours in the brain. They cannot be cut out. They can be shown a better way, however, to achieve what everyone wants: to be noticed by God.

With hope for a better day, Colin.

*

14th January 2013

Dear Friends,

Sincere thanks to all of you who have recently encouraged your own friends to join us: and welcome to them all!

After all that excitement, the world did not end in December, but, sadly, this is not great reason for celebration. The problems that beset our world in 2012 are still here, and no one seems to have any sensible idea how to solve them: except, as usual, by blaming others. I am often reminded of a photograph in a National Geographic magazine that used to fascinate me as a boy. It was of a river in, I suppose, British Columbia, on which thousands of logs had become locked immovably together because one had got stuck on the bottom. A caption explained that the only way to release the jam was to find and free that log. The rest would then be able to move. A more recent idea in Chaos Theory is that a very minor change within a complex system can cause everything to change: unpredictably, it is true, but with a new future. The solution we have found involves simply asking your friends if they have heard of the latest game of imagination. It requires just two questions: "What do you believe must be true?" And next: "What if you are wrong?"

Colin

*

14ᵗʰ January 2013

Dear Friends,

I have told elsewhere the story of the unfortunate Professor Frege: that, as he was about to complete the final volume of his memoir to demonstrate the colossal importance of his mathematical logic, he received a short note from a then minor academic called Russell, containing a simple question. It destroyed his life's work.

I have just come very close to this. I asked an even simpler question of myself.

When in his later years Bertrand Russell was asked why he had abandoned mathematics for philosophy, he replied that he wanted to understand the world rather better before he died.

Ever since I discovered him as a boy, I was very much affected by his contempt for shallow thinking, and by his atheism, and I have no doubt that this was a major factor in preparing me for my own experience. I am sure as well that a major reason he was never fully satisfied with his understanding of the world is that he never had any experience similar to mine.

How I wish I might have been able to talk with him about it!

We, meanwhile, have achieved a great deal in realising that the behaviour of young minds, which we began to explore when you were learning mathematics in my classroom, is able to explain the behaviour of entire adult societies. However much they may wish to be different: they are not.

The first question that I originally wanted to answer is: why is it so difficult for these adult societies peaceably to combine: and why, further, is it apparently so nearly inevitable for them to resort to aggression, for one to feel that it must defeat the other?

We have answered this question. The reason is that nearly all societies are dominated by leaders, religious and political, who find it impossible to admit publicly, and in many cases even privately, that they might be wrong.

This absolutely simple and fundamental question is precisely the question that religions, above all, hesitate, if not refuse, to address. But it has even wider applications. If only answering this question in the affirmative might be understood as proof of intellectual and moral strength, rather than intellectual or moral weakness, far less blood might be shed.

But here I find myself in a quandary. On the one hand, I wish to declare that I have experienced a very similar theophany as that which the majority of religions continue to celebrate. On the other hand, I must also explain that the reason why, for example, Catholic and Protestant Christians are so easily provoked to kill each other is that both of their religions are hopelessly corrupt.

The evidence and proof are obvious. Both claim to be loyal to the teaching of Jesus Christ. If this were true, they should find it easy to combine. But they do not.

A short while ago I was offered the possibility of moving from near the centre of Oxford to a perfectly idyllic cottage in a beautiful valley, miles away in the countryside. The rent would be nominal. I could become the perfect model of a modern anchorite.

"But, of course," I was warned, *"you will lose touch with all the new friends you have made in Oxford."* *"Oh,"* I replied, not entirely flippantly, *"I have very few friends in Oxford now. I have mostly made new enemies."*

Here now was an opportunity to make some very serious new enemies. For whatever I may say about the Christian religion can equally well be said of virtually all the intractable religions of the world, and all their leaders, and all the politicians, and all their incorrigibly entrenched political programmes. They are all captives of their Colonial—or, as my 'sauna seminarians' suggested, of their Habitual, or Imperialistic, or Unreflective—Minds.

Did I want this? I remember Professor Donald MacKinnon, many years ago, telling me, *"There are killers in this university!"* But he meant academic assassins. Some of these would be real assassins.

I was still debating this with myself when I asked the fatal question: 'Could I be wrong?'

And as Chicken Licken always feared would happen: The Sky fell down.

Of *course* I could be wrong. Of *course* I could be wrong: totally, hopelessly, pathetically wrong, wrong, **WRONG!**

I could not refuse to accept this. But what must then happen to the colossal importance of my own life's work, to my magnificent all-encompassing world-explaining theory, if this is true?

What if, all this time, I have been building nothing more than a bag of gas, a punctured balloon?

For the first time I looked for help from one of the very sources I had just reviled. I found a website of a Christian theological college and its list of generally accepted theophanies. Four biblical: Abraham, Moses, Jacob, Jesus; and one extra-biblical: Muhammad.

So, the entire construction of the major monotheistic religions of humankind, together with all the problems they have with each other, is built on the testimony of just five men! How could this possibly happen?

I retired to my hut to think: then resorted to my library.

'This book, and this man's ideas, may be the most influential, if not to say controversial, of the second half of the twentieth century. It renders whole shelves of books obsolete.'

This is a reviewer's comment of a book that I have mentioned before, with one of the catchiest titles in all scientific literature: *'The Origin of Consciousness in the Breakdown of the Bi-Cameral Mind'*. Its basic thesis is that before about 3000 years ago people were not able to think of themselves subjectively: that is, literally, to know: 'this is me thinking about myself and my predicament' but were forced to think consciously, or as we now say, subjectively, by a series of major catastrophes.

Before this, he says, the human mind was entirely 'bi-cameral': that is to say, no-one could, or even needed to, reason about what to do hour by hour, day by day. As I noted in beginning these essays, this was because the majority of their decisions required no new ideas. They were based entirely on habit. When, however, these catastrophes occurred, obliging entire societies to leave their accustomed territories and to subdue or eliminate weaker societies, they forced human minds to learn to reason, and also to learn to explain their actions. This they often did by declaring that they were told what to do, first by the hallucinated auditory command of spirits or gods, then by only one God, and only through the voices of socially recognised and accepted prophets.

In the Bible the most vehement and noisy of all the other 'bi-cameral' humans, apparently always men, are called *'nabiim'*. Eventually they became so many and their raving such a nuisance that the last of them were massacred by order of the prophet Elijah (I Kings 18.40).

And a little later the parents of children who had not learnt to keep their thoughts to themselves were ordered to put them to death at once (Zechariah 13.3-4).

'This,' Jaynes notes drily, *'is a serious injunction. If it was carried out, it is an evolutionary selection which helped move the gene pool of humanity towards subjectivity.'*

But surely, at that time this movement would be true only of Jews' gene pool? Since creative intelligence is a function of the left hemisphere, and habit of the right, could this early advantage explain the precocious intelligence of individual Jews, whilst the right hemisphere continues to support their collective belief in themselves as a unique people?

Colin

*

14th January 2013

Dear Friends,

Thanks to you all for your encouragement.

I have now posted the second part of my final essay. [This is getting to be a joke!]

Please note that it contains another suggestion that I don't believe has been made before: namely, that there is only one characteristic unique to human beings.

We have more imagination than any other species of animal; and, indeed, far more than most of us ever use. Darwinian evolution is not supposed to work like this. Notice that I do not say that imagination is not useful, but that it is hard to understand why everyone has far more than they may ever use. We must also notice that anyone noticed in most societies to be using their imagination in any distinctly unusual way is most likely to be murdered. This is happening now to poor girls simply demanding to be educated, but you may be quite sure that just a few centuries ago, if I had had courage enough, I would have been hung in iron chains on an iron post and burnt. I have always been a member of the awkward squad. This is why I got into trouble in the Army.

It is impossible to imagine now anyone being burnt alive for having the wrong ideas in any Western society, and although I am grateful not to live in fear of any other dreadful death, it is impossible to fear it for a reason which actually runs counter to my thesis.

Until a few centuries ago, virtually everyone in virtually all societies was enormously fearful that God would not choose to take them 'to heaven and eternal life'—reference to which you may read on many tombstones over many centuries. So great was this anxiety that people would eagerly demand the killing of anyone who seemed to threaten their selection. So sure are many impressionable young men in Islamic societies today that, entirely contrary to their faith, they will kill any number of blameless people to ensure their own selection.

This fear of missing God's attention has generally vanished in most Western societies, because belief in any God, in any power sufficiently interested in the human race, and able to make this promise, has also vanished. A major exception is the belief of several tens of millions in the United States that they will be selected, although this has diminished in recent years as dozens of predicted Last Days have disappointed them.

Although there is still a great deal of lip-service to this general idea, although many still derive a kind of vague comfort from it; and whilst religious orders are still very major social institutions, no-one—well, almost no-one—will try to kill you if you tell them that their selection cannot happen. The vast majority of educated Westerners have now been persuaded by the disclosures of science that there is no need to deny it. They will simply point at the nearest image of the universe, of billions of galaxies containing trillions of stars, and shrug: *"Look at this,"* they explain, perhaps regretfully, *"it's all got just too big for Father Christmas."*

Which is a pity, in a way, because I claim that it is not too big: but that we are simply not using enough imagination.

*

Also 14ᵗʰ January 2013

Dear Friends,

I bought my copy of Jaynes' book in 1992, and I must have read most of it by 1993. Now I took it from its shelf to look for his help. Here he offers an instance of the loss of the bi-cameral commands which made life less demanding for these early humans. In the following, he suggests, we can hear their anguish at being no longer prompted to act by their mind's previously clearly heard auditory commands: *"Now do this! Now do that"*—which they identified as any one of a variety of gods, telling them how and when to act.

Here instead they are being made to learn to think for themselves.

'As the stag pants after the water brooks / So I pant after you, O gods! / I thirst for gods! For living gods! / When shall I come face to face with gods?'

Their lamentation is preserved for us as Psalm 42. Later translators have turned 'gods' into 'God', and I have used my freedom to substitute 'I' for Jayne's 'mind'. However it may be translated, I feel some pity for that unhappy soul of so many millennia ago: but no less pity for the many souls still unable to free themselves from habitual thinking, who even persuade themselves and others that there is no such thing as free will, that we act: *'This way! That way!'* only because we are prompted to do so on different occasions.

One may wonder, as I have: how many bi-cameral people are with us today? They would be likely to declare that they *must* act as they do: that they have no choice!

I found Jaynes hugely important when I first read him, and I revere him now. Years later Professor Sheldon Hackney, then President of the US National Endowment for the Humanities, told me that he and his colleagues at Princeton had been astonished by his boldness.

Still more years later, I turned hesitantly to his Index. I wanted to find what he has to say about . . . about . . . here we are: 'Idols'; 'Iliad'; 'Imaginary Companions'; 'Immediate Experience' . . . nothing, nothing at all under 'Imagination'!

But dear, darling Doctor Jaynes: don't you see? It is only imagination that makes subjective thought and action possible! It is only imagination which can presage an action: exploring 'What if I do this; or, what if I do that? What if he does this, or he does that?' And, of course, most difficult of all to explain without free will: 'What if even "*I* think it's possible" may be wrong, but continue to follow my imagination?'

Knowingly and also unknowingly, the whole of science has been built upon this premise. *"It may be wrong,"*—Charles Darwin said of his and Wallace's theory of natural evolution—*"but it would appear to be the best explanation of the evidence."*

Imagination is the strangest product of human evolution.

Why strange? Strange because, as we have seen, and as we can observe today, the great majority of people simply do not want it or require it. They may even find it frightening.

From Zechariah's time to the present, the majority have always been content simply to continue to behave precisely as their cultures demand they behave, insisting that those who show the least inclination to behave unusually, which almost always means in using their imagination, be cruelly discouraged, even murdered: this is the basis of the so-called 'honour killings'.

We see once again the continual conflict between the habitual and imaginative mind. The seductive power of habit is very great. Whatever form the habits may take, they constitute a universal human comfort zone. To its power may be ascribed the otherwise deeply puzzling abandonment by Muslims of the tremendous advances they had made in every branch of science since their Prophet stopped them fighting each other and gave them a stable polity.

For five hundred years the simplicity of Islam as a faith, but equally as a system of equitable justice which free and slave could equally trust, swept aside the sad muddle of other faiths and other judicial systems.

But Muhammad's inspiration was sadly betrayed. Islam was soon bitterly divided into Sunni and Shia. In an attempt to bring them together, the most famous philosopher and theologian esteemed by both, the Persian Al-Ghazzali, proposed that they abandon their attempts to imagine differing interpretations of their sacred texts. To do this, they should eschew using their imagination altogether. All they needed to do was to learn, beginning as small children, to recite their sacred texts without fault: they would then be guided infallibly by God.

In the twelfth century Al-Ghazzali was one of the most enlightened men of the time. The effect may not have been what he intended.

Almost at once it was as if all the props of Islamic science were removed and a great stifling blanket of silence descended on the most advanced universities in the world.

In the twentieth century, when Churchill spoke of an 'Iron Curtain descending over Europe', the similarity of both its purpose and effect were striking.

Imagining any different meaning from the official Communist Party line was severely discouraged. In a curious twist, it was common to declare that anyone who dared to do so must obviously be mad, must therefore be in need of psychiatric treatment, and was so treated.

But then the difference is also very striking. Al-Ghazzali's injunction has remained stifling of Islamic intelligence for almost a millennium, whilst all the ingenuity of the implacable Soviet state in forbidding its citizens to use their imagination could not be sustained for a single lifetime.

'Mister Gorbachev, tear down this wall!' Ronald Reagan demanded in 1987 of the General Secretary of the Soviet Communist Party, and behind that wall rose the shout of the

indomitable people which he and his Party were supposed to represent: *"WIR sind Das Volk!"*

Twenty-nine months later, on November 9, 1989, its destruction began. I have a piece of it here on my desk as I write. It is just a rough piece of grey concrete with some paint on its only flat surface. I imagine it was chipped out of the Wall with a hammer.

Rebellions like these are beginning to happen in other parts of the world, very often to the dismay of other supposedly popular leaders. I will suggest that this must happen.

I shall now dare to propose an addition to Darwin's and Wallace's theory of natural evolution: which, to remind you, predicts that mutations will at first occur in only a few individuals. I suggest that the necessary mutation of our species to prompt and effect social transformations is made apparent in the ability to imagine.

Since mutations only reveal their beneficial character in new generations, we must expect that young people are likely to demonstrate their imagination: imagining a future no longer trammelled by the bi-cameral directions that previous generations ascribed first to gods, then to God, as here in Genesis 1.26: *'Then God said, "And now we will make human beings, they will be like us and resemble us."'* With the difference that they will do as we— or as I—tell them.

This time I will not be discouraged by the possibility that I may be wrong.

I have already suggested that the most effective test of anyone's imagination is their response to one question, also simplest: *"Could you be wrong?"* Anyone still in thrall to the belief that ancient records of bi-cameral commands must govern their lives to-day, must not only reply that they cannot possibly be in error, since these are the words of God, but that they must continue to obey God's instructions or risk being consigned to hell.

This is another way of declaring that they are unable to exercise free will.

I also reported in an early essay my disappointment at the level of the debate in Oxford between Professor Richard Dawkins and the then His Grace the Archbishop Rowan Williams. If both had begun by asking each other this question, they might have been able to achieve a more interesting conclusion.

But let me step aside from the difficulties that religions have in understanding other religions except to predict that unless they learn to accept and accommodate the imagination of new generations, they will fail.

Unless one wishes to believe that the 'gods' of Psalm 42 actually walked the earth, it must be obvious that the entire pantheon of the earliest gods was the product of early man's imagination; that these gods coalesced into the single jealous, wrathful, genocidal monster still believed in by many, and later still that the far more adventurous imagination of the Greeks led them to believe that the world is not ruled by gods but is ordered— and ruled —by numbers.

Cautious step after step, and failure after failure, mathematics was built from this early beginning. After the elementary processes of arithmetic, which are so easily made habitual that we can teach them in public schools, all later mathematics had first to be imagined. Some modern mathematicians remain convinced that their mathematical world is more real than the world we lesser beings perceive.

Every contribution to science has first been imagined. Imagination is sometimes only fantasy. But determined imagination, the fundamental proof of free will, overcoming failure after failure, set-back after set-back, is the key that unlocks the secrets of the universe.

When I write that I have imagined the events I have reported, I do not mean invented.

However impossible they may at first appear to be, imagining descriptions of the world that they would like to be true is what scientists do.

However improbable or impossible some of the events I have described may appear to you, as indeed they now appear to me, they were as real as they occurred as anything I have experienced in my life. This being so, it ought to be possible for others to experience them as well. I shall try to tell you how. In this way they will become part of science.

What do modern philosophers imagine of God?

I find that few philosophers like to commit themselves to a definite opinion. This, for them, is the philosophical equivalent of *kamikaze*. More commonly they enjoy playing word games in which they can insist, as soon as any risk appears of major error, that the other has committed the equally important but unfortunate error of misunderstanding their words!

I have found, and you will find, that modern philosophers, with very few exceptions, do not imagine very much of God.

The majority have effectively joined forces with the majority of modern theologians, who have either accepted the classical evasion that everything they need to imagine is to be found in their library; or are content with the kind of statement I once elicited from a very famous Oxford theologian, who declared his private knowledge of God to consist of *"an Indescribable Apprehension!"*, leaving me speechless with admiration at his effrontery, although I had to respect his honesty; or in joining the very modern scientists, with some theologians, who are beginning to argue that all spiritual experience is delusional—which claim, you might suppose, must be especially hard for Christian theologians to accept in respect of Jesus—and that all religions must therefore be understood as social constructs: like, for example, atheism.

What is remarkable is that no serious consideration is given by these great minds to the possibility that perhaps something extremely important to the evolution of humanity may actually have happened to the dim and distant figures of Abraham, Jacob, and Moses, and to the far less distant and far clearer figures of Jesus and Muhammad, and that it should be their responsibility, not least as scientists, to attempt to discover what it was.

I think we are getting closer to being able to tell them.

*

14ᵗʰ January 2013

Dear Friends,

Many philosophers are committed today to struggling with a word game invented by the Austrian Jew, Martin Buber, called the Second Person Perspective. In his game, anyone else, or any thing, can either be regarded by an observer as an object, in the I-It perspective; or as a living entity, in the I-Thou perspective. In the former instance only the observer is supposed to possess intelligence, emotions, even the right to be alive. In the latter, the observer possesses the prerogative to grant some equivalence to the other. Their game is to define which situation fits which category.

In my case, like Pontius Pilate in my 'Game', I am most likely to be wrong if I believe my truths must be well defined. I must think instead only in terms of probabilities. All events are possible. This is basic quantum physics. As in that austere realm of applied imagination, we must attempt to estimate which possible event is to us most interesting.

Most interesting to me is the possibility of the Second Person Perspective in which our intelligence, emotions, and right to live may or may not be recognised by God.

It appears to me, incidentally, that this was Buber's real concern. He abandoned Zionism when, regarding the Palestinians, it switched from the second option to the first. He considered this an abdication of the moral and social duty given to the Jewish people by God.

I think we live in a universe that has in it another far greater form of intelligence, of which ours may be a faint, imperfect copy. This is basically what all the monotheistic religions claim. What they do not all claim, at least consistently, this greater intelligence is capable of communicating with every other form of intelligence anywhere, instantly. It is capable of taking any form, including the physical form of a powerful male who embraced me. In this form it will also manifest emotions: from delight to contempt to anger. It can turn space-time into any shape. I believe, as do most Jews and Muslims, that we should be fearful of its anger. I think it must be getting tired of waiting for us all to grow up.

I think also that the main obstacle to being noticed by this intelligence is the thick carapace of habits that directs us to behave, and believe, as if we are not individual.

It is obvious that behaving as a true individual requires great courage; always moral courage, often physical. Many women, men, children, are today reviled, condemned, tortured, murdered, simply for being individual. Children may be murdered by their parents.

I think it is clearly essential: but it may not be sufficient. It is also possible that there may be some degree of selection. This is, after all, how a football team is decided. Why not a God Team to move human evolution forward?

But, since you cannot decide this selection yourself, you may decide that the effort is not really worthwhile; that it is far better to remain unobtrusive; to obey the big men; to keep in with the crowd; to stay, you hope, out of trouble.

If you are brave enough to try, however, you must decide for yourself how much you can afford to invest in being individual: in public; in private; even secretly. This will at once require you to learn to develop and use your imagination.

At first it may appear that at every turn you will be more alone.

You will be helped here to learn how to pray properly. If brought up in a strongly prescriptive religion, you are likely to have been taught that collective prayer is a necessary activity by which the people of your religion make themselves noticed by God. You are likely to have been persuaded, with them, that the most effective prayers involve the simultaneous effort of as many as possible, and that this will ensure their prayers succeed.

This is a double mistake. I am not the first to point it out.

The first mistake is to suppose that God is impressed by multitudes. Far wiser, more compassionate minds have realised that there will always be individuals who know how to address

God correctly, and that they will be best protected if hidden within activity of a multitude of others who may not. Mass activities give them an opportunity, if necessary, to do so in public without danger. Best of all, however, as Muhammad also remarked, is the extraordinary joy of a prayer answered alone.

The second mistake is to suppose that an active soul needs to demonstrate to be noticed. Once again, wiser minds have long realised that there is a level of personal identity, independent of any social control, which even older cultures called angels.

Socrates called his angel his *daemon*.

I have preferred to call it your soul.

For obvious reasons priests do not like angels, daemons still less. Although they may claim to have prior responsibility for your soul: they might once have insisted that they cared for it so much that setting you on fire was the only way to save it.

Although you may ask for an ability to do something for others, the correct form of prayer is not to ask God to do anything at all for you: such presumption of importance after all! It is rather to calm your soul—angel or daemon—to forget for a moment all your fears; to forget even who you are, for be assured that God does not know you by the name your society has given you; to imagine that you are nothing but an empty vessel; to tell it that you are ready, and then ask it to: *'Fill me with God's grace!'*

If nothing happens, try again, perhaps beginning this time with: *'Please'.*

You have no right to expect that anything will happen. If it does, it may be very gentle. It may be powerful. In either case it will be unforgettable.

However, I must warn twice. First of all: if you are rewarded, do not suppose that you are either special or privileged. This will immediately destroy the sense of unimportance which made it possible. Second, but just as important: do not abuse such a spring of joy, such inspiration, such happiness. It is not to become addictive. It will then also disappear.

I imagine that many men and women have taken Jesus' advice and found unique support for their courage in this way. Although there is nothing secret about the advice, those who have found this support are likely to have kept it to themselves. They might otherwise have been accused of trafficking with Satan. Of course!

But this is not the past, and I have found this not true. At every turn I have found more active spiritual support, more encouragement, more stalwart friends: and, of course, here we are, connected by the magic of imagination, to millions of others with the same ideas. We are the people of the future.

Here, finally, is an unintentionally funny description by the 19th century English poet Keats (son of a livery-stable keeper: how's that for England's class-ridden society?) in which he likened his emotions on reading the 8th century BC poet Homer in the original Greek to those of Hernando Cortez on his first glimpsing the vast, apparently limitless expanse of the Pacific Ocean: *'Or like stout Cortez when with eagle eyes / He star'd at the Pacific and all his men / Look'd at each other with a wild surmise / Silent, upon a peak in Darien.'*

Generations of children have giggled over poor stout Cortez. Since I am sensitive about my own physique, I sympathise. Keats need not have held him up to so much infant ridicule. He was also wrong, for the first to glimpse the Pacific was not Hernando Cortez but Vasco Balboa, his countryman—and rival plunderer.

Even so I feel a thrill in reading those lines—aloud, of course, as all poetry must be read aloud—for I feel that I have been allowed to stare across our vast universe, to know that it is not limitless, to judge that it is not as important as we may be told: and to imagine, with wild surmise, a greater purpose.

I think, quite simply, that this is why we are made as we are: to imagine. Only through our imagination can we have new ideas; only imagination values honesty above vanity, humility above hubris, compassion over self-righteousness.

Life is still a lottery. But imagination is a winning ticket.

Colin

*

Dear Friends,

Getting to the bottom of the mystery of existence takes a lot of digging. Perhaps that should be 'refining'. I am reminded of the efforts of the Curies to reduce several tons of pitchblende, which looks as it sounds, until they reveal the blue glow of nuclear radiation that had never been seen before.

Although it may be seen to complete my earlier suggestions, like all the most exciting discoveries, the argument that follows appeared unexpectedly.

I have called it aesthetic for the same reason that Darwin and Wallace's theory of survival by natural selection is aesthetic.

Their theory is not persuasive simply because it can be either proved or disproved. It is persuasive because of its apparent simplicity and economy. In a sentence: it argues that natural evolution is haphazard.

My proposal is that human evolution is subject to tests no less stringent and cruel as any suffered by other species, but is not entirely haphazard. It will explain that the kindest and also the vilest aspects of human behaviour are entirely natural within what I have called the First Person's Perspective. I suggest that these are tests to select for human survival.

This is not very different from the selection for survival of other species. Many animals display an aesthetic sense. The human aesthetic sense is demonstrably far more adaptable. I shall suggest that this explains why, if not how, human evolution can be directed.

Human evolution need not be haphazard. It can be directed with intelligence. This is not to suggest that it cannot fail. It is to suggest that the First Person's Perspective can be understood as the aesthetic inspiration of all human endeavours, monstrous as well as divine, and of all human intelligence, subjective and objective.

Since this theory of the First Person's Perspective offers to connect science, philosophy, and theology, I believe it is likely to be as new to others as it is to me. But this does not mean that it will be noticed.

A little later I shall recruit the eminent historian Theodore Zeldin to explain how naturally difficult it is for modern scholars to acknowledge the value of unexpected ideas. But, if they will not, he offers the encouragement that '*anyone, however modest,* [may] *become a person capable of making a difference, minute though it might be, to the shape of reality. New attitudes are . . . spread, almost like an infection, from one person to another.*'

This idea emerged, like the glow of radium emerging, after many months of hard work, from its mass of pitchblende, just as I was about to post the third and final part of my final letter.

As has happened several times before, my old friend Spinoza, clearly determined to prove the integrity of The Programme, introduced me abruptly to the work of a psychologist and philosopher called Dr Piers Hutchinson.

I soon learnt that he has developed a remarkable theory to explain and repair the defects of all modern physics. He calls it his '*Physics of Plain Words*' and attributes its origin and intentions to the influence of Ludwig Wittgenstein and A. J. Ayer, the two most famous critics of the twentieth century of what they saw as deliberate academic obscurantism concealing professional mediocrity.

It was a shock. It was as if I had been introduced to a minor clerk in an unimportant government office with no substantial academic qualifications who offered to show me that light can travel only at a constant impossible speed, in any direction, however bright its source or fast it might be moving, however it might be observed. Clearly an absurd proposition!

This was a similarly crucial moment. It was not the elegance of Dr Hutchinson's theory, but rather his courage, not unlike that of young Einstein, in presenting his theory in the face of hundreds of years of others' endeavours.

It was this that made me recognise, suddenly and with full force, that *all* human explanations are fallible; that, as my old friend Andrew would insist, no explanation is scientific if it is not provisional; that we must listen more attentively to those, such as another vital iconoclast, the Cambridge mathematician Dr Jerome Ravetz, warning us to be more aware of our uncertainties.

It is not that scientific explanations may not be trusted: only that it is usually dangerous to suppose that they are *ever* complete.

'*Know thyself*': γνῶθι σεαυτόν: (pronounced 'gnothi seauton'), was inscribed above the entrance to the temple of Apollo at Delphi. Apollo was the Greeks' god of healing, and therefore of life. Being even-handed, like radium, he could also bring plague and death. The inscription was in Greek, naturally, but if your computer cannot produce either an omega or a nu, you have it here in the language of our mothers and fathers.

Countless writers have noted how exceedingly hard this is: 'to know oneself'. We would all like to believe that we are as innocent as newborn babies. But we have found in these essays that there is a beast in everyone: a monster of ego, lust for power, and brutality.

This has surprised many ordinary persons given power of life, pain, or death over others. Have you ever imagined how you might behave as a bored demoralised guard in a concentration camp full of scarcely recognisable human wrecks; or as a doctor given the freedom 'in the interest of science' to do whatever you like? These and other scenarios are excellent tests of imagination.

It was actually one of my most distinguished sauna seminarians, John, an historian, who introduced me to Dr Hutchinson, asking me to judge whether his friend's theory made any sense to me 'as a polymath'.

I am far from being a polymath, and I soon discovered that my knowledge is insufficient to judge his theory competently. It was evident that Dr Hutchinson knows far more than I do of many branches of modern science, and that he dislikes all religions, but he endeared himself to me immediately by asking: "*What was it that drove the majority of twentieth-century scientists to believe in* [a] *mysticism more extreme than the religion they had outgrown?*"

Dr Hutchinson's theory, of which he sent me a copy from Canada, treats their achievements as little more than an imperfect creation of their imagination, supported by mathematical explanations, which are then held to be the reasons why the universe exists at all. He appears to believe that such explanations should not be treated as fact.

This is a very old problem. I am reminded of the Zen monk Hotei, who lived about 900 AD, reproaching his students for mistaking the words of their scriptures for the truth that the words can only describe imperfectly 'as if mistaking the pointing finger for the moon'. Hotei, incidentally, is always remembered as a fat little man laughing, which is how most of us, mistakenly, picture the original Buddha.

So, Dr Hutchinson is clearly behaving like a bull in a china shop. Not content with trampling on its best pieces, he then produces an apparently completely coherent explanation of his own of the same evidence, supported, he believes, by the same mathematics, without any of the 'mysticism' he identifies in science to make demands on our trust and our faith.

Now, it doesn't really matter whether we believe his explanation; just as it does not really matter whether enough energy to develop our universe and its trillions of stars jerked itself into existence out of nothing 13.72 billions of years ago, or whether it happened last Friday.

It is admittedly a little harder to explain last Friday; but last year a Gallup survey found that 46 percent of Americans believe that the universe was created six thousand years ago by God: also, of course, from nothing.

Meanwhile—this is the best part—the same survey discovered that 42 percent of American university graduates have the same understanding of why this happened that we have.

Professor Christof Koch is a Professor of Biology and Engineering at the California Institute of Technology. He is described as 'one of the world's leading neuroscientists' by Dr Hutchinson, who is then amused that in a recent book, *'Consciousness'* (MIT, 2012), Koch explains: *"I do not believe that some deep and elemental organizing principle created the universe and set it in motion for a purpose I cannot comprehend. I grew up calling this entity God."*

Presumably 'I grew up' means that young Christof was brought up in a good Christian family; but his 'some deep, elemental organizing principle' is a far cry from God the Father, Son, and Holy Ghost, and even more from the Virgin Mother. He has moved on. Nor am I being sacrilegious. I am following the precepts of Bishop Ian Ramsey, another Oxford man who became one of the most influential of twentieth-century theologians, who ultimately decided that *'humans come to encounter God by way of personal disclosure . . . The religious words that humans create are always involving the language of analogy.'* (From notes on his life in Wikipedia)

Setting aside the dismay of worried atheists and educationalists, it really does not matter that the majority of the citizens of the world's most scientifically advanced societies do not care that the mathematical formula created by Professor Max Planck in 1900 was found in 1990 to provide a precise explanation of the background temperature of inter-galactic space as measured by the COBE satellite.

It is to be noted as well that, despite the efforts of the same atheists and many educationalists, the majority of Americans continue to believe, as do most people worldwide, that life has a purpose: even if all are not sure what it is.

I imagine that this worldwide majority would have been disappointed, but unsurprised, by the conclusion of a presentation late last year by the Ian Ramsey Centre for Science and Religion (IRCSR) of Oxford University, entitled *'The Ambiguity of Cosmic Purpose'*. This was an examination by its Director of Research, the Reverend Doctor Andrew Pinsent, on the long history of attempts to discern purpose in the universe.

Before being ordained as a Catholic priest, Dr Pinsent had a distinguished career as a theoretical physicist. He is undoubtedly one of the sharpest intellectuals in Oxford. His conclusion was not that there is no purpose in the universe: *'only that we cannot discover that purpose (or purposes) without divine help. As* [Cardinal] *Newman said, by nature (without grace) we perceive cosmic order and glory but not God's will'.*

His own analogy of finding 'purpose in the universe' is perfectly appropriate if purpose is being sought *in* the universe. It may still be considered appropriate if the source is outside, but its effect is *within.*

Following Ramsey's lead, it seems to me that this fits the otherwise deeply puzzling evidence of the various 'God experiences' throughout history. It should also cause no one to feel personally diminished. I suggest, further, that we can perceive 'God's will' in ourselves: that just as there is cruelty and kindness elsewhere in nature, so too is it naturally in us.

If we are indeed 'made in God's image', and if we therefore understand God as that First Person on whom we are modelled, his will would appear to be for us to learn how to recognise and repair our defects, and to behave as he expects. This requires not only our imagination. It demands that we disengage our inclinations from the dominance of ancient appetites and habits: that we choose to behave every day a little differently from previous days: nothing extravagant, only different.

That many are called, but few are chosen, is another analogous explanation for both the extraordinary transformative power of these experiences and their apparent randomness: an unpredictability which leaves many deprecating their importance whilst simultaneously declaring: *"I will believe only if it happens to me!"*

I have suggested in previous essays that we may be part of an experiment, and that its aim is not to discover, as previously imagined, who can be helped to an eternal heaven, and who is doomed to an eternal hell, but rather, and more realistically, whether our species *as a whole* is breeding to a useful outcome.

And it seems to me to be fully supported by analogous evidence that the occasions when the First Person's Perspective has become evident in human consciousness mark the beginning of major epochs in human history.

In every instance the First Person introduces itself to a person, usually to someone with no special position or power, to tell him, occasionally her—I would like to include that wonderful Maid of Orleans, Jean d'Arc—that they have been chosen to act as its agent.

The point of the test is simple: to see how the agent then acts.

Given that our species have been marauding, plundering, enslaving, and killing others for as long as history has been recorded, it is apparently of interest whether the agent inspired will attempt to create a more peaceful and kind society, or one that is more unforgiving and brutal.

The results so far appear to be about equal.

"I Am that I Am" is a common English translation of how the First Person introduced itself to Moses (Exodus 3.14), who then returned to Egypt to lead the Hebrews out of slavery, to persuade them that they were the most favoured of all people, and to give them the code by which most Jews still live today.

This is an unusually clear result. But it is important to recognise, as history also shows, that how the inspiration is interpreted is not equally demanding.

It may be argued that the first interpretation requires more imaginative effort and moral courage, that the second may require greater physical effort and more physical courage. But we have also found that the Habitual, Unreflective, Colonial mind is far more powerful in most people than their Adventurous, Imaginative, Inventive mind.

It should not surprise us, therefore, that as a very general outcome a powerful people may be persuaded to make peace with a weaker people and allow them their freedom. But a no less powerful society may be persuaded that weaker people can eventually become too dangerous and decide to end their existence.

Moses is presented by history as an agent of the first sort. So is Jesus. So is Muhammad. Leap forward: here is Abraham Lincoln; here is General Marshall and the US Congress of his time; Mandela is even closer. You can fill in the gaps.

But this is not the only choice. Israel's King David, incidentally another 'son of God', reported that God had ordered him to exterminate the Israelites' enemies totally: *'And David would leave neither man nor woman alive, but would take away the sheep, the oxen, the donkeys, the camels, and the garments.'* (1 Samuel 27.9)

This sense of God-directed mission is fearsomely echoed in the words of another three millennia later: *'Hence I believe that I am acting in accordance with the will of the Almighty Creator: by defending myself against the Jews, I am fighting for the work of the Lord.'* (*Mein Kampf,* Hitler, A., 1922-23)

We can also see that this difference is a major reason why democracy is so difficult to achieve and sustain. Most people believe that most people cannot be trusted with freedom; that they may become dangerous; and, naturally excepting themselves, that most people must therefore be controlled through fear.

Religions have generally been very effective in this respect, although not more than atheistic regimes. Meanwhile, in his delightful *'An Intimate History of Humanity',* which everyone should read, Professor Theodore Zeldin comments on the modern limitations of academic and scientific freedom: *'Few scientists are able to reflect on the assumptions of their work, because the competition to obtain recognition is so intense; without the support of those in power, they cannot continue; and those in power are experts at politicking as much as in research.'*

I think the lesson to be learnt from Dr Hutchinson's description of modern scientists' acceptance of their own mysticism as being more extreme than any religion is profoundly important. But I do not see that we will ever escape from mysticism of some kind. Every one of our explanations is 'a finger pointing at the moon'.

This is not because we are all simpletons. It is rather because, as I heard my favourite empiricist, Professor Lord Rees, comment once upon a time: *"It is likely that human intelligence will never be sufficient to understand everything!"*

Since we may therefore allow ourselves some degree of uncertainty as to what we should believe, we may be mindful instead of the possibility that we—and I do mean *you*—may at any time be engaged in this experiment.

What matters is not what we believe: what matters is how we act!

This is the great value of imagination. It allows us a freedom that others may have lost or, most sadly of all, they may not want.

There is little point of arguing with those who tell us that they cannot possibly be wrong. This will only create more excitement.

You may, of course, respond to those who tell you that they have no soul by agreeing that this is possibly true; and if they insist that they possess no free will, that this is probably true too. Be assured, however, that you have both, and that you should enjoy and use them.

Love to you all, Colin.

*

23ʳᵈ-28ᵗʰ February 2013

To Professor Dov Waxman,
At the Oxford Centre for Hebrew and Jewish Studies.

Dear Professor Waxman,

As I announced at the end of your lecture at Yarnton Manor in American Jewish identity, I found yours the most rewarding of all the Patterson series I have attended. You could clearly enthral an audience by reading a telephone directory aloud, but what your surveys suggest is truly fascinating. They appear to show, as you observed, that the more Jews observe the minutiae of religious regulation, the more Jewish they believe themselves to be.

This prompted my somewhat muddled question (which I will now rephrase) whether this means that those who depend more on the regulations of any religion are actually treating this as their relationship with God: and are they missing the possibility of a more intimate relationship? The following was actually prepared for Dr Jack Templeton of the Templeton Foundation, but I hope you—and Mrs Waxman, whose company I also briefly enjoyed—will not mind if I send it to you otherwise unchanged.

*

To: Ms Roseann Wolf,
The Templeton Foundation.

Dear Ms Wolf,

Thank you for your kind note. Please let me add a few details to the letter you have offered to show Dr Jack Templeton. The scholars who took me under their protection in Cambridge, and who asked me to write the report of my experience for publication in their journal, also urged me never to tell anyone else about it.

I had actually no intention of doing so. It was already evident that very few people have the depth of knowledge, or the compassion, or indeed the self-confidence, to accept that another person has had a direct experience of God which they have not had, and most likely never will have.

This was the first obstacle. Another was that besides the industry of established religions, there are always far too many self-declared messiahs exploiting the credulous and lonely. I would never cheapen my experience by appearing to play such games. But the most important obstacle was still, as I had told Cecil King, apart from knowing that: *'He is real; and He cares'*, I had no more to say.

Even so, was I frightened that its inspiration would fail? Not at all. It then remained, and it has remained ever since, as real and as thrilling as in the moments in which it occurred. With another few years, however, I had become a mathematics teacher, which is always tiring, sometimes exhausting. Sadly, my sojourn in the army's asylum had destroyed much of the trust on which a marriage depends, and I was eventually in the midst of an unhappy divorce. But, by this time, I had learnt to pray properly: that is, effortlessly to receive God's grace, rather than continuing the exhausting attempt to project one's ego into God's presence in the hope of being noticed. This was a constant comfort.

Naturally I wanted to tell others: but there were still very real obstacles. I knew that I would have to find entirely independent evidence that *something* was driving religious and secular cultural evolution forward: something attempting to lift human behaviour from its too frequent impulse to subjugate, rape, and destroy.

It was only after I had been a mathematics teacher for a few years that I began to realise that the instruction to me that I had supposed entirely personal: 'Be honest!' is an instruction the rest of the world needs to hear: but that this is precisely what is *not* being encouraged in mathematics, the very subject which should teach it first.

It was about this time, I believe, that I met your Dr Paul Watson, and he suggested that I make a proposal to the Foundation.

But this was when I believed that I had found the Holy Grail of education, and had neither time nor the need to seek any other help.

This was not pure vanity on my part. There could surely be no doubt that once people realised that the Ancient Greeks had perfected what we now call 'mathematics arguments'—terse, efficient, eminently transferable to almost any context—*not* so that more people could do more mathematics, but to give all the people more confidence in their own intelligence, more confidence in the value of inquiry, more confidence in democracy—then all the authorities would want all their schools to teach it to all their children!

Wouldn't they? Wouldn't all those educational academics and government advisors, and secretaries of state and so on, *want* more of their nation's children to have more competence in democracy?

It took another ten years to discover, as my Danish deputy-director told me one day (and the Danes pride themselves on not being another Hamlet), that this ain't necessarily so: *"No,"* he told me carefully, we were watching a school cricket match at the time, *"they do care. But they don't care enough. They really want only their own children to be educated, to be able to think independently. Other people's children are to be persuaded that they are stupid, and to believe what they're told."*

So, why do I now ask for the Foundation's help when I have failed?

History is the reason.

History changes things. I grew up being trained as a scientist, and therefore to believe that religions only exploit people's fears and credulity. I have not changed my mind about this essentially. The scandal of paedophile priests being sheltered for generations by their church is one example of this exploitation.

But I have realised more recently that religions are overall far more a force for good, than for bad. They are far more likely to encourage millions of people to behave compassionately towards others, even of other faiths, than the thousands persuaded that they can win special favour with God by making war.

I am naturally thinking here of our own Anthony Lynton Blair and your own George W. Bush: but also a sad quarter of young British Muslims, born and educated in England, arrested recently before they were able, as was their plan, to exceed in England the attack on the Twin Towers in New York.

Whilst it obviously escaped those angry young Muslims' attention, science has revealed a universe in the past hundred years many times greater than any that human minds ever needed to comprehend before. It is so vast that it may contain billions of worlds like ours. How are we ever to believe that the God to whom so many honest men and women, and so many little children, address their prayers, may still be aware of their existence: and that He cares?

Most religions describe human existence in terms of an experiment in morality. In other words: they offer us opportunities to justify our existence morally. To those who succeed sufficiently well, they offer the reward of further existence in another happier world. Those who fail may expect an eternity in hell.

Despite the enormous success of the later Christian clergy in claiming that they could decide who would be resurrected after their death, their promise appears never to have been made by Jesus. He was concerned to help people recognise that they would be rewarded for acting compassionately towards one another in this life. This would be their resurrection, their spiritual rebirth, and the world they would then create would be God's Kingdom. The latter claim is pure invention.

Once this is understood, any attempt to decide which religion is superior to others becomes futile. Most religions are based on a founder's original spiritual experience. Most have survived by adapting to their society's priorities and environment intellectually until a relatively stable orthodoxy has been achieved.

Its continuing stability will require the suppression of further individual inquiry or expression. Insisting that elaborate daily rituals must be followed, not merely as an accompaniment of everyone's personal life, but as the actual purpose of their personal life, leaves very little room for either.

This process of development seems not to have occurred to Charles Darwin, who never attempted to apply his theory to more than plants and animals, but his theory explains the evolution of religions just as well.

Perhaps he did notice, but was unnerved.

Once this development is understood, it becomes unsurprising that the sciences have evolved very similarly.

Many early scientists were motivated by spiritual ideals and ambitions. Isaac Newton, who secretly rejected the Trinitarian dogma whilst continuing to study as a Fellow of *'The College of the Most Holy and Undivided Trinity'*, was sure that he was discovering how God made the universe work. Later scientists achieved a more stable orthodoxy by demanding that both their moral and their intellectual rigor be open to scrutiny by other scientists, and by discouraging any individual insight which appears to threaten their collective and tightly woven orthodoxy.

The consequent struggle of scientists to have their *personal* ideas recognised by *collective* agreement is the cause, on the one hand, of the great fecundity of science. On the other, it is sometimes also a cause of its collective blindness.

One kind of experiment: two great systems of observance.

Only the very rarest individuals will risk being outlawed by both. But, as I attempted to explain in this essay marathon for my ex-pupils, we may need many of these individuals to save our species from its suicidal addiction to its habits.

I have come to realise, finally, that the key to our survival is imagination.

Einstein once declared that imagination is more important than knowledge. I believe he meant more important in science and life.

Many years ago a man called John Wisdom likened our world to a garden so long neglected that it is now uncertain whether its owner will ever return.

This would mean that its gardener has decided it is not worth saving. When surgeons decide that someone's injuries are too severe to be treated, this is called 'triage'.

If our God has also to care for millions of worlds besides ours, I think it very likely that Wisdom is right. Our species cannot hope to survive if we cannot even begin to agree on how to agree. Faith is no answer. A form of triage may be applied to us.

Atheists are right to mock faith in God that leads people only to disaster. *'Where has this god of yours been for millennia?'* they ask. And: *'Do his latest witnesses include that Reverend Jim Jones who persuaded nine hundred of his followers to take cyanide in Guyana, or David Koresh's 'Branch Davidians' at Waco?'*

More soberly: if this decision has been made, how might it be revoked?

Religions depend almost entirely on their followers' imagination. Inevitably this means that they also depend on the limitation of their imaginations.

Recently a professor of Tel Aviv University decided to research the period of history—which still powerfully shapes the modern world—in which the Romans expelled the Jews from Palestine.

Knowing that the University's library contains many thousands of books of Jewish history, he asked the librarian to direct him only to the shelves of books describing their exile. *"There aren't any,"* the history librarian replied. *"Well, alright, just the one!"* *"No, you don't understand. There are none."* *"But,"* spluttered the professor, *"every young Jew on this university campus believes that their parents returned to a homeland from which their ancestors were expelled two thousand years ago! This is believed by all Jews everywhere."* The librarian shrugged. *"That's not the historians' fault. If it happened, there'd be books. If they've written no books, it never happened."*

Such celestial irony! Imagination creates worlds: and it causes wars.

Scientists also depend on their imagination. Of course they have the advantage of being able to check their ideas by experiment. Even here, however, as David Hume pointed out three hundred years ago, human thinking is usually far more habitual than it is rational. The success of even a series of experiments is no guarantee that they are leading anywhere. Researching new ideas may employ some of the best human talents, but the results may not improve the lives of the rest of humanity by even a fraction.

So what can we *imagine* might be the possible purpose of this supposed experiment? Wisdom suggests that it might prompt us to realise that we are not going to be saved by instructions from Heaven. We must save ourselves.

But this will require an almost spontaneous, almost universal, unprecedented change in the habits of billions of people. Most are simply trying to get food into their own and their children's bellies. If made to change their habits, most will die.

There is one other possibility, however. Being too unorthodox is not a healthy option in any society. This is why my Cambridge friends feared for my future.

But being subliminally conscious of being different can be communicated to others. Army sergeants are especially attuned to this. They call it dumb insolence and they do not like it. It signals a resistance to their orthodoxy.

And perhaps *this* is the point of the experiment. If so, it was announced over two thousand years ago, and is recorded in three gospels, and one apocrypha. I shall use only one, but the others are virtually identical: *"Show me the stone which the builders have rejected. That one is the cornerstone."* (Matthew 21.42)

Suppose now that this is your experiment. We are, after all, supposed to resemble our experimenter. Would you really want to spend aeons visiting billions of worlds to discover that no species has evolved beyond its primitive ability to devour all other species or has succeeded in curbing its habits of destruction?

According to Darwin, this is all that any organism may be expected to do.

Or is it? In my *'Educating Messiahs'* essays, I found in the opinion of the philosopher Karl Popper support for my suggestion that organisms may be able to improve their chances of survival by altering themselves. Popper calls this *'enriching Darwin's theory'*!

We might turn again to an older authority, claiming: *'Those who say they will die first and then rise, are in error; they must receive resurrection while they live.'* (Gnostic gospel of Philip, found in the Nag Hammadi collection.)

I think it is always important to try to set human hubris aside. To realise, as J.S. Haldane urged us to accept: *'the universe may be not only queerer than we think, it may be queerer than we **can** think'.* Or, as I have heard Professor Lord Martin Rees explain several times: *"There is no reason to suppose that human minds are capable of understanding 'everything'"*.

But as queer as our universe is, and as limited as our understanding of it may be, we can at least be aware that, in every possible way, everyone is unique: genetically, biologically, neurologically, mentally, emotionally; and that not only are we made so very different, every one of us is capable of making ourselves, if only secretly, just a little bit more different again.

If we can do this in sufficient numbers, it is just possible that this may be enough to rescue our wonderful world, this sorely neglected garden, from ourselves.

It appears to me now, therefore, that if my experience were made available to young people in the form of an animation or film: presented in a form in which they are encouraged to see themselves, as I saw myself; to understand their predicament, as I understood mine; to demand directions, as I did; to receive a direction, as I did, this might raise their imagination to a new level: a new level on which they feel the inescapable responsibility to be personally honest in every situation, moral as well as intellectual, and, whilst doing so, to feel the presence continually—as I did, and still do—of God noticing, and applauding.

Whether in the sciences or in the religions, it appears to me that this is what we are challenged to do: to be honest. It isn't easy, but it is worthwhile.

Colin.

*

19th **March 2013**

To Ms Roseann Wolf,
The Templeton Foundation.

Dear Ms Wolf,

The most serious obstacle to dialogue between science and religions is not religions' fear of the contempt of science, or scientists' remembrance of Galileo and Bruno. It is the fact that neither side will admit how little it knows. With forty years' preparation behind me, I believe I can do a great deal to remedy this. If scientists can be persuaded to abandon their pretence that human experience is not 'objective' enough for them to study, and if religions can be shown to science to be based on repeated experiences like mine—by which instances Aquinas and Pascal were clearly moved, but left no record—a way might be found to open the minds of billions of young people to this possibility. They would be then able to judge whether a fresh attempt should be made to reconcile science and religions: not on the basis of knowledge and pride, but of humility and belief in God based on experience. Peace on Earth could follow.

Best wishes,
Colin Hannaford.

[Neither Dr Templeton, nor Ms Wolf, replied.]

12th **March 2013**

Dear Friends,

Ziauddin Sardar is a very courageous and thoughtful man. For several decades he has been risking his life reminding Muslims of the essential spirit of the Prophet Muhammad which they seek to emulate and promote in their children: *'his spirit of generosity, the respect and devotion he showed to the elderly, the children and marginalized in society, his concern for justice, equity and fair play, his dedication to inquiry, knowledge and criticism'.*
These, he says, are the traditions all Muslims should follow.
He has not had a great deal of success. Instead, he notes sadly, the greater likelihood is of modern Islam producing *'narrow-minded bigots absolutely certain that their way is the only way of living'* and, of course, of serving God.
Christians were once equally fanatical. Some still are.
I first met Ziauddin at the 80th birthday celebration in the Said Business School in Oxford of my friend Dr Jerry Ravetz. Jerome is a Cambridge mathematician, also of Trinity College, to which I belonged for a year, but he is the real deal. As a distinguished Oxford academic, he was one of the first scientists to question the truth of global warming: not because he believed it could not be happening, but because he found its data and predictions uncertain.
He is, therefore, a fully-fledged member of The Awkward Squad. I should have realised that Zia must be another. As usual (and this is usual), I felt too unimportant to speak with him, and missed this opportunity. More recently I have read his book, from which I have quoted above, and amongst other important insights, I am infinitely grateful to discover that Islamic theology has a place for me.
It is to be found in that branch of Islam called Sufism, which traces its origins back to the most trusted companion of Muhammad, Abu Bakr, and to Muhammad's cousin, Ali. I have therefore some claim to be recognised, in both Sunni and Shia

Islam, as what Sufis refer to as one who has experienced direct knowledge of God.

Sadly, but as my friends in Cambridge predicted forty years ago, nothing appears to produce such a frisson of dismay through modern Christian theologians as someone who offers actual evidence of the faith *they* have learnt from their books. I have therefore been only faintly amused that even Oxford University's Centre for Science and Religion has shown no theological interest, but more bemused that it has not evinced any scientific interest either. In my view, the latter is more discreditable.

There is precedence. My closest Christian colleague would seem to be the great Catholic theologian Thomas Aquinas, who, in the very last year of his life, appears to have had a similar experience to mine.

In Italy in 1273, after a lifetime creating a vast scholarly compendium on the correct behaviour of Christians, still mandatory for priestly candidates to study to this day; and, incidentally, a mediaeval counterpart to Islam's Sharia, it appears to have occurred one night as he prayed alone in his cell.

The next day he could only tell his secretary, who begged him to leave some record of it for future theology—or, indeed, to illuminate the world: *"I cannot, because all that I have written seems now like straw to me (mihi videtur ut palea)."*

One is irresistibly reminded of the use of straw most familiar to him in his time: that it is thrown into stables in order to absorb dung.

What Ziauddin Sardar needs to know is how the essential spirit of Islam described above can return to Islam. I believe I can tell him. Let me try.

In my previous essays I have tried to show that the primary obstacle to experiencing God directly is exactly that which was explained to Sardar in a simple sentence by a Sufi teacher: *"You must empty your mind of all you know."*

This is clearly what I was forced to do in that small bedroom of the Army psychiatric hospital forty years ago. Sardar was surprised, but doubtful: *"Wiping oneself clean of information and knowledge seems a perilous path, a giant leap into the void, even if the objective is a form of wisdom."*

I may reassure him that it is not such a *'perilous path'*, nor is it *'a giant leap into the void'*. Both of these overly dramatic assumptions betray a fear of being never able to return to normal life. But they may betray perhaps an even more elemental fear: that of discovering that a 'normal life' is essentially not more interesting than an insect's. Both may be guided by habit alone: from birth to death.

We may suppose that it was what Aquinas learnt that night in his cell. His secretary found him in tears. Could it be that after a lifetime of working on a rational proof of the existence of God and the purpose of life, acclaimed for centuries since as 'the Angelic Doctor' and as the greatest Christian theologian, he may have asked in his prayer: *"What more, dear Lord, do I need to know?"*

What if this admission of deep humility and trust opened to him, not more extensive *objective* wisdom, but the deepest *subjective* wisdom: the realization, in the most spectacular fashion, that we are all, fundamentally, of God.

I rather hope that he may have had a similar experience to mine. But remember that this would have been three centuries before Galileo built his telescope and discovered that Jupiter has moons and Saturn has horns! How bewildering to a thirteenth-century mind—and how terrifying—to learn that the universe is greater than any heaven ever imagined: and is filled with stars.

Could this be what caused Aquinas' tears: his realization that there is no *Summa Theologica,* nor any formula, however pious; but also no scientific method, however careful, which can disclose this truth for everyone? That it can only be discovered subjectively? That science cannot grasp or deal with it, precisely because it is not objective truth? Much of history is also subjective.

There is, however, a simpler means to begin to achieve what Ziauddin Sardar wishes to achieve. It is certainly not by denigrating Islam. If one looks at Islam for the fundamental spirit of Muhammad, if one judges its importance to peace and justice after the collapse of Rome, its inspiration remains magnificent.

There is no real value in criticizing any of the religions. They provide societies with essential moral and social foundations. They are supported by billions for this reason alone: not because they make it possible for them to know God directly.

It must not be supposed that I have always known the reason why.

The first intimation was prompted when I was invited to speak to an evening class at a small college in Georgia in the United States. Among the students were a number training to be teachers. I supposed that my lesson would last 45 minutes. This was what I was used to. I was soon horrified to discover that I was expected to talk for over three hours!

I had talked for over an hour about teaching mathematics, when Professor Duane Davis, my host for the evening, realised that I was running out of material.

"Now," he suggested kindly, *"why not talk to us about your ideas of identity."*

I was astonished. The majority of my audience were ladies: mainly black ladies; mainly mothers; mainly working mothers in their late thirties or early forties; all giving up precious evening hours with their families to achieve a bare qualification to become teachers themselves.

They sat in rows, arms folded, and very dignified. Some of their grandparents had certainly been slaves.

These were people to be deeply respected: and the night before, my host and I had agreed that this topic was like a box of grenades. They would have very clear ideas about their identity. As I had discovered all those years before, some Catholic and Protestant Irish find their different identities reasons to kill. I had found since then that children who feel their identity is being threatened can hate others, and their teachers. Recent events have shown that they can kill too.

"Well," I began, somewhat nervously, *"Everyone has first what I call a mass identity: male; female; child; adult; old; Asian;*

African; European; American; Japanese. And then those related to belief: Hindu; Buddhist; Jewish; Christian; Muslim; Animist; Atheist; and so on.

These are rarely important enough," I said, *"for people to kill or be killed for them alone."* But they do. I did not need to say this. My audience would know it as well.

"And then everyone has a social identity. These are given to us by societies. They are believed to define exactly who you are. Even more important, they are likely to define who you think you are."

My audience of mainly black, middle-aged, working-class mothers, aiming to become teachers, now looked as if they could dislike me a lot. Their social identity had always filled their lives: as does ours. Many had clearly never looked for any other: except possibly to hope, as they filled their chapels and their churches with prayer and song, that this might be how God would know them.

"Is it possible," I continued, *"that you have another identity: an identity entirely personal and private: an identity that only you know?"*

By now the silence was intense. *"That is what I mean,"* I said, *"by your intrinsic identity. It is not decided by where you are born, by your family, tribe, nation, or religion. It is entirely private. It belongs to you only. You must be aware of it privately, protect it, and you must help it to grow."*

I did not suggest that this could be how God would know them. My host told me later that I had made an impression: but no-one asked me how to help it grow. At that time I would have been hard pressed to answer. We talked of other things: mainly, I remember, about chickens.

Since then, however, as you will know from my previous essays, I have become convinced that the most serious obstacle to achieving this sense of identity is our addiction to habit: and that this characteristic, which we share with all other species, is all the more dangerous in us because we confuse our habits with morality.

Since established religions are also mainly social habits, they can fall into both categories. They can be major obstacles to recognizing intrinsic identity. They can also create beliefs about social identity which declare other beliefs heresy.

The learning of habits is essential to our survival. But in our species the habit of learning habits has evolved into an addiction so powerful that it can paralyse cultures for millennia. The example of Judaism is both exceptional and typical.

Like many addictions induced by recreational drugs, addiction to habit creates a preferred state of regressed childhood for millions of people wanting only to be told what to do, what to think; how to act, what to like, avoid or dislike, whilst being assured that all this is what God will eventually reward them for doing.

Their reward is undoubtedly a sense of euphoria: of relief.

Ziauddin reports being told on the same occasion: *'Three snakes harm human beings: to be intolerant and impatient with the people around you; to be dependent on someone you cannot leave; and to be controlled by your ego'*.

Strange to learn that Sufis have adopted Freud's ego!

Let me try to describe the three snakes in modern terms.

A solipsist, for example, is a person who believes that he alone has the right to exist: that the universe exists only to support his life. He is very likely to be impatient of others: to believe that, although they are decidedly unimportant, scarcely human, they can still irritate by refusing to acknowledge his importance.

The empathic human mind belongs to a person who believes it can share the emotions and thoughts of other human minds, and that it must act to show its identification and care for them. It is unlikely to examine itself objectively: but it may insist that it can—and must—do this for others.

Other egos annoy teachers who don't like questions. This can be ignored.

Cultures, societies, nations can be solipsistic or empathic. Usually the two characteristics are mixed: but I am sure examples of extremely solipsistic or empathic cultures—and nations—will easily occur to you. They are equally important in an individual context, when they must only be prevented from swallowing each other.

To this extent: I agree with the Sufi.

Meanwhile, the *cognoscenti* amongst you will know that Ziauddin's 'leap into the void' was suggested in the 19th century as a cure for existential anxiety by a permanently unhappy but very influential Danish Christian theologian called Søren Kierkegaard, who suggested that people might cure their anxiety by making a 'leap of faith'. It is not apparent that this succeeded for Kierkegaard: or, since his time, whether it was a success for anyone else. I imagine that it is rather similar to leaping into the sea holding an anchor. If they had been able to meet, I am sure the Sufi would have warned him to empty his mind of everything: e-v-e-r-y-t-h-i-n-g!

To make Sardar's leap without holding on to one's faith: and to return, even if disappointed, with wit and soul intact, requires both serious solipsistic strength and great empathic courage.

What may often be very bad for cultures is essential for the individual.

Great solipsistic strength means accepting, at least as a working condition, that there is one universe; and that this universe, and everything and everyone in it, is yours; and that you are an agent of God.

Amongst other occasionally awkward consequences, this means that you never need to be deceitful or lie. It does not mean you cannot do either. It only means that both will be beneath you. (This used to be called *noblesse oblige.*)

Great empathic courage might appear to be a contradiction. But this is only if the first condition is rejected. Otherwise, everyone you will meet belongs to you: just as you, and they, belong to God. You can learn from their emotions and their thoughts as if they are your own. Neither can ever harm you. They can certainly never harm God. The whole notion of heresy is ridiculous. It belongs to lesser egos.

So those are the two, and possibly the three, snakes.

When wondering how to finish this, it occurred to me that persuading people to empty their minds, and leap, must be very similar to persuading small children to swim. Next day I approached a swimming instructor, whose infant pupils were splashing and diving around her like manic tadpoles, and asked for two minutes of her time. I explained the background to my question, which she accepted as perfectly appropriate, then asked her: *"What is it that persuades your pupils to let go of the side of the pool and learn to swim?"* She answered at once: *"Their confidence in me."*

Which seems to be the final piece of our puzzle.

Aquinas had certainly a great burden of ideas in his head, the most important of which he had spent decades painstakingly refining or creating himself.

But he must also have had an uncommon confidence in his instructor to let it all fall: and then to declare that it was all straw.

Everything can only mean e-v-e-r-y-t-h-i-n-g.

*

22ⁿᵈ March 2013

Dear Friends,

I have recently received a wake-up call: when a friend asked me where I would like to celebrate my birthday.

I was astonished: *"My birthday?"*

"Yes, you'll be seventy next week."

"What?! Last week I was only twenty-nine!"

But I've checked the calendar. It's true. On June 3ʳᵈ I reach three score and ten. The hard part, I find, is not the prospect of death. I don't really believe in death.

It's the likelihood of not being able to do any more thinking.

I must have mentioned how thinking is addictive. There is a very special kind of pleasure in realising: *"Ah! So that's why that happens!"* or *"Now I know what this means!"* For this to stop doesn't bear thinking about. What else is a guy to do?

But, let's look on the bright side. We have done pretty well.

I was naturally flattered when asked by you to *'teach the rest of the world what you taught us in your classroom'.*

Then I was puzzled.

Sure, I had tried to teach you to be honest; to say if you didn't understand; to ask questions without fear of being humiliated. But this is hardly going to transform the world of education: not when education is controlled by so many wankers.

What is it, I asked myself, that might be sufficiently frightening to everyone: even sufficiently frightening to persuade the multitudes of wankers in education to abandon wanking to concentrate on teaching their pupils, of all ages, always to be honest?

I have just used some British slang. Cassell's Dictionary of Slang explains: *'To wank': verb from late 18C Scot dialect whank, to beat, thrash; hence 'wanker', anyone primarily, even exclusively, given to solitary self-gratification: a lazy, incompetent, unpleasant person.*

So, it's really Scottish slang. All the better. As Robert Burns once wrote: *"O, wad some Power the giftie gie us / To see oursels as ithers see us! / It wad frae monie a blunder free us, / An' foolish notion."*

Apart from the wankers, who very rarely see themselves as others see them, I decided that the main aim of good teachers should be to teach how to prevent wars; and, since the nastiest wars are religious—see Bertrand Russell's 'dictionary' of a few essays past—that they should be primarily concerned to teach how to prevent religious wars.

Addressed explicitly, this would clearly get a lot of good teachers in a world of pain.

Eventually I realized that the basic reason for many wars is that our species has a special aptitude for rapidly learning habits necessary for survival. This is what the neurological structure that we have called the right brain is supremely good at.

If, however, the right brain is not continually required to justify its choices by the structure that we have called the left brain—and which I have identified as religion's soul—it will control us. The least dangerous result includes the many social habits: accents; vocabulary; dress; dietary preference, which essentially harm no-one. The most dangerous result is that different tribal groups convert entirely unnecessary social habits into moral markers, and are prepared to prove their exclusive importance by hurting, oppressing, torturing, and killing.

On the morning that I wrote this I was amused to find it echoed in a collection of Albert Einstein's remarks: *'It is of vital importance that conflicts be avoided when they arise from subjects which, in fact, are not really essential for the pursuance of religious aims.'*

When last year I told an audience in St John's College that the greatest threat to human existence is that 'the right brain is programmed for extinction', several students later approached me who were delighted to have understood this at once.

My previous essays appear to have won a readership of many young people, amongst them many young Muslims. When many tell me that they have rejected their religion, I understand them to mean that they believe that God must be true for everyone. So say I.

It is actually very difficult to write a simple sentence so that everyone will understand what it says, but will also understand what it means. Its value must be measured by the degree that it makes its hearers think. Following young Albert, I shall try this here.

'Good people go wrong because they learn inessential habits.'
Does this mean everyone? It means everyone.

Does it mean that all religions include inessential habits?

Most religions comprise little but inessential habits, which are then held to be essential.

This is why religions can never agree.

If you find this disappointing, you are clearly misunderstanding what religions are for.

What it means, however, is that teachers can aim to show their pupils what is, and what is not, essential to an adequate understanding of any subject.

Since all religions attempt to convey the subjective experience of meeting God, I must close with a final best guess as to how objective reason can help us to avoid the inessential.

One of my most valued friends wrote to me recently about this:

'In other cultures it [the subjective experience] *is recognised and managed some way or another. Our culture is unique in that its importance is simply denied. Even those whose studies deal with it, can't—as you have seen—handle it when confronted by it.'*

The last is by far the most perplexing.

One of the most important Catholic theologians is the 13th century Saint Thomas Aquinas, the so-called 'Angelic Doctor'. His *Summa Theologica,* on which he worked through the most celebrated period of his life, containing his five proofs of the existence of God, now represents the general teaching of the Catholic Church. This must also be true of most Protestant churches.

The witness I call in my defence is therefore *Saint Thomas Aquinas!*

Read on!

Colin.

*

Dear Friends,

I am now posting the last *'Educating Messiahs'* essay in Facebook.

I have also signed a contract with a publisher to produce them as a book. This will mean that I must stop!

This last essay is, as usual, too long for Facebook entries. Nevertheless, I hope you will try to read them all. Once again I must thank you for all your encouragement; but I must especially thank my editor.

You met him introducing me to my first evening class. He is now an emeritus professor of philosophy and religion at Mercer University in the United States. I was introduced to him by the chair of the mathematics department in one of the colleges of the University, who contacted me initially to find out more about the Socratic Methodology in order to teach its approach to Mercer students of mathematics. My first little book, '473959', is mainly the result of his invitation to me to address his colleagues and students.

Whilst he has been a constant support for nearly ten years, is a man of saintly patience and now a dear friend, he has always been my sternest critic. *"I dig deep,"* he warned me when he first offered to be my editor, and I have learnt to expect this.

You may imagine, when he telephoned me the other day, from five thousand miles away, to tell me: *"Colin, I've just finished reading your last piece; and it's"*—there came a pause, in which I stopped breathing. Until he continued: *"wonderful"*.

No praise could be more precious.

On the wall beside me is encouragement from the German poet, scientist, and philosopher J.W. von Goethe: '*Whatever you can do, or dream you can do, begin it. Boldness has genius, power, and magic.* '

Many fridge magnets tell us much the same: every journey starts with a first step. The question in philosophy is not: *'To be, or not to be?'* It is: *'When to start?'*

I remember reading somewhere: 'good physics requires too much time for young minds; the best mathematics is of young minds; and good philosophy needs the most time'.

In other words, it should be the product of a slow maturation: of not learning about the world from books, still less from others' opinions; but from living it.

This may take an unexpected but vital spark some time: even all of seventy years.

Even then one can only try—essay—to show that what appears to be possible to understand in only one way, has a very different aspect, even an entirely new meaning, from a new perspective.

Whether our world is the product of an intelligent design, or four billion years of random evolution, it still appears that our lives are an experiment. Virtually all religions actually agree about this. We are created here to prove something. Although there is some confusion about the details, we are required to behave a certain way to be rewarded. This has produced many remarkable claims. Never mind about the seventy-two virgins. There is scarcely a town in Europe without a memorial to those who died in the past century of wars which does not promise that they have received a glorious reward in heaven.

Microbes in laboratory trials might wonder what is expected of them. Most are likely to be tipped down the sink. Perhaps we can do better.

Our own experiment may not be especially intelligent, or benevolent.

But let us be brave. The experiment may be a dispassionate study of the increase from around 4 million years ago of a few thousand specimens of *Australopithecus afarensis*—apparently our most likely ancestors—to the seven or more billions we have become at present, and whether we will continue to outbreed and to starve slowly, or will suddenly exterminate ourselves in one or more of a variety of possible disasters.

A second possibility—admittedly less likely, but more interesting—is that some individuals may be noticed as being worthy of further study. They may be decanted from the first test-tube to another, with even the prospect of further selection.

This last, after all, is no more than the rationale of a whole spectrum of enlightenment religions offering life after death. But *Tempus,* as you will notice, *fugit.* I rather favour another possibility—admittedly still only just imaginable—that increasing global communication via the internet may make possible the enlightenment of an entire generation. Difficult: but do-able.

A crucial lesson that modern soldiers learn is that a mission without a clear, simple, and achievable aim, agreed by everyone, is the most likely to fail.

We late descendents of *Australopithecus afarensis* have pinned our hopes on two major investments of collective belief: that we will be sent another saviour, as many Hindus, Jews, Christians, and Muslims still hope, or that our scientists will be able to solve all our technically manageable problems, then send settlers to Mars.

Religions and scientists have also serious aims: but none that is clear, simple, and agreed by everyone. Neither recognizes that they share a common aim which can be described clearly and simply, and which will be agreed by almost everyone!

I shall describe this common aim presently. You will recognize its truth.

In the second part, I describe again: for those with a well-developed sense of humour, the very nearly funny fact—but for the rest of us, a very terrifying fact—that our likelihood of being exterminated by someone who has never had a sense of humour can be illustrated by the rabbi who was mistaken for Jesus Christ.

In the third, and finally, I praise the poet Shelley and explain how all this can be changed as if by a butterfly opening its wings.

Love to you all, Colin.

*

Dear Friends,

In this final essay for *'Educating Messiahs'* . . . Ouch! How many times have I written that? Let's start again.

In this final last essay for *'Educating Messiahs'*, and *'Children for an Honest, Just, and Fair World'* in Facebook, I will describe the basis of a programme of education to end the war between religions and science. This part is easy.

I shall also explain how a mind perceives God. This is not so very difficult.

Since our Facebook space is limited, my explanations may seem crude.

My real task will be to show that they are the right approach.

Since religions are all far older than science, we will first need a new understanding of the aim of religions; next, a new understanding of the aim of science; then to show that their aims are identical. Not similar: identical.

The aim of religions is to alleviate depression.

The aim of science is also to alleviate depression.

The primary and secondary causes of depression are the common sense of being helpless in a world of relentless, universal change.

Both religions and science attempt to deal with this depression by describing a universe governed by laws which do not change.

Religions make these laws their articles of faith.

Scientists seek to identify features of the universe which they call invariant.

Both are attempting to deal with depression. What both seek is invariance. There is no possibility of showing that the features which the scientists find invariant are even similar to the articles of faith which religions make invariant.

It is precisely *because* articles of faith and scientific laws are found in entirely different ways that attempts to end the war between religions and science in this way will always fail.

We need first to understand why depression is so much a part of the universal human condition that it has given birth to religions, and then how depression has also engendered science.

Depression is one of the oldest human illnesses. The practice of trepanning: of boring open holes in the human skull to let out evil spirits—or, as we might now conjecture, to relieve low spirits—was common in many prehistoric cultures as early as 10,000 BC. The Greek philosopher Hippocrates, who has been called the first modern doctor, gave specific directions for the procedure around 400 BC.

Galen, an equally famous follower, did the same around 200 AD.

In mediaeval Europe, depression was called melancholia. In his *Summa Theologica,* Thomas Aquinas called it 'the sorrow of the world.' If a patient could afford it, the operation was common much later. In the 18th century, Prince Philip of Orange, who must have

303

been spectacularly unhappy, is reported to have been trepanned seventeen times. What it did for his unhappiness is not recorded.

In industrially developed countries, in which depression is now generally recognised as an illness, it is the most common of all medical health problems: as the cause of every kind of private and social dysfunction, from apathy to despair, violent crime, and murderous rape.

In these countries the licit response is a multi-billion dollar pharmaceutical industry and the illicit response a multi-billion dollar drug trade. It is doubtful whether either is more effective in alleviating depression than religions. All that is certain is that they cost more together than boring holes in skulls ever did.

But what is the cause of an affliction as old as this, a cause as active, possibly now even more common? To find this cause we must reflect on the most basic human response to being human.

It is likely to be very ordinary, very simple, very obvious. To some degree or other it is likely to affect everyone: child, woman, man. Most of you should be able to recognise it as soon as it is described.

The changes which affect everyone immediately, and usually irrevocably, are simply the addition of more children into a family.

The response is a child's realisation that more of its parents' affection will now have to be shared with yet another sibling. It is to be found in the mother's realisation that her survival, and the survival of her children if she should die, is at risk once again. It is to be found in the father's realisation that the burden of his family has increased once more: whilst he is becoming less able, and perhaps also less willing, to support them.

Depression grows from this common root.

This is the origin of religions. It is also the origin of a fundamental mistake concerning the nature of God: a mistake which religions may not acknowledge; a mistake which bedevils our lives today.

Marx was wrong that religions are always imposed on people. Later, yes; originally: no. Since not everyone could have holes bored in their skulls, which is an inevitably expensive and risky business, ordinary people expected their religions to alleviate their depression as soon as they were sufficiently organised to support them.

In general, their religion provided the needed relief in three forms:

God was called upon to appease children's fear by offering them unconditional affection. God was called upon to offer mothers moral and emotional encouragement in having more children. God was called upon to tell men that they have a duty to marry, and to inseminate their wives, but must never confuse either duty with pleasure. They need not, therefore, as a general rule, love a wife. And this, we may surmise, is where gays lost the social cachet they had enjoyed in Sparta, in Greece, and in classical Rome, and got a firm shove in the direction of Hell.

The general response to this universal depression is an industry which declares that all its people are guarded by a God: a God who could change, but never does; which tells people that their faith must also never change; which promises children God's affection in return for continuing obedience; which promises mothers His moral and emotional encouragement to have more children; and which tells fathers they have a dual duty: to defend the tribe and increase its number. (But not by taking too many wives at once. Solomon had 700 wives and 300 concubines, the dear man. This was one of the reasons why God abandoned him.)

Such gods, as Muhammad would make plain, are incorrigibly tribal: and they soon become their tribe's idol.

It does not matter if the tribe is ten million strong; or fifty, or a hundred, or a thousand million strong. This is where Marx happened to be right. Because they want a God who is their own, and invariant, tribes soon become stuck with a specific set of beliefs which cannot—and, in some cases, must not—be shared with others.

And, once again: because of right brain addiction to fixed forms, fixed habits, fixed thinking, their idols are very likely to be any kind of fixed form, fixed habit, fixed thinking. In any society in which ultimate authority is claimed to be derived from an unapproachable god, the idol will eventually become the whole settled pattern of fixed religious rituals, unchanging prayers, incorrigible history, hierarchical religious, social, domestic relations; all almost invariably accompanied by an all-encompassing and very vicious fear of inquiry, humour, and thought.

Inquisitive thinking began in Greece about two millennia ago. So, remarkably, did theatre, and satire. Apart from Pallas Athene, that brawling, incestuous, disgraceful family, the gods of Olympia, never regained their prestige.

Having its origins in a society in which the old tribal gods had largely lost their powers, the Greeks began to search for invariance for much the same reason as before. Their manner of doing so, however, was entirely different.

Their most notable stroke was to refuse to acknowledge the need to alleviate any of the forms of depression described above.

They did this heroically. They refused to admit that subjective reality is important at all. One of the most influential, a man called Heraclitus, pointed out in around 500 BC: *"No-one can step into the same river twice."*

*

Dear Class,

I was delighted yesterday to read a comment in a book by Stephen Jay Gould, a very famous American scientist, concerning the question I am addressing in this last essay. We are living at a time when the challenge that science seems to present to religions and religions to science has become so fierce that sooner or later some seriously angry and depressed individual (it is almost sure to be a man, but it may be of either gender) may decide to prove the truth of his own ideas by playing God. If you doubt my belief that this could happen, you will find a very similar warning in this month's *'Nature'*, the world's foremost scientific journal.

To encourage our effort to prevent this disaster, Gould quotes the words of an equally famous colleague, E.O. Wilson, with whom, incidentally, he usually disagrees, that: *"The greatest enterprise of mind has always been and always will be the attempted linkage of the sciences and the humanities."*

In the first part of this last essay I show how to succeed in this 'greatest enterprise'. My solution may not be entirely welcome to, say, the President of the Royal Society, the Archbishop of Canterbury, or the Pope, but linking science and the humanities (which must include religions) is actually quite easy.

It is achieved by subtracting much of the self-importance of both, by showing that both are engaged in a far simpler enterprise than either seeking advice from God, or help from a Theory of Everything, and suggesting that they try relieving depression with humour instead!

I hope you enjoy my examples.

Love to all,
Colin.

*

Entracte (again)

If it is true, as Heraclitus and his followers believed, that *"no-one can step into the same river twice,"* invariance must be sought in the features of the world which they held to be impossible to change: in proportions, in geometry, in numbers.

They became the first Western mathematicians. Although unable to eliminate change in the actual physical world, they bravely insisted that the physical world has the same relation to the real world as the constantly changing light and shadows thrown on the wall of a cave by a fire outside would have to the things themselves that cast the shadows. This play of light and shadows is always unpredictable. It is always confusing. It is never to be trusted. It is not real.

They believed that the real world could be detected only through thought: that everything in this real world has some kind of counterpart in the physical world. The essential difference is that in the world in which we live, everything is imperfect, changing, dying. In their real world everything is perfect, invariant, eternal.

Scientists have been attempting to perceive this changeless world ever since. They have had immense success in relating it—through the application of their theories—to our actual world. They have succeeded in changing our actual world to a degree impossible to imagine being achieved by tribal idol-worshippers.

But just as tribal idol-worshippers have generally failed—or perhaps it is better to say, have made no attempt—to understand that worshipping their idols is equivalent to boring holes in their heads, so scientists apparently also do not care to examine what urges them to take such risks in seeking their invariant understanding of everything—notice that it has precisely this name: 'The Theory of Everything'—that whilst they are footling about, one of their misfits, or one of their accidents, may destroy the world that, effectively, they posture to despise.

Knocking heads together by the billions is beyond even our powers. But we can easily explain why idol worshipping and theories of everything have the same appeal. We discovered it over thirty years ago—times does fly—in our classroom.

Which reminds me of a story to lighten our mood.

I was sitting alone in a dark corner of the sauna a few days ago in which I have held so many useful seminars when the door was flung open and in fell a mountain of a man who, not noticing me, plumped down heavily in the seat opposite and said, as he did so: *"F—me! I thought it was still mornin'!"*

"Tempus fugit," I offered in my helpful fashion.

He peered at me in the dim light. He seemed affable. He had a big belly but also huge biceps. Not a man to annoy. *"Eh?"*

"Tempus fugit," I replied. *"Time flies. You find it often on old grandfather clocks. Latin. Time never stops."*

"True enough! I thought it was still morning'." He held out a vast hand. It swallowed mine as a whale swallows a sardine. *"I'm Darren."*

He told me he was a builder: *'and in security'.* I told him who I was; and then: *"It's like a lot of entirely English expressions which don't seem to make a lot of sense. I have a German lady staying with me, who asked me this morning, 'What do English people mean when they say: "Well, really." '?"*

"Ahah," said Darren. *"Hard!"*

We spent a short while dissecting it grammatically, semantically, even syllogistically. And then I added, *"There's another expression, just as difficult, that I didn't like to offer to the lady."*

"Oh. What's that?" asked the man-mountain.

"It's 'F—me!'"

His response could have been ugly: *"You makin' fun of me?"* Instead, there was a pause; then a great bellow of laughter, then his massive paw again enveloped mine in a bone-crushing grip: *"Yes! O'course. F—me, you're right!"*

Habits of thinking, behaviour, reaction—as we discovered in our classroom and have now explored exhaustively in these essays—are the main preoccupation, possibly the sole preoccupation, of that neurological structure (as my friend the award-winning Cambridge physiologist has advised me to say) that less cautious physiologists still call, as we have, the right brain.

The right brain has no sense of humour. It cannot afford a sense of humour; for humour, even in the most minor instance, is triggered by one confident expectation being supplanted by another which is unexpected. The right brain can only remember, and recall, information that experience has planted there before.

There was once a rabbi who boasted to a priest that, being also Jewish, Jesus Christ must have looked like him. *"Hah!"* said the priest, *"I don't believe you. Prove it!"*

So the rabbi took him through the city to a somewhat rundown apartment building where they took the elevator up to the third floor. There the rabbi approached a certain door and briskly rang the bell. There was a momentary pause, before it was jerked open by a voluptuous woman in a skimpy negligee, who stared at the rabbi and exclaimed: *"Jesus Christ! Not you again!!!"*

What, exactly, did you expect? Only the left brain (this is with apologies to my Cambridge friend) can hold two or more expectations of an event simultaneously until further information appears. You knew, as the priest knew, that the rabbi could not possibly resemble Jesus Christ, because you have been conditioned to visualize Jesus Christ as a tall, handsome guy, possibly with pale blue eyes.

This is what your right brain expected: which is why it was surprised.

The only essential difference between the right-brain hunt for invariance in religion and that in science is professional. It has to do with ambition.

The priest will be respected only if he is able to confirm to the faithful that absolutely nothing has changed to affect their faith: that, in the universe over which he is bound to preside, what was declared to be eternal a thousand, two, three thousand years ago, is still eternal; that all the promises made and all arguments used to establish and maintain their faith remain unchanged. Their tribe's idol is intact.

Although several such tribes are now capable of nuclear war, there is nothing essentially dishonourable about keeping their idols and temples ready to serve the faithful. The aim of religions is to alleviate tribal depression. They do this well. If the aim is well intentioned, their methods cannot be fairly impugned.

And of course scientists have their own idol to defend.

'*By standing on the shoulders of giants*', as Sir Isaac Newton once explained his own success, scientists have established theories which now appear to explain the universe with astonishing accuracy—or '*pretty well*', Sir Isaac would say—across unimaginable scales of space and time.

Many would like to believe that eventually they will achieve a theory that will explain everything: eternally; unfailingly; completely. Imagine that! Imagine never to be shown that you are wrong again: imagine writing the last text-books; learning to fish; improving your golf; opening the first camps for dissenting scientists!

Perfect theory, perfect practice: always a fascist dream!

The main functional difference between priests and scientists is, of course, that priests already have their theory of everything.

They only have to learn it. However they spend their idle hours, their textbooks have all been written. Everything knowable is known. (*"Here come I, my name is Jowett. All there is to know, I know it. I am master of this college. What I don't know isn't knowledge."*—Remember?) They cannot doubt. They can only no longer deal with dissenting priests as they once did. It was also useful to fine those who did not go to church.

A scientist, in contrast, can win the respect of his peers, notice, and advancement, only by finding new details or correcting errors others have not noticed.

They are fortunate professionally in inhabiting a universe which may also be suspected of having a sense of humour. Its most recent cosmic joke has been to disclose that they have been puzzling for centuries over a universe of which ninety percent has never been noticed before. It is full of dark stuff.

They are back in their cave. Actually they are not. They are trying very hard to look unperturbed, and to read over others' shoulders what they are scribbling.

Could it be that our new friend Dr Hutchinson is right: that the universe is filled with particles so small that no earthbound experiment has ever been able to detect them, but that they are responsible for gravity, and carry light, and diminish light's frequency over cosmic distances: so that all those thousands of man-years of work proving that it is caused by the expansion of the universe beginning, for an unimaginable reason over thirteen billion years ago, has been wasted?

'Certainly not!' scientists will say. They expect theories to fail. As a dear friend of mine liked to say (as you will recall): *'If it isn't provisional, it isn't science.'*

But it will be useful at this point to notice another theory beginning to show its age. I mean the theory that, because the most advanced intelligence known to exist in this vast universe belongs, to borrow from Lord Russell's history of Western philosophy, to *'the minds of tiny lumps of impure carbon and water impotently crawling on a small and unimportant planet'*, no greater intelligence can exist.

This has become embarrassingly similar to notions of the universe before the invention of the telescope.

If a cosmic intelligence exists, such scientists are most unlikely to detect it.

Being intelligence, it will be alive. It will best be able to communicate with the left brain, not with the right. It was not only for its ability in inquiry that I suggested we should identify the left brain as the soul.

Our ancestors, our forebears, and our immediate predecessors developed two principle ways of dealing with depression.

One may be characterised as the fascination of religions with their past: I am here reminded of Albert Einstein's comment on witnessing the worship of his fellow Jews before the remnant of Herod's Palace in Jerusalem that is called the Wailing Wall: *'Where dull-witted clansmen of our tribe were praying aloud, their faces turned to the wall, bodies swaying to and fro. A pathetic sight of men with a past, but without a present.'*

The other is our scientists' fascination with the future: for it is only by ignoring everything ugly and inconvenient in the present that the majority of scientists can hope to win glory in the future.

'The good' wrote Shelley, *'want power, but to weep barren tears. The powerful goodness want: worse need for them. The wise want love; and those who love want wisdom.'*

I found this, as usual by chance, and thought it appropriate for what I am trying to say.

It is certainly compressed. It is poetry.

My understanding of it is this: there are four kinds of people:

There are many who would like to improve the world, but are realistic enough to know that if they ever achieve power, the situation is likely to be beyond rescue.

Those who are powerful now have usually achieved their power through deceit and corruption, and can think and act only in this way.

Those who are capable are not sufficiently attended.

The love of those who care most for their own religion and their own world prevents them from seeing what must be done.

Only poetry can translate itself immediately into the mind. Shelley was a poet of genius, and I felt at once that these three lines perfectly describe our situation:

Scientists will never achieve enough power to undo the damage being done by religions.

Political power is largely controlled by industrial interests wanting profits now. They have very little concern for the future.

There are people who see what must be done, but have no more power.

The great majority of the faithful of a religion love it so much that they cannot imagine it harming anyone. Only other religions can do this.

Religious tribes are no longer separated by empty deserts, steppes, or seas.

They now declare the primacy of their own idols everywhere. They challenge each other with bombs, assassinations, with armour, and from the air. When Muhammad ordered the destruction of the three hundred and more idols in the Kaaba, it was not because he feared these ancient lumps of stone and wood. It was because he saw, presciently, that their continued existence would ruin all his hopes of uniting his people's ever-warring tribes. He also foresaw that they would invent new idols.

But science had also better start pulling in its horns.

Are scientists who prostitute their minds to pursue what seems often like pointless research more to be respected—more than soldiers, I hear you mutter: who prostitute their minds *and* their bodies? A fair point. Are scientists who spend their lives enjoying their privileges and freedom to pursue their interests, with no care for the world, more to be respected than those priests who sacrifice their entire lives in attempting to comfort and rescue thousands from life's sorrows? I think not.

Many scientists are at least honestly selfish. For the most fortunate there are prestige, prizes, and public acclaim. It may not be well-informed acclaim: *"Why did I win a Noble* [sic.] *Prize? If I could just tell you, buddy, it wouldn't be worth a Prize."*

This was Richard Feynman's response in 1965.

But we, of course, the great unwashed, and seriously uninformed, are rewarded with better health, hygiene, comfort, nominally more safety—and, of course, with a staggering amount of knowledge most of us will never use.

Knowledge can hurt and help. Dr James Martin, a most successful and remarkable scientist, has spent much of his fortune to create the Oxford Martin School in Oxford. Attached to the University, it is the first of its kind in the world. Its purpose is to reduce the dangers to your children's future.

He has pointed out that crusades no longer need armies. A single modern science graduate may now be capable of creating a virus capable of killing every human; or of hacking into the computers to launch one of the tens of thousands of nuclear missiles still operational, causing others to launch automatically, entirely beyond human control. This is our reality.

In September 2013, Professor Lord Martin Rees and Professor Stephen Hawking have recruited others, from the Universities of Cambridge, Oxford, Harvard and Berkeley, to found the Cambridge Centre for the Study of Existential Risk.

Several of the risks they envisage as being capable of wiping out much of the human race could result from religious conflict. It is not apparent that this is being taken seriously.

This is presumably because it is far too difficult. We can certainly sympathise. But we are getting closer to a very general solution: a kind of religious armistice.

In my introduction I wrote of primary and secondary causes of depression. We have now spent sufficient time on the primary. The secondary form is not so widespread. But, since it inclines adults to be suicidal, it is more dangerous. Since the sufferers are more conscious of it, provided they are helped before being persuaded that others must be killed because of it, which, as we now know, is how most suicide bombers are recruited, it is fortunately much easier to deal with. We have only to tell them it requires more courage than to kill oneself, or others.

And there are pioneers.

Not long after his twenty-ninth birthday—oh, this *is* a dangerous age!—a brave young man experienced a typical collapse of right-brain confidence.

He had learnt, we may suppose, to think all the right thoughts, to behave in the right way, to expect the success this is supposed to provide. Now, suddenly: *'The most loathsome thing of all was my own existence. What was the point in continuing to live with this burden of misery?'*

This young man was Eckhart Tolle. In the report that he has written, bought by millions, he also explains how he discovered a totally different way to experience his life. He calls it *'The Power of Now'*. Dismissed by Time magazine as 'mumbo jumbo', it is not: although Tolle has not tried hard enough to curb his enthusiasm for calling others to his promised land.

Although he does not actually explain what it is that produces relief from such terrors, I am fairly confident that you can. You will find it perfectly easily, and without buying the book!

Recall my experience in that night-school classroom when I asked my audience of mainly black ladies to think first of their social identity.

In the moment that followed, what did they do?

They consulted the store of memories in their right brain. Those memories told them how others had identified them in the past, and how they should think of themselves now. But when I asked them whether they could recognise another very private identity, an almost sacramental silence fell. One by one, they nodded.

Sixty years ago the writer Aldous Huxley took mescaline to do this. He called it 'opening the doors of perception'. I suggest that it allowed him for a time to perceive with his left brain all the complexity of the present that the right usually makes humdrum, and to recognise his own identity. But no drug is needed.

And how might a butterfly begin to transform these thunderheads of hate into peaceful white galleons, bringing only shade and rain?

Could it really do this by only opening its wings?

Open! Let us tell children about their right brain: that its addiction to habit is natural, but that some habits are dangerous.

Close! Religions comfort, but also divide. Anyone sufficiently ambitious can turn divisions into hatred, then war.

Open! A good religion is like a cup of tea: unexciting, inexpensive, refreshing.

Close! A bad religion is like a hard drug: addictive, controlling, destructive.

Open! Fly away. Children can work the rest out by themselves.

And finally: I promised to explain how to open one's mind to God.

This is very simple, although it requires practice.

Find a quiet place. Pack all your thoughts and anxieties in a box; place it carefully to one side, for you will need to deal with them again. Close your eyes, compose yourself; and say to yourself: **"I am that I am."**

Moses believed that this was God's name. I believe he was being told how to do this. In January this year—the 14th I think—I told you how to pray.

I think this is all you really need to know.

But another fascinating possibility appeared as I was writing this.

In a treatise he composed after his discovery of gravity, and although he does not record it as his experience, Sir Isaac Newton wrote, very, very carefully (he is now supposed to have been autistic): '[D]*oes it not appear from phenomena that there is a Being incorporeal, living, intelligent, omnipresent, who in infinite space—as it were, in his Sensory—sees things themselves intimately, and thoroughly perceives them, and comprehends them wholly?'*

On reading this for the first time—I had wanted to check that earlier quote—I wondered whether he had had an experience like Aquinas's, or Pascal's, or even like mine.

My suspicion increased as I tried to write a description of my own which might possibly satisfy modern scientists and theologians.

I soon realised that I could do no better than Newton. His great mathematical rival, Gottfried Leibniz, poked fun at Newton's belief that the Earth's orbit could become erratic. God, Leibniz insisted, would not allow this. Newton calculated the year: 2060. You may want to mark this in your diary.

Another of Feynman's statements is one of the best known in science: '*If theory is not proved by experiment, it's wrong.*'

Could it be that Newton, fearful of the immense row with the Church if made public, buried an actual report in the huge collection of papers he left behind in Trinity College: all in Latin, much of it still untranslated?

What if he hoped that his report would be found in a more rational era? What if it is still there amidst his notes on alchemy and biblical numerology?

The proof of a real experience might be found in the differences between that airily imprecise: '. . . *does it not appear?* . . . and the hard facts in this secret report.

The 'Being' I experienced was not *in*corporeal.

He was very physical, vigorous, and powerful.

Most important and totally unexpected, however: for nothing in any solemn history of previous experience in any culture could possibly have prepared me for it, was that, as this very solid, vigorous, and powerful 'Being' embraced me, *he laughed!*

He laughed with pure delight.

He laughed uproariously.

I felt him laughing: as if I had solved his favourite riddle.

Then he was gone.

He has other worlds to visit, I imagine.

*

THE FINAL CHAPTER OF 'EDUCATING MESSIAHS'

in which all is explained.

PART ONE: God of the Gods

Dear Friends,

Last week our second old pupils' reunion was held in our dear old European School, in the village of Culham, outside Abingdon. Founded as a school in 1978 to support a major EU project to achieve fusion energy in nearby Harwell, it was provided with the Gothic pile founded as a college for missionaries by Bishop 'Soapy Sam' Wilberforce. So called because of his nervous hand-washing habit, he is best known today for his debate with Thomas Huxley in 1860 over Darwin's theory of evolution in which Huxley told him that he would prefer to be descended from an ape than from a bishop. Men roared; ladies fainted.

No ladies fainted at our second reunion. It was once again organised by the redoubtable Liz Fraser, a.k.a. 'The Noodle', and was another splendid success. It may also be the last, for this, the only official European School in Britain, will close in 2016. This has more to do with cost than politics. The European Schools are an excellent idea; are hugely successful academically, but are also hugely expensive. The cost of our relatively small school simply became prohibitive.

We must wish it well after it is reorganised on a less ambitious scale. Meanwhile we may comfort ourselves that there are still no official European Schools in France. This is reputedly due to an historic *ukase* of General Charles De Gaulle, aimed at preserving France's intellectual purity.

Ah well. Our school served us well. It lasted long enough for me to learn how to teach better than I had been taught: and I hope most—no, I hope all—of the several hundred girls and boys from whom I was privileged to learn will remember me as fondly as I do them.

Or, more directly, you.

"I remember," one told me, holding her young son on her hip, *"how you taught us all English by having us read 'Animal Farm' in turn; and how we all used to wait to see whether Benoit Froget would pronounce 'orse' with an 'h'!"*

In the first year I was one of only two British teachers, and was required to 'teach': EFL, English as a foreign language; Physical Education (girls and boys: a strange experience for a grammar school boy then soldier); Science; and, but only finally, Mathematics. My classes would always contain several nationalities; several different age groups—also girls and boys— all with very different levels of English.

Reading Orwell together worked like magic. After we finished *'Animal Farm'* we read Gerald Durrell's *'My Family and Other Animals'.* I would have liked next to have tried one of the Shakespeare comedies: *'A Midsummer Night's Dream',* or *'Twelfth Night',* but I was then replaced by a 'proper' English teacher.

From then on, I had to use my mathematics lessons.

"And I remember," said another, *"that when we got bored with mathematics, one of us would be told to ask you about the Army, and you would happily spend the whole lesson"*—this is definitely libellous!—*"telling us wonderful stories!"* It also got their attention: see, as an example, *'Catching the Bus in Oxford Street'.*

Sadly, I never did get to tell them of the *'Terror Ride of Grafenwöhr',* which involves the attenuation of light by dust—as from distant galaxies—and how to measure it by the sweat on a German army major's brow.

Looking around at so many familiar faces, and some that are *almost* familiar, at all of you who are now parents, and at several of my old colleagues, all in good health, I was moved by our enormous good fortune that we are still able to enjoy such a happy day together.

And then, and then: I found myself thinking. 'How wonderful it would be if, on reaching the age of, say, 12, children everywhere were given my experience of meeting God. Would this be enough to stop so many idiots killing each other?'

I think it might do just that. Of course I know it is impossible. Wiser minds have written that many are called, but few are chosen. I know as well that it is not really necessary to ascribe such an experience to being selected by some wonderfully caring supra-cosmic identity.

It may also be explained as due to a rare combination of unusual emotional and intellectual pre-conditions; of unusual momentary mental stress, if not distress; and a very unusual, yet very fortuitous, situation.

My situation was extremely fortuitous. That may be the sole reason why nothing like my experience of that first evening has been reported, or has dared to be reported, in at least the past few hundred years.

The conditions were perfect.

Being closely examined subsequently in a military mental hospital, where, after many tests and lengthy observation, I was found to be in no sense mentally, or emotionally, or psychologically unbalanced: these conditions could not have been bettered if carefully arranged. Above all, they made it impossible for me—never mind what the rest of the world might later suppose—to dismiss my experience as being an idiot aberration or due to drugs.

It is possible also that I was so shocked by its importance—for this I understood very soberly at once—that I realised that I must now appear extraordinarily sane!

Anyway, 'nuff said. Apparently I did indeed manage to appear extraordinarily sane. I am rather proud of this. When, some years later, I watched Jack Nicholson in the film *'One Flew over the Cuckoo's Nest',* which showed me the horrors which I may have escaped, I wept.

The fact that all these factors can be categorised as 'unusual' is sufficient to explain the rarity of their combination, and its possible culmination. The last may not be inevitable. If it occurs, it may take different forms. There may or may not be a sensation of physical presence. There may be no impossible cosmological insight.

Even so, I will argue, the importance of such rare events to human consciousness—and human history—cannot be seriously doubted. They have transformed entire societies, created new cultures, have even founded new empires. To understand why and how they happen is, very arguably, far more important than sending settlers to Mars.

Whether they are delusional or not, they are clearly far more important in giving lives a purpose than popping pills or sniffing cocaine. However they may be explained, education can certainly do much to prepare the appropriate conditions which may allow them. We have explored this preparation in earlier essays. The fundamental aim is to protect, sustain, and promote the child's awareness of being uniquely individual, and of having, therefore, uniquely individual responsibilities. These must include not wasting one's life as a pawn for others.

A thought came to me as I wrote this: surprising, because it cast a sudden light on that uniquely challenging advice of Jesus to respond to personal attacks by 'turning the other cheek', or, as Muhammad advised, with kindness.

It came to me that to be fully aware of being individual means being aware that one's own beliefs are unique: and that the beliefs of others must also be unique.

This is essentially what Kant and Wittgenstein attempted to point out. There is, essentially, no such thing as an observable public reality. Scientists attempt to model such an objective reality, but our minds do not perceive their artificial reality. We perceive instead our own personal mental construction of reality. Some of these constructions may be nearly identical to others'. Many, especially those we think the most important, are not.

This is why the only way to agree about anything important to oneself and to others is to treat personal affronts as trivial, and to sit down and talk until you and the others agree on what both find most important. In some occasions it may be sensible to start with survival.

Applying their advice is not easy. It requires considerable empathy and humility, strong critical and inventive powers. The essential stages in promoting these qualities are to encourage all young children to question; to require older children to express their opinions intelligently, but never carelessly; for the older still to accept their responsibility for their own decisions. This will produce maturity.

But this is getting ahead of our game. In our first pursuit of the Woozle, then of The Beast, we saw both monsters eventually metamorphose into the simple, universal, indispensable, and only occasional psychotic habit of *habit*.

We realised that virtually all human behaviour, especially its wars, can be understood in terms of people's preference everywhere for being told what to do.

I had first noticed this all those years ago in our classroom. It is demonstrated by the fact that mathematics may be taught, and it may certainly be 'learnt', almost entirely as a matter of habit, without any real understanding at all. But every capable teacher will recognise the phenomenon that I may call 'awakening'. This happens when a teacher's response to a question or to anxiety produces a change of expression in a pupil's face of sudden insight and comprehension.

This is almost always unexpected. It is always delightful. It is what makes teaching worthwhile. Children engaged in constructive discussion can also elicit this response in one another. This is what makes such discourse so enjoyable, and fruitful, for them. Once experienced, this habit will last.

Two days ago I had made over twenty different attempts to write this final chapter, and I was hopelessly stuck. Being completely unable to still the whirling confusion of beginnings, and middles, and ends in my mind, I sought distraction in my garage, bedroom, and library and noticed there a book which the flyleaf tells me I acquired in 1986.

Its title is *'God of the Gods'* and it has probably remained unread in the twenty years since I bought it. Looking into it briefly—*thank you, Baruch: I have it now!*—I found that it told me what I needed. It was written by a biblical historian called Walter Beltz, then employed as a mere 'assistant in the archaeological section of the University of Halle' ('*God of the Gods*', Beltz, W. 1975; trans. Heinegg, P. 1983)

The ancient city of Halle was then in the German Democratic—that is, in the Communist—Republic. It must have been hard for any biblical historian to find employment anywhere in a society in which atheism was official polity.

*

PART TWO: Gods of the Past

Outside the confines of the then German Democratic Republic, Walter Beltz was recognised as a major biblical scholar. In his '*God of the Gods*' he explains that the early Semitic tribes which eventually combined to form the nation of Israel were originally either pastoralists, long settled in the area that we now call Palestine, or nomadic warriors, who invaded and settled there later.

The pastoralists worshipped a god called Elohim. Beltz describes Elohim as being a god: '*very lofty, very kind, who dealt directly with men*'. He adds that: '*Elohim would have nothing to do with war. He loved the order and harmony of agricultural society, still closely connected with matriarchy.*'

This last observation will be important later in the case of Jesus' mother.

Meanwhile we must note that in the original Hebrew *Elohim* is often used as a plural. The still highly influential 13th century rabbi Moses Maimonides suggests that this merely reflects the many appearances of one god to different men at different times, thus implying that these many appearances were always of one god.

The difficulty here is that in Jesus' time and earlier, any Jew—and this, naturally, includes Jesus—would know that they worshipped two gods. Although the reason for this may now be as fiercely debated as any of their other complex beliefs, modern Jews may still address their god as '*Adonai*'. *Adonai* is also plural. It means '*lords*'.

There are no accounts of any visitations to women by either. This is not so surprising. They would almost certainly have been deleted because of the later dominance in Jewish nationhood of the second. His name is Yahweh.

Yahweh is described by Beltz as not only definitely masculine, but the god for whom it became: *'an act of virtue to wage war'.*

This would seem an entirely adequate description. Four decades later, Dr Dawkins offers more details, as: *". . . arguably the most unpleasant character in all fiction: jealous and proud of it; a petty, unjust, unforgiving control-Freak; a vindictive, bloodthirsty ethnic cleanser; a misogynistic, homophobic, racist, infanticidal, genocidal, filicidal, pestilential, megalomaniacal, sadomasochistic, capriciously malevolent bully."* (Dawkins, R. *The God Delusion*, Houghton Mifflin, 2006, p. 51)

Yeah, right! That's old Yahweh alright! What a character!

But why is Elohim not mentioned in this diatribe? Could it be that he—or she—is the inspiration of Dr Dawkins' determination to deal only with the reality perceived by the five physical senses; and, since this is the reality that all people can recognise, this is the only reality which should concern us; nothing else matters? (Dawkins, R. *'The Magic of Reality'*, 2013)

But this is not only hopelessly mechanistic and sterile. It is extremely dangerous. Since he sets aside all feelings as being only the products of our minds, his description is not sufficiently mature to make any sense of war.

And war, I suggest, is a bloody important feature, in every sense, of everyone's reality. I recall telling H.H. Sheikha Mozah of Qatar: *'Your Highness, you should understand that war, for many men, is a necessary spiritual adventure.'*

Until we understand and share the feelings that drive men to fight and to kill as if this is a truly spiritual compulsion; and can understand them, and share the feelings impelling others to encourage them, we do not deserve to be called, or to think ourselves to be, intelligent.

Dr Dawkins is undoubtedly right when he notes that: *'rocks don't feel joy or jealousy, and mountains cannot fall in love'.*

This is true. But it is also so facile as to be extraordinarily silly. Our species is not in danger of being made extinct because of our knowledge of atoms and molecules, or because we dare to guess how galaxies are made. We are most likely to be killed because of our and others' feelings.

Amongst the most dangerous of these feelings—and this exists purely *as* a feeling—is the belief that certain acts of extreme violence will be rewarded at once by a further delightful life in heaven. No delay. Their reward is expected to be granted immediately. There is, curiously, no suggestion of meeting Muhammad in this heaven, nor any of the earlier prophets: only all those virgins—or all those raisins.

There is some confusion about this item. But does heaven exist? If we can understand the first reason for believing it does, then we might also understand why other cultures have come to believe it too; and why Christian nations promise their warriors that they will receive a heavenly reward for killing and dying in battle.

Warriors who expect to die, who may also be determined to die, are most likely to glorify killing, conquering, and plundering. Sooner or later they may even claim that this is by divine command. Such commands need not be direct. They may be told by others that this is a divine command: that this is the purpose of life.

But their love of death, their reason for dying, is also the reason for such warriors to believe in heaven: as a further painless level of existence, in which they will continue to enjoy wine and song and orgiastic roistering with other undead heroes, rewarded for their loyalty by a grateful Yahweh. They may also invent hell, incidentally, for their enemies' eternal torment: another happy reality.

It is significant that several other warrior cultures have done much the same.

The Vikings, for example, invented Valhalla: but omitted hell. For these Northern warriors it was sufficient punishment to fail in battle. When the early Christian missionaries told them that hell

325

was waiting to punish them for their sins, they responded gleefully: *"Then we shall be warm!"*

It is certainly attractive to imagine heaven as a kind of bucolic Las Vegas with endless room service of a happily physical kind. Conveniently forgetting that 'the Kingdom of God is within you', Christianity was soon promising its crusaders a similar reward for killing every Muslim and Jew their swords might find.

But what then of the god called Elohim?

The more practical and, to my mind, more feminine god of the early Jews might be supposed to have inspired the joy of those early pastoralists in the fecundity of their fields and herds. They had no need of heaven, or hell; no endless search for the enemies of their god; no drive to conquer; to exterminate; to enslave.

This was all commanded by Yahweh.

The worship of Elohim was very much quieter. It might involve no more than heartfelt thanks at the continuity of life, a calm acceptance of a life's rewards, courage to accept its occasional perturbations, with its inevitable end.

Besides much else, in other words, these early Jews may have invented Zen.

We like to think (to feel) that Western societies inherited the rationality of the Greeks. Even more fundamental is that we have inherited Jewish spirituality.

I hope you will agree with me that Elohim is the only god that Jesus can be sensibly imagined to be inspired by. In contrast to his love of order, harmony, and peace, the psychotic bully Yahweh seems only capable of inspiring violence.

Some of this violence was certainly in self-defence. But by the time the Torah (and the rest of the Old Testament) was finally written down, its compilers had not only edited Elohim almost entirely out of sight, but had also developed the belief (the feeling) of Jews that they are the most important people in the world: even of the universe.

That this belief (or feeling) has cost the Jewish people a long and bitter history of vilification and suffering seems only to have made it all the more impossible for them to think of abandoning it.

They have instead developed a remarkably resilient and successful culture, nationally as well as internationally.

We should now try to recognise the source of their resilience and success. This is actually very simple. Every morning a truly observant Jew gives thanks that he was not born a woman: then his wife—or his mother—tells him what to do with his day.

This was a joke, of course. A very Jewish joke.

According to Beltz, Elohim appears only once in the Bible; and then only as Yahweh's partner; and only in the account in Hebrew of the story of Adam and Eve in Genesis.

Here, Beltz remarks, Elohim seems to be more in sympathy with Eve than with her somewhat dopey spouse, and he suggests: '[This] *served as yet another justification of the older, matriarchal social structure, where woman plays the clever, decisive, enterprising role.'*

I recall making a similar observation in an earlier essay. Not bad.

But what does this signify to us today? First, we should notice that the matriarchal principle was still active in Jesus' time. Jesus was recognised as a Jew because his mother was a Jewess. His paternity was far less important.

Modern Judaism preserves this tradition. I was identified as a Jew when I once mentioned a family rumour, never confirmed, that my mother's mother was a Jewess. *'Then'* cried my Jewish listeners, a rabbi, a diplomat, and an historian, and all, I think, with relief, *'you are a Jew!'*

Second, and far more serious, is to ask whether this brings us any closer to the solution to our problem: how to transform the cultures currently at odds with each other into the cultures they might be if every child at the age of twelve, as if in a bar mitzvah, experienced meeting Elohim, not Yahweh.

No-one could possibly imagine this could be easy. And times have changed.

Until nuclear weapons made major wars unwinnable, most governments liked to settle their differences using their armies. But, as I and the rest of the British Army found in Northern

Ireland, and as is now being experienced in Afghanistan, a modern enemy may be just a few hundred young men determined that their own religion must direct the moral behaviour, the order, and the harmony, of their nation's entire population.

They are likely to be sure that this is God's plan.

Even more problematic is when the enemy is a small boy or a young woman who appears beside a road, in a mosque or a crowded bazaar, sewn into an explosive vest. Neither they nor their dispatchers are interested in debate. They are purely instruments of death.

Meanwhile our preference is also violence: although our emphasis now is on the 'surgical precision' by which our enemies can be eliminated by noiseless missiles falling from an empty sky. Most of the time they may do this unerringly: turning the bad guys into charred meat.

Just like the Bible! More of God's plan!

*

Entracte:

Dear Friends,

I have frequently commented—possibly too often—how my thinking has been repeatedly directed, redirected, even corrected, by information, almost always textual, that I have not been looking for, or have expected, and sometimes that I have not even wanted.

Virtually all of these events have been useful. Some have been crucial. But the fact that many have been so essential, and that they happen so often, is also deeply disturbing, for the only sensible explanation is that something is happening in my thinking to somehow create these opportunities: which is obviously absurd.

So absurd that you have seen me invent a ghostly librarian, whom you know now as Baruch De Spinoza, in order that I might at least imagine them to have an agent. Most of these events are ridiculous. The next was crucial.

I had made twenty—no, let me count: over twenty-five—separate attempts to continue writing; and I was stuck again. This was a typical Spinoza moment.

I have described how I found Walter Beltz's book and discovered from it that the earliest Hebrew tribes worshipped two gods: the first, Elohim, was worshipped by the pastoralists; the second, Yahweh, by the nomadic tribes.

This was not remarkable. Most tribal gods were of this kind.

But from Beltz I then learnt something truly remarkable. As the tribes combined to form a nation they combined their two gods to worship them as one. They refused to give this new god a name. Perhaps the reason was that doing so might have divided the tribes again. But this new god with no name now had two natures.

The first required the Jews to keep an ever increasing prescriptive social order, an order governing every aspect of their rituals, lives, and deaths. This pleased the pastoralists: and this obsession of Jews with precise observation of their rituals has lasted to this day.

The second ensured that the more prescriptive order was preserved through divinely legitimatized violence: directed by their priests; or occasionally by an especially forceful prophet; even personally by this new god.

Their social order could therefore be extended through conquest to include other tribes: or their remnants: for only the most attractive women were usually kept alive. This pleased the warriors. In fact their new god rewarded everyone. He was clearly superior to all others. For a time the Jewish nation felt unbeatable.

I soon realised—within the same day—that this pattern became the model for all the later Abrahamic religions: especially Christianity and Islam, including Sikhism, possibly Mormonism.

Their gods also exhibit two natures. One demands strict obedience to tradition and laws, promising punishment for failure, even beyond the grave; the other is compassionate and merciful and urges only more piety and sacrifice.

Which one to invoke will naturally be decided by their priests. They will also decide how severely to punish. Sometimes this may be purely psychological.

Little is so terrifying for a child as being beaten by a parent. Being told, as an adult, that you have angered God, that you have disgraced your religion, and dishonoured your family: and that neither religion, family, or society will therefore any longer allow you to belong to them, may be more terrifying than death.

This must be the easiest way to persuade young people to kill themselves and others. Almost all the hard work is done. They need only to be sewn into a vest.

I knew vaguely of Elohim and Yahweh before picking up Beltz's book. I did not know of their tribal origins, or their different characters. I certainly did not know what the early Jews would make of them. Equally important is that I would not have understood its significance had it not been presented to me at this time and in this way. On any other occasion I would probably have looked into it and shrugged: 'I read this in 1986', and put it back.

Instead, I opened it: and was at once transfixed. I have to confess, you see: otherwise it may seem that I possess an extraordinary range of knowledge and of scholarship that I do not have. I wish I felt that I was controlling these events. I know, however, that I am not. If an intelligence is directing this information to me, it is not my intelligence. I only receive it.

Events like these are called serendipitous, which means happily fortunate, or synchronicities. The last name was given them by Carl Gustav Jung who, with Sigmund Freud, was one of the earliest pioneers in human psychology.

Carl Gustav was a very strange man. He was fascinated by the unconscious and his oddity did not prevent Einstein and Wolfgang Pauli, who was Nobel Laureate in physics, from being amongst his friends. They were interested in his suggestion that intelligence, and therefore information, may be communicated by something like a quantum field: unlimited by either time or space.

This may be what is happening. Their ideas are undoubtedly important, but they are still insufficient. They may explain some kinds of serendipity: when, for example, no exact coincidence of material objects is involved without any voluntary actions.

When both are involved, a far more complex game is clearly being played.

Here is the Wikipedia entry that I have just read: 'Jung introduced the concept as early as the 1920s . . . and in 1952, published a paper, *Synchronizität als ein Prinzip akausaler Zusammenhänge* . . . . It was a principle that Jung felt . . . was descriptive of a governing dynamic that underlies the whole of human experience and history: social, emotional, psychological, and spiritual.'

The last category is most interesting. I have always felt that attempting to achieve peace is more of a spiritual than social duty. Jung's proposal fits. But still does not explain.

*

PART THREE: The Gods in your Mind

I hope I may be persuading you that old Yahweh has not packed his tent and slunk off to Bethlehem. (I have used this line of Yeats before. It is also fitting here.)

But hear this, friends! Yahweh is not dead. He is alive and well! He has a trillion dollar credit line; millions of workers in thousands of factories; many of the most inventive minds on the planet strive to please him; and he can still turn good people into killers.

A good example is when the Christian president of the world's most Christian nation is reportedly offered the names of those said to be a threat to his nation's security—at a distance of several thousand miles—and authorises them to be killed—at a distance of several thousand miles, by remote control.

No tyrant in history ever had such power. No Mafioso can do this. It may be unpleasant to accept that the president of the world's most powerful and Christian nation is a serial killer. If the reports are true, this is what he is. It would be good to know his feelings. Why does he not refuse? He is killing those whom others have decided to kill. I recall a friend, who has been in similar situations, telling me: *"No-one ever orders me to take a shot. I decide. The responsibility is mine."*

This is not pleasant: but it is mature.

Of course there may be danger in not accepting such advice. In 1963 President Kennedy may have been assassinated because he was not sufficiently eager to make war in 1962. This is only conjecture. What is certain is that in 1962 he and a young Soviet naval officer called Vasili Arkhipov prevented nuclear war.

This was in the so-called Cuban Missile Crisis, when Kennedy rejected his military chiefs' offer—echoing that of General Curtis LeMay's in the Vietnam war—to bomb Cuba 'back into the Stone Age'.

In October of that year Arkhipov refused to fire nuclear torpedoes into the US aircraft carrier, the USS Randolph, which had depth-charged his submarine.

All he had to do was turn a key: and he refused.

What no-one knew in the United States at that time was that there were several dozen Soviet nuclear missiles in Cuba. If they had been hit, or if the Randolph had been blown up, thousands of nuclear ICBMs could have been launched within minutes by the US and the USSR.

If only Vasili had turned his key . . . then, as the lovely Milla Jovovich declares as the delightful humanoid (not many know this) called Leeloominai Lekatariba Lamina-Tchai Ekbat De Sebat in the film *'The Fifth Element'*: it would have been a very big BADABOOM! We would not be here.

There may have been several other moments since then of men having to decide whether to push a button or turn a key, with Yahweh whispering: 'Do it!'

Even more chilling today, as James Martin, the computer scientist and founder of the Oxford Martin School, has pointed out, is that modern missile systems no longer allow humans to turn keys or push buttons. The process is now entirely controlled by computers. *"And in any computer program, however often it may be tested,"* Martin comments drily, *"there are glitches."*

The cleverest men on our planet who designed these systems are now trying to have them dismantled. They are too late. It would take only milliseconds for these computers to end our lives. Yahweh has control.

I have thought of a possible way to take it back again. It is simple and even cruel; but it is not hidden somewhere in a billion lines of code. If you refuse to use it, nothing will change. But if you agree, nothing will ever be the same again.

Rather than being caused by the things that Dr Dawkins accepts as real, like thousands of nuclear weapons, wars depend on feelings. And these depend on much the same questions as asked years ago by our old friend Socrates.

What is good? What is virtue? What is excellence?

It is now obvious that the worshippers of Elohim and Yahweh have been at odds throughout all human history. What kind of gods are they? Do they really exist? If so, do they care about us? How can we understand them?

And there's more! Why has evolution made us all individual? Why does this matter? What is its purpose? What is its survival value?

So many questions! I suspect there is just one answer: and it is simple. It must be so simple for all cultures to understand and value it, and despite the fact that no-one has noticed it before, it must also be obvious. Above all, it should prove to young people that life has more promise than they have ever been told. This is a tall order!

Meanwhile I had previously suggested that mothers should be responsible for teaching their children never to be afraid to be honest and to ask questions.

I have realised that this is unworkable. In many cultures it is still too dangerous for women, especially for young women, to challenge cultural norms. Older women may demand that young mothers accept the treatment they have known and treat their children just as they did. We have still not found the key to give them freedom.

Recently I tried to enlist Judaism. Despite the huge moral cost of allowing Israel's national-religious core to force its terms on Israel and on the US Congress, the influence of modern Jews is still great. A few weeks ago I suggested to a very eminent Jewish statesman and scholar that Jews might increase peace in the world greatly by sharing the secret of their strength with others.

He gazed at me suspiciously. To him it was clearly inevitable that any strength that Jews might share with others could only increase the possibility of another Holocaust. His own concern was much more limited. *"Bah!"* he decided finally. *"Israel doesn't need this. Israel can make mincemeat of all the countries around it."*

Yahweh, obviously: in fine form.

Some weeks later I made the same suggestion to another almost as important Jewish scholar. He was more cautious. *"And what exactly,"* he asked slowly, as if dreading my reply, *"is our secret?"*

"You teach your children to ask questions," I told him. *"No other culture does that as systematically as you do. That is how yours survives."*

It is also, I might have said, but this would have taken too long an explanation, how Jews still contrive to worship Elohim with Yahweh.

He sighed. *"Any Jew who said that would only increase, not decrease, anti-Semitism."* But he wrote to me later: *"You do it. I encourage you."*

Our children offer a solution.

We can depend on the fact that any child called too clever may attempt to act the fool. A child called too feeble may learn to be strong. This is a generally reliable reaction. Any accusation is likely to provoke the exact opposite behaviour.

This is cruel. Young children can be very cruel. This is the habit we may use.

We can change the way they see their society: change the way that they behave, even very subtly, towards their society: and this will change their society. At the height of his early popularity,

Richard Dawkins coined the word 'meme' to describe any idea that is rapidly accepted for general use as if everyone has always wanted it.

We need a meme.

We can begin by describing how our closely related species behave: not necessarily, *pace* (contrary to the opinion of) Mr Huxley, our immediate ancestors but close enough: the apes.

Apes are highly sociable. They like to live in closely related groups. They are obsessively concerned that every other ape be like themselves: in appearance, in behaviour, in eating. All use the same language. Although they may accept those who pass their tests as an ape like themselves, they remain intensely suspicious of any strangers and anything that appears to them unusual.

If they notice anything of this nature, even if in their own, their usual tranquility is replaced by a ferocious reaction. This response will soon infect others. They will dig up the earth, tear down branches, throw sticks and stones, scream and gibber to excite each other further. The cause of their anger must be destroyed.

The ape brain is interested only in the present. It responds with unlimited aggression to any apparent threat to what it conceives to be the proper order of the world. It will aim to destroy any enemy, even if this may risk destroying its own nest, its own tribe, its own territory, itself. It may imagine heaven as another mango, and peace.

These characteristics, we may explain to our children, are not typical only of apes. If old enough to understand the connection, we may describe the Cold War: the trillions of dollars spent on nuclear weapons; the millions of men trained primarily to kill and be killed: the ships, submarines, satellites; MAD, Mutually Assured Destruction; etc.

Perhaps we should not add what Dr Martin told us. They may not believe this.

Now ask your children whether they see any similarities in the people they know. Of course they will. They experience everything we have described in the company of other children. Then, if we dare: "Which of our relatives is most ape-brained?" Prepare to be shocked. If told what to look for, children can be acutely perceptive.

The truth is that most of us are happy, most of the time, to enjoy our customary beliefs, routines, and pleasures: our habits. This, we may say, is what life is all about. To enjoy our lives everyone needs order and harmony. In other words, we are all perfectly happy to worship Elohim.

And it is precisely because of this that we may suppose that deliberate disorder is created only by what we may call disorderly minds. But we are simply being persnickety: using 'disorderly' when we really want to say 'defective'; imagining—as far more dangerous—that disorderly minds cannot be clever enough to plan and then execute major and complicated acts of mayhem.

This could not be more wrong. The early Jews worshipped two gods with very different natures because they recognized that most of us have two natures.

This hasn't changed.

Whilst a majority will always worship Elohim, the fraction who believe that some violence is always justified to prove the truth of their beliefs are also inclined to be worshipers of Yahweh; a still smaller fraction are the sociopaths and psychopaths who worship only Yahweh.

The last of these are the most dangerous of all, for instead of killing only here and there for thrills, one of them may decide that they deserve the greatest possible privilege of ending all life on Earth: and may find the means to do so. As Dr Martin has also pointed out, this is now more conceivable than at any other time in history.

But there may still be a way to dim the enthusiasm of everyone who is inclined to hurt those they disagree with. We may point out—gently, sympathetically, and diplomatically—that none of them are servants of some cosmic arbiter of righteousness. They are only the servants of a nasty little idol in their head.

I was once about to be bitten, unprovoked, by an enraged ape. Perhaps I looked at it too long: 'dissing' it in gang-speak. Spraying saliva through bared yellow fangs, it bit the bars of its cage instead.

My image of Yahweh is as an ape like that: furiously raging against the captivity of its own unimportance.

In contrast, my image of Elohim is as a plump and happy mother-figure: supremely confident in running her immaculate household; always ready to serve savoury broth and dumplings in her perfectly ordered kitchen; always ready to whack any ingrates with her ladle. It may be unnecessary to add that no-one is safe who messes with this lady. Few survive being whacked by her ladle.

Thankfully, our world is run mostly by ape-brains of the Elohim variety.

This, however, produces a different problem. When Thomas Jefferson's friends protested that democracy would ruin America: that hundreds of thousands—now hundreds of millions—of ordinary Americans did not know enough—about anything—to govern their own country, Jefferson replied calmly that they, who did believe they knew enough, had a duty to see that everyone receive the necessary education.

It was, and still is, a noble ambition. But what if education also comes to be governed by the ape-brained? Once they are in control of education, they will naturally insist that all children be taught to know and understand alike, and not to question.

Naturally: because this is in accord with their own nature.

Islamic schools do this. Jesuits boasted they could do the same. Hitler's *Jugendschule* achieved it perfectly. Socialism tried it for over seventy years. The result is always disastrous. The natural result of trapping youngsters in a cage of their unimportance is a psychotic distrust and hatred of those who are different. Conformity ultimately ruins all societies. Democracy requires diversity.

This is why I was so lucky to teach in our school. Just as in the army, it gave me room to think. It gave me time to realise that what I had been taught was wrong. Children are not items of industrial production. They must be allowed to learn as individuals. If they are not treated with respect, this, their most precious asset, dies.

I think we all know this. But the mystery remains. How can we ensure that all children everywhere know that they are uniquely important: as uniquely important as I am; for you may be sure that I know that I do know this. It is a very good feeling. It goes together with the nicest compliment I ever received, which was paid me years ago by a forcefully direct American lady I got to know in Cambridge, who said to me one day: "You know, what makes you so unusual is that you have a totally *unthreatening* personality."

This might not have been intended as a compliment from anyone else, but we had both recently met several monstrous egos, all of them eager to be noticed and admired. Her praise was given over thirty years ago, but I have understood why it was given only because of what comes next. Perhaps you can see what it may be.

In all our minds there are two gods. One desires tranquillity, and is relatively content with life; the other deeply resents its unimportance, and is ready to lash out on any provocation or pretext.

Every time we lose our temper, kick the dog, break the china, even—if this *ever* happens—get raging drunk, the second had kicked out the first and taken control.

Presuming that no-one is actually killed during his tantrum—although murder was once condoned in French courts as a *crime passionel*—Mister Grumpy retires to his den, full to the brim of moral righteousness, and Mrs Tidy returns with a broom, sweeps up the debris: *'Schrh, schrh, schrh'*, to restore order again.

This cycle occurs daily, at every human level, everywhere in the world. It may end with injury and death. It is responsible corporately for bad management; nationally, especially in supposedly 'multicultural societies', it is responsible for increasingly fractious relations, capable of becoming murderous; it leads to Western leaders who pray to their god for directions and to launch new crusades.

*

Entracte:

Dear Friends,

The prompts I receive from dear old Baruch are usually considerate of my weak scholarship—which I am sure he thinks entirely unsuited to the task—and gentle, for he knows as well that I am easily bruised.

Occasionally, however, he demonstrates a more splenetic temperament. I may be able to see the path I am expected to take only very dimly; and I am stumbling bravely along, when I feel a shove in the back, as if to say: *"Oh, do get on!"*

I admit that Baruch's task is immensely more difficult than mine, for he has somehow to arrange the entire history of the world, together with every material thing in it, so that, in the moment I decide to reach out my hand—and he can never be sure when this will be—he can place the right book in it, which will open at the right page, and that I will then read, and then comprehend what it is that he wants me to read.

You think this is all nonsense? I think so too.

There is a country pub near to me called The Fishes, which keeps a small library of books for its customers. Recently I found several unread books in my garage library, and decided to donate them.

One of the three redundant books I chose is a fat mystery novel called *'The Interpretation of Murder'*, written by Professor Jed Rubenfeld, a Harvard University don, and published in 2006. I have never read it. I open it, idly, at pages eighty and eighty-one.

The back cover had already told me that the story is set in New York, in the early 1900s; and that Dr Rubenfeld has managed to involve Dr Sigmund Freud, on his first and only visit to America, in investigating the murder of a beautiful young socialite. A glance at page eighty tells me that Freud is discussing the case with someone. I am not interested in who this is. I look now across at page eighty-one.

"So. You ask me a direct question," said Freud; *"I will give you a direct answer. I am the deepest of unbelievers. Every neurosis*

*is a religion to its owner, and religion is the universal neurosis
of mankind. This much is beyond doubt: the characteristics we
attribute to God reflect the fear and wishes we feel first as infants
and then as small children. Anyone who does not see that much,
cannot have understood the first thing about human psychology."*

I am shocked. Why did I never make this connection? You may
say that there is nothing untoward in people wanting an orderly
and harmonious society, nor in accepting—and even demanding—
that those who disturb its order or its harmony shall be punished.
Any secular society can be expected to support these desires;
religious societies even more so.

As we have just learnt from Dr Beltz's book, the early Jews
made these two desires the purview of two gods. As their tribes
combined, these two gods came to be worshipped as one. This god,
they insisted, had—and still has—no name. They then ascribed to
this one god the authority to order the despoliation, destruction,
enslavement, and even the total slaughter of all who offended,
threatened, challenged, or even seemed to offer a different
prescription of the order and rituals on which they believe their
social harmony to depend.

The last, Christians will recognise, is what made Jesus so
fatally unpopular.

I trust that you have become used to my hop-skip-and-jump
manner of writing commentaries between these sections. I cannot
help this. It is as if I am writing in a room illuminated with flashes
from a light-house, giving me just enough time to see what I need
to before leaving me scribbling in semi-darkness before it comes
round again.

I have already suggested that Christianity and Islam, in their
many often hostile forms, have both followed the Jewish pattern. I
have included Mormonism too.

This I already knew. Why was I now shocked by the real Dr
Rubenfeld's fictitious, yet perfectly credible, Sigmund Freud?

Because I realised almost at once—actually some hours later,
sitting in the North Oxford Esporta gym's sauna in 80 degrees of
heat—that the two most explosively destructive secular ideologies

of the past century—Hitler's National Socialism, and Stalin's Communism—did the same.

I am setting aside Mao Zedong's version of Marxist-Leninism. Mao inherited the tradition of the Chinese emperors and used this to the full. He killed upwards of fifty million people. Stalin's score is around twenty. Hitler's, as I once heard it described by an eminent Jewish historian, of less than ten purely racist and political murders, is 'small beer'.

To respond now as I did to Rubenfeld's Dr Freud, read here the symptoms of neurosis in an individual (once again from Wikipedia):

'[These] *may include some or all of: anxiety, sadness or depression, anger, irritability, mental confusion, low sense of self-worth, phobic avoidance, vigilance, impulsive and compulsive acts, lethargy, unpleasant or disturbing thoughts, repetition of thoughts and obsession, habitual fantasizing, negativity and cynicism, dependency, aggressiveness, perfectionism, schizoid isolation, socio-culturally inappropriate behaviours, etc.'* (Professor C. George Boeree of Shippensburg University, Pennsylvania)

What *'anxieties, sadness, depression, negativity and cynicism'* do religions try traditionally to alleviate in people? I am sure that most rabbis, priests, imams may attempt to do so. But may not religions also create neuroses involving *'anger, irritability, mental confusion, impulsive and compulsive acts, unpleasant thoughts, obsession, dependency, perfectionism'?*

Then what kind of punishment might a traditionally religious people demand, or accept, to be inflicted on those few who are identified by their leaders, better still by their one leader, as being responsible for all their misfortunes?

May I suggest that a traditionally religious people would find it entirely natural to believe that their nation's leader possesses virtues and powers of that god with no name: that he could never be wrong, never mistaken; that he would bring them unequalled order; search out and eliminate all wrong-doers?

All this happened. Twice.

Hitler and Stalin were opportunists. Their elevation to absolute power was a consequence of the work of countless priests over many centuries. Stalin trained as a priest. As a result of their efforts both German and Russian people were deeply grounded in the same traditions of belief that the early Jews first instituted: that social order and cultural harmony are to be regulated by divinely ordained rituals and rules, and—since the punishment of transgressors is also divinely sanctioned—such punishments may therefore be imposed without limit or mercy.

In Germany, Hitler murdered Jews, trade-unionists, homosexuals, gypsies. In Russia, all enemies of harmony and order—as Stalin defined them—were worked and starved to death, exiled or executed en masse.

All this is history: ancient to most of you. But once you see the pattern in these chapters from your history books, it is intriguing to see whether it remains active in countries in which a religious tradition is strong.

This may certainly include the USA, which I recall Professor Robert N. McCauley, in a public lecture in Oxford, declaring to be: '*the world's most Christian country*'. In an essay in the New Scientist's famous '*God Issue*' in March 2012, Dr McCauley remarks on the fact that '*the religions that the vast majority of people actually practice are not the same as the doctrines they learn and recite.*' (Director of the Center for Mind, Brain, and Culture, Emory University, Georgia, USA)

We may wonder why.

That all religions succeed in alleviating much unhappiness and insecurity is obviously true. They would hardly last if they could not do this. It is still important to ask: but what neuroses may they create?

Look again at Professor Boeree's list. I think you will find it is possible to identify a religion solely from the symptoms of its principal neurosis.

What, for example, can be expected from teaching children that they have inherited the 'sin' of Adam in their mother's womb?

This ludicrous story was invented in the first century, then written into history as fact by the saintly Augustine in the fourth.

The Catholic Church has maintained it to be true ever since. It is a major article of faith.

A cynic might also describe it as a nice little earner. Augustine was actually trying—manfully, you might say—simply to discourage fornication.

It is not at all clear why poor Adam should be blamed for this. Syphilis may have been far more effective when it became epidemic in Europe a century later after Augustine.

This terrible disease still infects millions world-wide. Men in some countries believe that they can cure themselves by raping virgins. All they do, of course, is infect traumatized young girls. Then their babies may be born syphilitic.

Catholic priests continue to teach that children are infected with Adam's sin in their mother's womb. In his chapter on St Augustine, Bertrand Russell describes Augustine's insistence that: *'Only God's grace enables men to be virtuous. Since we all inherit Adam's sin, we all deserve eternal damnation. All who die unbaptised, even infants, will go to hell and suffer unending torment. We have no reason to complain about this, since we are all wicked.'* (in *'History of Western Philosophy'*, Russell, B. 1946, p. 362.)

Such is faith. Let us not pretend to be surprised by this nonsense. At least your children were not infected with syphilis in their mother's womb.

This systematic creation of lowered self-worth is, however, much more than a nice little earner. It is as fundamental to Catholicism as believing that the mother of several children was always and remained a virgin. Such is faith.

Now let me test you!

Which religion springs to your mind if I suggest that the principle symptom of the neurosis on which it depends is *'perfectionism'*?

No, I don't need to know. What matters is that you have recognised one.

Here's another!

Which of the world's religions most depends on persuading its followers to engage in *'habitual fantasizing'*?

Is that too general? I suppose it is. Then how about this: which insists that its people's moral strength and racial purity destines them to be the rulers of the world?

No, sorry: that was Hitler's idea. His belief in the natural superiority of the Aryan people, as they were rather quaintly defined, was more an ideology than religion. You might say, rather sourly, that Hitler wanted the Germans to imitate the British in creating an empire; but Britain's empire was built on a class-system, whilst the Third Reich was supposed to be class-less.

Similarly, Karl Marx obviously believed that communism would produce class-less generations intellectually, socially, and morally superior to those of the deeply fissured capitalist societies with their dog-eat-dog mentality and careless social ineptitude. Seventy years of socialism in the late Soviet Union has produced a deeply demoralized people ruled by an elite of such brutality and spectacular cupidity as to make Western bankers and hedge-fund crooks seem like altar boys.

Professor McCauley's explanation may fit religions and ideologies. The vast majority of people rarely practise the doctrines they learn and recite because neuroses naturally produce contradictions. Socialists praise socialist honesty: but observe flagrant dishonesty. Christians praise compassion: but punish mercilessly.

Following the ideas of the psychologist and Nobel Laureate Daniel Kahneman, McCauley's explanation is that these contradictions are due to the collision of the 'fast' and 'slow' forms of thinking.

Fast thinking is for survival: slow is for comfort.

This is the difference the early Jews saw several millennia ago.

Religions are like ideologies—or, if you don't like the comparison: ideologies are like religions—in depending on cultivating neuroses with many active, but also erratic, symptoms. Some persons may present mostly one major symptom. Others may present several symptoms. These may change unpredictably.

Everyone infected, however, can be expected to display Professor Boeree's symptoms of *'schizoid isolation'* and *'mental confusion'*.

As much as being convinced that everyone is a robot, the two are likely to manifest morally. We have examined the reason previously. All who believe that they are certain of the truth are usually unable to understand why everyone else does not, or will not, agree with them.

Is it because everyone who does not agree is stupid?

No? Then perhaps they are evil. If they are evil, perhaps God wants them to be punished. Perhaps I, or we, or our nation's soldiers, must punish them for God.

All kinds of people may think in this way. It is infectious. People are killing and dying right now because of this kind of massively infectious neurosis.

Professor Dawkins coined a valuable word, 'meme', to describe infectious ideas. Copying him, we might use 'MINS' to describe these neuroses.

Fortunately there is an antidote to them all.

Each has its own creeping, crawling, fizzing swarm of symptoms. These symptoms invariably support the belief that their host culture is uniquely important.

The habit of fantasizing, together with their deliberate policy of cultivating their own particular brand of schizoid isolation, for example, another nice earner: has led generations of Christian theologians to declare that their Lord Jesus Christ is God: despite the fact that this is being specifically denied by all the Gospels, and, according to their account, was denied by Jesus personally.

No matter. Such is faith.

Satan's last trick, wrote the French poet Baudelaire, is to persuade you that he no longer exists. That was in 1864. It can't be true today. There are more little Satans running around today than you can shake a stick at. What they all have in common, however, is that none of them likes to be identified with one of Professor Boeree's symptoms. I leave it to you to continue. You should be able to fill a book.

Jefferson's Declaration of Independence: famously asserting the right of the future people of America to *"Life, Liberty, and the pursuit of Happiness"* has been called 'the most potent and consequential in history'.

Jefferson might have explained that the pursuit of happiness must entail the free exercise of humour; the freedom to think; to learn; to question; freedom to criticise; to speak—and, above all, to laugh at official chicanery, political pomposity, and individual pretension of importance.

Fortunately all of these freedoms are implicit in his declaration. They became the traditions of which all Americans can be proud. Recently, and most sadly out of fear of their own brand of Satan, they have allowed many of the most important to be curtailed.

Our world is dangerously full. One of the several major dangers facing us all is the inability of religions to accept that they incubate massively infectious anxiety, sadness or depression, anger, irritability, mental confusion, and, in many individuals, a sense of low self-worth.

In terms of its effect on our species' survival, this must be considered disastrous. How could evolution have taken such a wrong turn?

Alternatively, why is God not correcting our error?

Occasionally I have explored another possibility in these essays. It is, I admit, only remotely possible. But what have religions been trying to do all these thousands of years—as atheists like to scoff—but attempting to write a formula for creation, without even understanding why we are able to think?

Science prefers simple explanations. The following explanation is as simple as it gets. It also explains, as Charles Darwin once said, all the evidence fairly well.

What if we are part of a relatively minor experiment in social evolution on a very pretty but also minor planet orbiting a just adequate sun in the corner of an average galaxy? And what if the intelligence our species has learnt, with a great deal of confusion, to call God, is looking for something in us that is exceptional?

From time to time this god may appear to people—so our history tells us—to give sometimes puzzling hints as to how we are expected to behave. One of the earliest and most famous is the statement from Moses' burning bush: *'I am that I am'.*

This is all the more credible in being so cryptic. It has recently been convincingly explained to me by David Bohm, one of the foremost 20th century physicists, as meaning: *'Do not limit me with human terms. I am everything.'* (This is to be found in *'Unfolding Meaning'*, Bohm, D., 1986. Yes, another book on my shelves.)

Other than demanding that we be honest with ourselves and with others, I do not know what a universal intelligence should want of us. A major clue, however, may be that we have all evolved as unique individuals.

Religions, in contrast, are developed to treat us as all the same. It takes some courage to escape their neuroses; not least because we are made to accept them before we have discovered, as many of you have, that we need not.

It therefore appears to me not only important, intellectually, morally, and socially, to know that we are individuals, but that it is even more essential spiritually.

Be consciously as individual as you can be; and keep your sense of humour.

This is what I tried to encourage in your mathematics lessons.

If more teachers, of any subject, would do the same, I believe it would help peace to grow where wars still flourish.

Love to you all,
Colin.

*

PART FOUR: The Ape and Sophia

I believe that most children would still like to believe in a god.

We must tell them that their minds actually have two gods.

The more violent made itself known the last time they had a tantrum.

The more peaceful likes order. They will remember how they, sometimes, like to put their toys away and tidy their room.

We must also explain that both gods are worshipped in combination by many people, and that both can become nasty. One is invariably ready with violence. The other is not always 'Jesus meek and mild' they may have learnt about in Sunday school. Believing in the absolute necessity for order, it may also hurt.

These two gods are worshipped by billions of people. Feelings are made, directed, and justified by them. They are inseparable from us. They are part of our reality. Modern atheists are no less justified than Thomas Huxley when he berated Soapy Sam Wilberforce for teaching ancient fairy-tales. The harm they do to receptive minds is all the more culpable when they must know that scrupulously careful scholars, including Albert Schweitzer, have deciphered their meaning.

Coincidentally—*thank you, Baruch, I have it*—yesterday I found a 1952 copy of his *'Denken und Tat'* in the charity bookshop in which I work every week, in which I find Schweitzer declaring his belief that: *'Der Jesus von Nazareth, der als Messias auftrat, die Sittlichkeit des Gottesreiches verkuendete, das Himmelsreich auf Erde gruendete und starb, um seinem Werke zu geben, hat nie existiert'*. [Jesus of Nazareth, who appeared as the Messiah, who proclaimed the morals of the Kingdom of God, who established the Kingdom of heaven on earth and who died to complete his work, in fact never existed.]

Despite this loss of half the heavenly duo—and some will say removing the kinder of the two—I repeat my belief that most children wish there may be a god to watch over them, to hear their prayers, to inspire and guide them in life.

If this be called supernatural, so be it. Dr Dawkins believes in quarks because he and others infer their existence and nature by studying the history of energetic particles produced by atoms colliding at near the speed of light. Let him not mock us for inferring the nature of the gods that people believe in from our history.

By all means tell your children—on my authority, if you wish—that the god they wish to exist does exist. But you must also warn that he is just as modern as they are, and just as difficult to know as any quark is to be found alone.

When, in times gone by, I used to explain to my pupils the function of their left and right brain, I would tell them that they communicate with each other, through the thick bundle of nerves at their base. This, at the time, was the best I could manage.

Dr Dawkins endears himself to me by declaring, fairly often, that there are some aspects of science that he does not understand. This is even truer of me in neuroscience. However, I have it on very good authority that no-one understands how the mind creates the reality that we perceive. We may never understand this.

I can be more confident regarding these two gods. They can obviously function independently. Their differences will then be most plain. They may act together. Then they are capable of inspiring the destruction of people on an industrial scale.

Perhaps the earliest record of this is when the Israelites are said to have taken the city of Jericho: *'With their swords they killed everyone, men and women, young and old. They also killed the cattle, sheep, and donkeys'*. (Joshua 6:21)

Although archaeologists now say that this could never have happened, it does not diminish the relish with which it is recorded. If it didn't happen then, it is likely to have happened elsewhere. The Old Testament editors obviously liked this sort of thing. Many dead: lots of blood: keep all the virgins for yourselves.

You may heartily dislike my suggestion that for thousands of years people have been worshipping the projections into their reality of these two functions of their minds. Or that billions do so now. Or they have given them both images and names: *'the Father and the Son are One'*, for example, thus combining the two as the Jews did. Or that they install priests whose livelihood then depends on their claim to speak with their authority. Or that the priests send armies against armies.

All of this is still happening because no-one, until now, has been able to recognise the same pattern of behaviour appearing again and again.

Can these inventions of our minds really be considered part of reality?

Of course they can. Behind them are the functions which create, control, and direct our feelings. We cannot escape them. But we can learn to recognise and manage them: and teach our children to do the same.

But what, finally, of the ability of mind I have always lauded, and which I believe is always especially pregnant in children's minds: the ability to criticise, to discourse, and invent? What space is there for this precious ability between these two gods?

Surely you realise that in many cultures and in countless manifestations, Elohim was once revered as the Mother Goddess: as the ability endlessly to form and unform, to create and re-create?

She, like any capable housewife—let us finally reject the masculinity foisted on her by men priests—let us recognise instead that whoever keeps order can also create disorder; whoever arranges, can re-arrange; whoever tidies can make untidy; that she alone is able to recognise toys that are outgrown, damaged, defunct—and will throw them out!

The most critical, inventive, and creative function of our minds is more feminine than masculine. We may now understand why men in male-dominated cultures, usually with only male priests, are frightened by this ability. Being themselves controlled by that nasty little monster Yahweh, they are most likely to threaten violence or to use violence to prevent it from happening. The simplest recourse, once again, is to claim that God forbids any change of anything. This is then declared to prove their faith. It only proves they are frightened.

I'm sorry, fellers! Remember that the other god is in male minds too, and that another of her ancient names is Sophia, the Greek word for wisdom.

The day after writing this last line I walked into the Oxfam charity shop in Summertown, where I found a book by Philip Pullman, the famous Oxford author of the trilogy: *'His Dark Materials'*. This book had the curious title *'The Good Man Jesus and the Scoundrel Christ'*. I bought it for one pound.

I do not know whether Pullman is an atheist. Here, however, is how he describes the descent from spiritual freedom to religious tyranny. Remember that this is all intended for children. Mark his words. You will see that he means to be general:

'As soon as men who believe they're doing God's will get hold of power, whether it's in a household or a village or in Jerusalem or in Rome itself, the devil enters into them. It isn't long before they start drawing up lists of punishment for all kinds of innocent activities, sentencing people to be flogged or stoned in the name of God for wearing this or eating that or believing the other. And the privileged ones will build great palaces and temples to strut about in, and levy taxes on the poor to pay for their luxuries; and they'll start keeping the very scriptures secret, saying that there are some truths too holy to be revealed to ordinary people, so that only the priests' interpretations will be allowed, and they'll torture and kill anyone who wants to make the word of God clear and plain to all; and with every day that passes they'll become more and more fearful, because the more power they have the less they'll trust anyone, so they'll have spies and betrayals and denunciations and secret tribunals and put poor harmless heretics they flush out to horrible public deaths, to terrify the rest into obedience.'

Before buying his book, I had intended to look at still another puzzle.

As children you may have wondered, as I did, why Christianity is not content to make its God out to be two divinities joined as one: but insists that there are three.

Together with the Father and the Son, they include a Holy Spirit.

I could never fathom what this Holy Spirit is. It was never explained.

This is all the more curious because this Trinitarian doctrine, this belief in a Triune god, in a Trinity—celebrated in Cambridge in the name of the college that gave me shelter and helped to restore my confidence—does more to separate Christians from other religions than any other statement of belief. It is a major obstacle to peace.

It is easy enough for anyone to discover that this dogma was invented in the first century, then developed through to the fourth century, and that its purpose was to put an end to further heresies and to establish a Christian orthodoxy. Once decided, the bishops, by this time only men, declared it must never be questioned: never changed!

There is a danger, I have realised, in something I wrote a page or two back. Unless I correct it, I may be accused of anti-Semitism. More serious is that it may upset my friends of the Oxford Chabad Society, who have always treated me kindly.

It is extremely unlikely that this doctrine resulted from those first century bishops deliberately copying the Jews. I doubt that they knew enough history to do this. And they wanted desperately to be different from Judaism, from Jesus' own religion. But, just like the Jews as they brought their tribes together to form their nation, the early Christian bishops needed to combine the power of their nascent church to punish, as represented by the Father, and to reward, as represented by the gentle, forgiving Jesus. This, I suggest, is the simple and understandable reason for combining the Old Testament god they adopted, with the New Testament god they created: principally by traducing virtually everything he said of himself.

I am always ruefully amused, for example, that the advice that he gave to his own immediate followers and to us: the advice which was the most dangerous challenge to the Jewish tradition of his time; routinely ignored by the Christianity made in his name, that this alone makes me doubt that Schweitzer's conclusion is correct. This man lived!

"And when you pray, you must not be like the hypocrites who love to stand and pray in the synagogues and on street corners to be seen by others . . . . When you pray, go into your room and shut the door and pray to your Father in secret. And your Father who sees in secret will reward you." (Matthew 6.5-6)

I like this, in addition, because it was what I did: and I was rewarded.

Notice that once they had combined their earlier gods into the god with no name, the Jews did nothing more. They certainly made no attempt to curb their pleasure of arguing. *"What does a Jew do,"* goes a Jewish joke, *"when he wakes up alone in the middle of the night with a terrible desperate urge?"* Answer: *"He gives in to the urge, and tells himself, 'Oyoy, Mensch, you've got that so wrong!'"*

Arguing may once have been the only pleasure that the majority of Jewish men could afford; or, at least, engage in publicly. It is certainly why synagogues were constructed: and why their wives sat in them somewhere else.

Very much more seriously, I am convinced that it is this tradition which explains the intellectual success of Jews, although not often of observant Jews, in virtually every field they care to enter. They are simply very good at arguing, at seeing every side of every question, and then another, and another, not noticed before.

It also explains, far more unhappily, the disastrous consequences of the reluctance of Muslim parents and teachers to encourage Muslim children to question anything.

Quite apart from the remarkable behaviour of the eminent British professor of education, whom I had naively expected to support us, but who instead only attacked our initiative, I realize now that this was a further reason for the fiasco of the conference that I and my colleagues organized for the Qatar Foundation in the magnificent surroundings of Windsor Castle.

We proposed that Qatari schools should actively encourage children, not only to question their texts, but argue with one another over the meaning of their texts.

If I had not been so appalled by the bad temper, and bad manners, of the British professor trashing our efforts, I might have heard a number of Qatari spines stiffening with horror.

First, questions in their mathematics lessons!

And after mathematics, what next?

This reluctance to question is still as important in modern Islamic societies, and indeed in the average Muslim home, as it was before the Renaissance in European societies and homes.

It made it even more difficult to overcome when many eminent Islamic scholars seem set on following the British in justifying the creation of their Empire: by claiming that they were impelled morally to do so in order to spread God's true word.

As they were building their Empire the upper classes did not find it morally necessary to address the lack of education, the poverty and misery of the millions of ordinary British people on whom they depended. Far more important was spreading God's word: as Christianity.

Here today is one of Islam's eminent scholars, Sheikh Yusuf al-Qaradawi, on the necessity of offensive Jihad: *"Islam has the right to take the initiative . . . this is God's religion and is for the whole world. It has the right to destroy all obstacles in the form of institutions and traditions . . . it attacks institutions and traditions to release human beings from their poisonous influences which distort human nature and curtail human freedom. Those who say that Islamic Jihad was merely for the defence of the homeland of Islam diminish the greatness of the Islamic way of life."* (From the website ReligionofPeace.com.)

Sigh! I can hear British voices saying the same only a few centuries ago. With such moral certainty two thirds of the globe was soon coloured red. The irony is that the British that theirs was also a necessary jihad. Now it is called 'colonialism', and is abhorred.

In a moment we shall see how it happened that any kind of questioning is still regarded in Islam as anathema.

First, however, let us ask why the Christian bishops moved this wholly mysterious 'Holy Spirit' or 'Holy Ghost', presumably from our earthly sphere, in order to place it in that of heaven?

I did not intend that pun: the 'wholly Holy'. On reflection, it is apt. I have asked several thoughtful Christians what it means to them, and received several different replies. It seems very like a hole in their catechetical understanding which they are expected to fill with their own ideas. One lady explained: *"It's the nice part of all of us."*

Hmm. So why is it in heaven? *"That's to remind us to be nice to others."*

Hmm, once more. But these replies are immaterial. Sorry: another pun. What we need to know is what those bishops actually believed. Since they ain't never gonna' tell us, not no-how—my father used these double negatives—we must think.

These guys lived in tough times. Their Emperor was watching. What is it that they would want most urgently to remove from the aspirations of their own followers, now flooding into their new churches following Constantine's making his empire their parish? It was agreed at the first Nicene conference in 325 that the Holy Spirit must have been the power that inseminated Mary. I hate to think how these men worked out that this was managed. In the modern version of the Nicene Creed accepted by Catholics, the Holy Spirit is called 'the Lord, giver of life.' This sounds a little more interesting, but it is still pretty vacuous.

Pullman's book is not so big, but I had no time to read it. I had already found the passage I noted above, and flipped to the end where my eye was caught by the word 'Spirit.'

In Pullman's account someone called the Stranger is talking to Jesus' brother, here called Christ, after Jesus has been crucified: and is thoroughly, permanently dead. Together they have watched his body being smuggled from his tomb to create the belief that he has survived.

"Now I must tell you," says the Stranger to Christ, *"about the Holy Spirit. He is the one who will fill the disciples, and in time to come more of the faithful, with the conviction of the living Jesus. Jesus could not be with people forever, but the Holy Spirit can, and will."*

This was already surprising, and puzzling. I dropped my eyes a few lines.

"The Spirit is inward and invisible. Men and women need a sign that is outward and visible, and then they will believe. You have been scornful lately when I have spoken of truth, dear Christ; you should not be. It will be truth that strikes into their minds and hearts in the ages to come, the truth of God that comes from beyond time. But it needs a window to be opened so that it can shine through into the world of time, and you are that window."

'Strewth!' was my first thought. *'Absolute crapola'* was my next.

'The truth of God, that comes from beyond time.'
Just what is *this* supposed to mean?
'You are that window'.
This is terrible. This is a blatantly cynical rip-off. Philip Pullman is a highly intelligent man, a hugely successful author. He is just three years younger than I, but infinitely more successful commercially. He has no need to write this tripe. Although reported once to have said: *"I'm trying to undermine the basis of Christian belief"*, his *'Dark Materials'* trilogy has won many prestigious awards. It has been recommended to be read in schools as religious commentary. Surely he should know what this third god of the Christian Trinity represents.

Slowly it dawns on me: he hasn't got a clue!

This is far worse than being dismissed by all those modern wiseacres, some of whom are quite nice people, as a cupcake.

Surely I cannot be alone in understanding what Constantine's bishops were up to. Sherlock Holmes once said, famously: *"Once you've eliminated the impossible, whatever remains, no matter how improbable, must be the truth."*

Let me, respectfully, rephrase that: *'Once you've considered all the nice reasons that people may have had for agreeing to anything, but then remember that they all actually hated each other, the greatest likelihood is that they will have agreed to something of benefit to them all. They are not going to tell you what this is. But they knew why they agreed. They are also likely to have agreed on a symbol for it.'*

This may read like an abbreviated Dan Brown, but I suspect that those three hundred bishops really did hate one another. Remember that Constantine's empire covered the entire civilised world. To decide the precise form of the religion of this empire, the settled agreement that their Emperor demanded was a prize of immeasurable value. The man—or the men—whose opinion was decisive, would be elevated to positions of immense authority and power, and would be remembered by millions with gratitude: for ever and ever!

But it was precisely because of this that they must have hated each other. They could not agree how to agree. But they must agree. They decided instead on a pact.

The symbol the majority agreed should represent their pact was the Holy Spirit. The Holy Spirit has nothing to do with inseminating Mary. What a grotesque impiety! These were grown men. It has nothing to do with 'giving life'.

That their pact has been magnificently successful cannot be denied. Two millennia later, after almost two thousand years of not questioning their decision, the Holy Spirit, or the Holy Ghost, remains safely cloistered in heaven, and no-one has any sensible idea of what it is actually intended to signify. Everyone seems to think this is so obvious that they need not ask.

I should not be so surprised. Baruch rarely wastes an opportunity. I was really looking in Oxfam's bookshop for a Jack Reacher thriller by the British writer Lee Child.

Instead I found Philip Pullman. I should not be so hard on him. His is certainly sloppy thinking. But I think we can be fairly sure that a billion church-attending Christians, who should know better, actually do not. If they did, they might attend church for the same reasons, but with far less confidence in their understanding of their reasons, than they do now.

The truly great irony is that those not-so-very-stupid old men, back in the third to fourth century, certainly knew what they wanted; and their cheap little trick to conceal it has crippled Christian belief for over sixteen or so centuries. It is substantially what they invented.

A little over a thousand years, I believe, after they must have agreed on their pact to give Constantine what he wanted, the most influential Islamic philosopher of his time, still widely influential today, achieved exactly the same for Islam, for just the same reason.

He was Abu Hamid Muhammad ibn Muhammad Al-Ghazzali, known in the West as Algazel. He lived from around 1058 to 1111, and what he succeeded in doing—to, it must be said, the obvious relief of many Muslims then and ever since—was to trample underfoot the most important inspiration of their Prophet.

'The ink of the scholar,' the Prophet Muhammad is said to have declared, *'is weighed on the Day of Judgement, and outweighs the blood of martyrs.'*

It is actually hard to dislike Al-Ghazzali. In his *'Alchemy of Happiness'*, he wrote, very wisely: *'Declare your jihad on the enemies you cannot see: on egoism, arrogance, conceit, selfishness, greed, lust, intolerance, anger, lying, cheating, gossiping, and slandering. If you can master and destroy them, then you will be ready to fight the enemy you can see.'*

Unfortunately he did not take his own advice. As a result of his far more influential book, *'The Incoherence of Philosophers'*, he is credited—although perhaps this is not the best word—with ending Arab pre-eminence in virtually every field of systematic inquiry: in astronomy; medicine; mathematics; science.

This single work dropped on Islamic science like a kybosh, the heavy metal plate used to smother flames, turning Islamic light into Islamic darkness, persuading pious Muslims from that time on that the ink of the scholars should ever be used endlessly only to copy the same permitted texts over and over and over again.

Al-Ghazzali's argument was far simpler than that of the inventors of Christianity a thousand years before. It was perfectly explicit. It was also so cleverly framed as to be very difficult, if not extremely dangerous, to argue against it. *'Questions,'* he declared, *'sully the purity of our faith. Therefore, question no more!'*

Until the present day his interdiction has preserved the divinely prescribed order and harmony of Islam. From that day, the spirit of inquiry in Islam, of criticism, of invention, was dead, and has still not recovered: and the authority of whole legions of arrogant, selfish, greedy, intolerant, angry old men, Christian and Islamic, has never been more secure.

The Holy Spirit is Sophia, once known, as you may guess, as Elohim. The Holy Spirit is indeed inward and invisible: in individuals. But the outward effects are often powerful and visible.

The Holy Spirit is the spirit of inquiry: a very real and constant danger to all arrogant, selfish, intolerant, and—above all— consciously fraudulent old men of no true confidence in God at all.

It is the spirit of science, of the search for the truth, of the knowing that this search can never end. It is the spirit that led us here.

This was the spirit that these old men removed, figuratively, but also inspirationally, far beyond the reach of ordinary mortals; placing it in heaven, exactly as if they were placing temptation, like a cookie jar, out of children's reach.

They were wilfully wrong. We can see why. They wanted what their Emperor wanted: a monolithic church which he would control through them: a religion to stifle imagination; a church in which no-one would be allowed to question their authority, or his.

Their error was to divide Christianity for many centuries into warring tribes, each insisting that only it is right. But this continues. Without any example to correct it, the same error divides Jews and Christians. It incites Muslims to murder Muslims; Buddhists to murder Hindus; Hindus to murder Sikhs. There is so much confusion and so much ill will.

The truth is so much simpler.

What they should have said is: 'God the Father, God the Son, God the Holy Spirit: all three are not in heaven; they are in you. The Father is in you, demanding that you agree with others how to keep your own society safe. The Son is in you, expecting you to forgive as he forgave. The Holy Spirit is in you, leavening your soul with imagination. Only through your imagination can you truly know the other as yourself. Only through imagination can you transcend your mortality. It is only your imagination that allows you to know that you are uniquely individual, and that you can do more than only exist.'

The effect of Dr Dawkins and his contemporaries—Sam Harris, Daniel Dennett, and the late Christopher Hitchens—has been to blow a lot of pure dross from religions, especially from Christianity. This can only help to reveal their source. Perhaps not so surprisingly, it is the same as that of their science.

The source of all religions, and of science, is the Holy Spirit: indeed the gift of life, of individuality, of inventiveness and creativity, of talent, skills, of potentials of every kind, some never yet known or explored, all waiting to bloom, to give pleasure and to astonish.

The signs of its awakening are many.

Young people within Islam are beginning to ask: why is their education so limited? Presently only a few Muslim nations are following the leadership of the Emir of Qatar and his remarkable lady, Her Highness Sheikha Mozah, in showing their youngsters the respect they deserve. More nations will follow. The Holy Spirit demands it.

More Muslims are beginning to recognise that they must read the Qur'an with more care: that whoever ensured that it contain those splenetic outbursts of Muhammad, venting his anger—as Jesus also did—on those who doubted his sincerity and reviled him, bequeathed Muslims with a propensity for violence which undoubtedly pleases that bad-tempered god called Yahweh, but now is responsible for Muslims daily massacring Muslims by bomb and bullet, whilst making it perfectly impossible for them to follow the Prophet's essential inspiration in achieving peace.

The latest fright word in Judaism is *'individualism'*. It means questioning. More young Jews are beginning to question whether they really want, or really need, to be Jews; whether Israel is really worth the cost, the danger, of maintaining an illicit nuclear arsenal, which can only ultimately be used to destroy itself—more celestial irony—with a nuclear suicide vest. *"It's a great show of principle,"* and here's another Jewish joke, *"but you still look dead."*

Young people are beginning to question. The Holy Spirit is coming back to life. Let us celebrate its renaissance in them. They need the Holy Spirit to be new messiahs.

"But!" they may yet complain: *"This is all very well. No doubt it's all very true. But, if you say God exists, when am I going to meet him?"*

It cannot be achieved only by getting into a cupboard and inviting God to join them. But, if my own experience may be a guide, this is when their imagination will be vital.

Before attempting anything, however, they should be warned that the most common error is to suppose that the imagination should be used to conjure up the kind of wishful thinking in which the Pharisaic doctrine of resurrection is amplified, as in the Revelation to John, to predict that: *'God will finally and totally defeat all his enemies, including Satan, and will reward his faithful people with a new heaven and a new earth when his victory is complete.'* (From its Introduction by the American Bible Society)

This kind of final victory has been expected many times. It is still expected by many Jews, by many Christians, and by many Muslims. One wonders why they suppose that God has to wait to defeat all his enemies, including Satan.

This was, of course, an early example of the use of the imagination. It is a bad example because John expected others to believe what he imagined.

If, however, one realizes that the word 'imagination' was not available until the 14th century, there is a perfectly clear explanation by Jesus himself of how to use it properly, and how not: *"The eye is the lamp of the body. If your eyes are good, your whole body will be full of light. But if your eyes are bad, your whole body will be full of darkness. If the light within you is darkness, how great is that darkness!"* (Matthew 6.22)

If one's imagination is to be used to enable us to receive an entirely personal and private revelation, what more might Jesus have told us?

I suggest that he would have explained that it is needed to achieve a very difficult degree of humility: difficult, that is, to achieve voluntarily; not so difficult if involuntary; more difficult again if one is threatened or hurt.

Quite simply it requires imagining, in the moment, that one knows nothing of any value; that there is nothing of any value in anything one has been taught to believe; that there is no-one one can trust. No-one.

What Jesus actually said was: *"If anyone comes to me and does not hate his father and mother, wife and children, brothers and sisters—yes, even their own life—such a person cannot be my disciple."* (Luke 14.26)

I prefer to imagine that he said *'anyone who still trusts his father, mother, wife, children, brothers and sisters—who still trusts anyone, or anything, he has trusted before'*—but his original words are lost. We must use our imagination.

This, then, describes my situation, seconds before the experience that changed my life. In the next moment it came to me, very swiftly, that I was not in this situation because I had tried to stop a religious war. It was because I was the agent of an infinitely greater power. Just a few seconds later: long enough to kneel like a child, but with a mind entirely clear of junk and clutter, and with perfect assurance that it must respond, I declared: "I need some help."

The help I received changed my life. It would change anyone's life. It has ruled my life for over forty years. It is not to be sought light-heartedly.

There may be other conditions that Jesus never mentioned. And there may be a matter of selection. But there is one last condition that I believe may be decisive.

It is knowing how to love.

Although I do not have much chance to do so, if I did, I would tell children that meeting God is very much like falling in love: deeply, completely, and forever.

It appears to me, therefore, that one may know this only if one is capable of falling in love, deeply, completely, and forever.

If this ever happens, they will certainly know it.

But if, then, when you find that you have fallen as deeply in love as I have, there is one final test to be passed.

You must know that love, if it is true love, involves letting go.

All parents know this in letting go of their children.

Ours is the child that we will have imagined.

Yes, this was indeed a last nudge from old Spinoza, who led me to read of the great Hindu epic *Ramayana*.

This is a story—and it is also, as we shall see, a powerful moral parable—dating from about the 5th or 4th century BC. It tells of a heroic young man, Rama, and his love for a beautiful young woman called Sita.

Just as he is about to marry Sita, she appeared to him in a dream, offering him a life of happiness as her husband.

In this moment, however, his guardian angel—or his daemon—whispers in his ear that he must choose either a long life of private delight with Sita, or to fulfil his duty to his people. He chose duty, and was never to see Sita again.

We may also have decided that the god we imagine is God. We may also be deeply in love with his image. The meaning of Rama's story is that we must choose between private happiness and public duty: and the second requires us to claim no preference for any image at all.

This recalls to mind—without Baruch's help this time—the wisdom of another prince who gave up a life of private luxury for public service, the 'awakened one', known to us as Gautama Buddha, possibly the first to detect the failings of his bi-cameral countrymen.

Buddhism preserves a famous, if also slightly macabre, saying to warn against anyone supposing that they have seen their saviour: *"If you meet a Buddha in the road, kill him!"*

My own reservation is far more easily expressed in a very much shorter version, which may indeed have come from the Gautama himself: *"Not this, not this."*

It simply seems to me unreasonable—if not extremely foolish—to suppose that human minds will ever be capable of understanding God as he truly is. We must instead be prepared to let go of any image we have formed, even more certainly of any image that our society has foisted on us. They cannot match reality.

You, who are reading this, are amongst the most evolved human beings in all of history. Darwin was not the first to bring down the Holy Spirit from heaven. Galileo had protested four centuries earlier that 'sense, reason and intellect' are given by God.

We have now still more imagination.

We can imagine, for example, an intelligence able to take a mind across the universe, to show it what science has theorized must be exits out of our world into others. Science may therefore be understood to support most religions in showing us where our souls may enter other worlds. This was also Al-Ghazzali's intention, to keep our souls sufficiently pure.

Our present duty, as adults, parents, and teachers, is to do our utmost to stop our species from destroying **this** world: especially over religions. We can do so by helping children to distinguish what is essential in an argument and what is not. We should help them to see that religious arguments have always some essential social purpose. In general, however, they are relics of our earlier bi-cameral ancestry, in which the commands of earlier manifestations of God have been made impervious to sense, reason, and to intellect. They need rework.

Our generation of new messiahs will explain to others, quietly, that they believe God must be for everyone; and that they demonstrate God's inspiration by being as honest as they can, and by asking questions—of anything, and anyone.

*

That's really all, folks. But with much to do!

I will end—hah! finally!—with some lines I noticed some time ago in a new book by an anthropologist, William 'Chip' Walter, in which he explains how we, *homo sapiens*, have so far survived for around seven million years.

These lines, by Loren Eiseley, another anthropologist, who died in 1977, seem to me to say all that I have tried to explain here.

'The need is not really for more brains, the need is now for a gentler, a more tolerant people than those who won for us against the ice, the tiger and the bear. The hand that hefted the axe, out of some old blind allegiance to the past, fondles the machine gun just as lovingly. It is a habit man will have to break to survive, but the roots go very deep.'

(In *'Last Ape Standing'*, Walter, C. 2013.)

Love to you all, as ever,

Colin.